PRAISE

An emotionally difficult read that will gnaw at your value system, jerk at your humanity, and light a fire under you to take action. This book tears down the prevailing societal scaffolding which reveres war and violence, and with oh-so-gentle hands reconstructs a future built with the utmost respect for the individual, unwavering wisdom of collective nonviolent action, and dogged demand for accountability. It's packed with horrific, gut-wrenching personal accounts of what we all know goes on in war and behind prison walls but consciously choose to ignore; it also boldly lays out the global system of governance which emerged out of manmade human tragedies that left entire peoples, like mine, hemorrhaging to this very day; and, overarching all of this, it chronicles two longtime activists trying with every breath they have to right the wrongs of our time. Bottom line: break the cycle of violence before it breaks us all!
—Sam Bahour, coeditor with Staughton and Alice Lynd of *Homeland: Oral Histories of Palestine and Palestinians*

Read this book for an accounting of the horrors and sordid motivations for America's unending wars. Read this book as a guide to resistance. Read this book to heal. Share this book with a high school student, an active-duty service member having second thoughts about the mission, a veteran struggling with PTSD, or a prisoner lost in the criminal injustice system. They will see they are not alone, and that there is hope and precedent in their urge to resist and overcome their injuries. And encourage that person to pass the book along to their friends, because as Alice and Staughton Lynd masterfully demonstrate it is more powerful to resist and recover in a group than alone.
—Rory Fanning, author of *Worth Fighting For: An Army Ranger's Journey out of the Military and across America*

Staughton and Alice Lynd once again serve as emissaries for a rational peace. They lead us as insightful, capable, and stalwart nonviolent combatants in the struggle to achieve a more compassionate society with subtle reminders of the battles already waged. They design a path to understanding for all who seek to heal their souls. I respect them most for their tenacious devotion to opening the hearts of those who have not yet lear_____ ___science is speaking. This book challenges us to fa_ greatest challenge to us is that we dare to
—Monica Benderman, coauthor of *L_ Conscience*

Read Alice and Staughton Lynd's new book, *Moral Injury and Nonviolent Resistance: Breaking the Cycle of Violence in the Military and Behind Bars*, and understand their concept of "moral injury," which poisons all social relations and institutions in our society. The Lynds trace the malaise to its sources. They not only expose and condemn ever-expanding militarism and death culture, but offer spiritual and practical guidance to non-violent resistance.

—Roxanne Dunbar-Ortiz, author of *An Indigenous Peoples' History of the United States*

Alice and Staughton Lynd's study of moral injury is an indictment of war and an indictment of America's prison system. Society commemorates wars but tends to forget its veterans, who often return home plagued by shame and guilt for killing; many prisoners also carry the weight of their violent actions and the Lynds do a remarkable job in connecting the struggles of the two without equating them. The individual stories in this book are riveting and painful, but they are also stories of redemption, of those who followed their individual moral conscience and rejected a cycle of violence that was imprinted on them either through the horror of war or a shattered life history. This book urges us to rethink social movements and people's history, of how individuals—through their moral example—can make history. It should be read by prisoners, soldiers, activists, social and diplomatic historians, social workers and counselors. Alice and Staughton draw their conclusions not only from detailed research, but from their on-the-ground commitment to soldiers and prisoners for decades. Like the people presented in this book, they too stand as exemplars of a moral conscience.

—Carl Mirra, associate professor, Adelphi University, Marine Corps resister and author of *Soldiers and Citizens: An Oral History of Operation Iraqi Freedom from the Battlefield to the Pentagon*

Alice and Staughton Lynd provide war veterans with a much-needed touchstone for making sense of their lives after they have returned from the battlefield. For many of us, PTSD doesn't quite capture our lifelong malaise. Moral injury does. The concept of "moral injury," so powerfully outlined and then enriched through their elegant choreography of data, personal anecdotes, and medical definitions, brings us all some solace. And the Lynds have masterfully offered veterans from all wars a bridge toward each other—moral injury plagues all of us. We who have gone to war and have come to realize that our moral compasses were purposely dismantled by our so-called leaders know that we cannot justifiably evade our own personal responsibility for the damage we have done. But now at least we can understand ourselves a little better. We owe Alice and Staughton Lynd a great debt.

—Doug Rawlings, cofounder of Veterans For Peace, Vietnam veteran

Understanding how being pressured to go against one's internal moral voice, in the midst of violent actions that contribute to conditions of PTSD, can be extremely valuable for soldiers as they seek healing and for those assisting them in the healing process. In this book, Alice and Staughton Lynd help us see how valuable and possibly lifesaving this understanding can be for people suffering longtime abuse or someone who, in the midst of threat of violence, wants to reach the humanity of those who are threatening violence against them. To know that even for the so-called hardened criminals, there is an internal moral line they will not cross to inflict violence on another human being, can give us hope and deepen our commitment and creative exploration of nonviolent action.

—Peggy Faw Gish, worker for peace and justice in Iraq and Palestine and author of *Iraq: A Journey of Hope and Peace* and *Walking Through Fire: Iraqis' Struggle for Justice and Reconciliation*

The oppressor learns from the Roman Empire, which ruled the oppressed by the punishment of decimation whereby every tenth man was to be put to death by the other nine. Thus by murder and shame were armies made and the oppressed denied humanity. Staughton and Alice Lynd have accompanied today's executioners and victims, the soldiers and prisoners of today's empire, on and off death row, in and out of court, by law and by direct action. With decades of experience, courage, patience, and intelligence they listen, learn, and record individual human beings in the belly of the beast who struggle to forgive and to resist. The collaboration results in the highest human faculty of moral reasoning that promises to link the individual, suffering human conscience to restored humanity. Empire cannot withstand even the hint, much less the fulfillment of such promise!

—Peter Linebaugh, author of *The Incomplete, True, Authentic, and Wonderful History of May Day* and *Stop Thief! The Commons, Enclosures, and Resistance*

When I speak against war people tell me that war is inevitable because natural. Then I ask them to name a single case of PTSD resulting from war deprivation. It is participation in war that requires intense conditioning and that usually creates horrific suffering even among those on the side initiating a war with superior technology and killing far more than dying. The suffering is hidden in part by misnaming it. This book names it accurately and in doing so identifies war as a criminal outrage, as a barbaric institution that must not be continued. Recent U.S. wars have been largely one-sided slaughters of foreign civilians, with the greatest dying among U.S. troops coming through suicide. But this book goes further and points to courageous examples of the sort of resistance that can help make all war a thing of the past.

—David Swanson, author of *War Is a Lie*

In this thoughtful book, Alice and Staughton Lynd have gone to great lengths to introduce people to what modern clinicians, philosophers and theologians have attempted to describe as "moral injury" and what St. Augustine of Hippo called "anguish of soul" or "heartfelt grief" following combat. Chief among the many laudable aspects of this multi-faceted text are the numerous and particular conscientious objector and veteran stories and testimonies that are at the heart of this concerned and attentive work.

—Shawn T. Storer, director, Catholic Peace Fellowship and its David's Heart Ministry for veterans and their loved ones

From the Israeli "refuseniks" to the hunger strikers in the Pelican Bay supermax prison, the Lynds give us the voices of those struggling with "moral injury." Their courageous choices help them heal but also lead to creative strategies for nonviolent change. The Lynds also provide us with the key points of the relevant international treaties and domestic legal frameworks that support them. A reality check and source of inspiration for all contemporary advocates for social justice.

—Cathy Wilkerson, author of *Flying Close to the Sun: My Life and Times as a Weatherman*

Alice and Staughton Lynd are relentless nonviolent resisters to the cycle of human violence that threatens the Earth and all its creatures. The Lynds' latest work, *Moral Injury and Nonviolent Resistance* is based on the ineradicable inner light of morally wounded soldiers and prisoners. Through the Lynds, we learn nonviolent transformation from the beaten souls and struggles of veterans of combat and solitary confinement. Their stories, drawn from the Lynds' careful documentation and analyses of campaigns of conscience especially in the U.S. and Israel, are a flame of revolutionary hope. Florence Nightingale said, "I stand at the altar of the murdered men and while I live I fight for their cause." Alice and Staughton Lynd stand at the altar of the murdered and morally injured in our wars and prisons. They are one with them, fighting their cause nonviolently for the sake of all. Let us join them.

—Jim Douglass, author of *Gandhi and the Unspeakable: His Final Experiment with Truth*

If this were only a book about moral injury it would be an extremely important book. We have been bombarded with accounts of people who suffer from PTSD yet few of us ever heard of the more frightening reality of moral injury, which we suffer because we have been forced, cajoled, or willingly entered into actions that violated our deepest sense of what is right and what is wrong. The strikingly profound thing about this book, though, is how the Lynds contrast moral injury to nonviolent resistance. Surely, if there is a "cure" for moral injury, it is to be found in courageous acts of nonviolent resistance taken with, and on behalf of, friends who are still being injured. In doing so, we not only find redemption from our own ghosts but we relieve the suffering of those who continue to inflict harm, whether voluntarily or against their will.

—Denis O'Hearn, author of *Nothing but an Unfinished Song: Bobby Sands, the Irish Hunger Striker Who Ignited a Generation* and coauthor of *Living at the Edges of Capitalism: Adventures in Exile and Mutual Aid*

This book is filled with insights: that somewhere within every person lies the possibility of redemption; that it may take a long time for causes to produce effects; that ultimately people are driven to resist not by external forces but by their inability to live any longer with themselves as they are; and, perhaps most important, that we are all, every one of us, perpetrator and victim. The accounts of individuals who have confronted in their own lives the meaning of right and wrong are inspiring even if one does not share the Lynds' commitment to nonviolence.

—Noel Ignatiev, editor of the journal *Hard Crackers: Chronicles of Everyday Life*

This book demonstrates how moral injury results from asking young people to do things that go against their deeply held values. There has been much discussion of PTSD in recent years, but this text goes farther. It links the damage done to soldiers and prisoners: the complex ways in which our society uses and abuses the generations we should be empowering rather than destroying. In true Lynd fashion, this book also shows us a way out. It is a must read for anyone concerned about survival with integrity.

—Margaret Randall, author of *Haydée Santamaría, Cuban Revolutionary: She Led by Transgression*

The Lynds' half century of work with soldiers, workers, and prisoners has embodied the concept of accompaniment. In the face of violence both here and abroad, the Lynds are documenting a way forward that eschews the tactics and language of violence and honors the agency and humanity of those caught in the chaos of war, poverty, and violence. Inspired by the act of truly listening, *Moral Injury and Nonviolent Resistance* documents the burgeoning success of this model. It offers critical strategic tools to a new generation who seek to dismantle the systems of oppression that create foreign wars and internal mass incarceration.

—Noelle Hanrahan, Global Audio Forensic Investigations, Prison Radio

The Lynds' life of commitment to make the world a better place is inspiring beyond words. I think it was my first year in college when I encountered a reader that Staughton Lynd edited on nonviolence and then a few years later encountered their book of interviews with Depression-era labor/radical organizers (which became the basis for Julia Reichert and Jim Klein's film *Union Maids*), and also found that little gem, *Labor Law for the Rank and Filer*, and on and on. It seems that whenever there was a "good fight," they have been there.

—Bill Bigelow, codirector, Zinn Education Project

In April 2010, I traveled to Washington, DC, to attend the Howard Zinn memorial organized by Historians Against the War at the annual meeting of the Organization of American Historians. I had pre-arranged a meeting with Staughton, who was circulating a call-out for historians and other scholars to organize teach-ins with veterans from Iraq and Afghanistan in the fall. In response to this call-out, I became involved with U.S. war resisters in Canada. I organized a conference in September 2011 in Toronto that Staughton attended and the following summer I visited the Lynds in Ohio. It was also the excellent collection published by Alice in 1968, *We Won't Go*, that gave me the idea that war resisters in Canada need their own book of oral histories, interviews, and public statements. Because of the Lynds' example of accompaniment with ordinary people exemplified in *Moral Injury and Nonviolent Resistance*, they have provided inspiration to me and countless others in the ongoing struggle for peace and justice.

—Luke Stewart, coeditor with Sarah Hipworth of *Let Them Stay: U.S. War Resisters in Canada, 2004–2016*

Moral Injury and Nonviolent Resistance

Breaking the Cycle of Violence in the Military and Behind Bars

Alice Lynd and
Staughton Lynd

Moral Injury and Nonviolent Resistance: Breaking the Cycle of Violence in the Military and Behind Bars
© 2017 Alice Lynd and Staughton Lynd
This edition © 2017 PM Press

ISBN: 978-1-62963-379-4
LCCN: 2016959586

Cover design by John Yates/stealworks.com
Interior design by Jonathan Rowland

PM Press
PO Box 23912
Oakland, CA 94623
www.pmpress.org

10 9 8 7 6 5 4 3 2 1

Printed in the USA by the Employee Owners of Thomson-Shore in Dexter, Michigan.
www.thomsonshore.com

This book is dedicated to
friends who made personal sacrifices in order to
break the cycle of violence:

Sam Bahour

Hector and Susie Black

David Dellinger

Barbara Deming

Art and Peggy Gish

Vincent and Rosemarie Harding

Lessley Harmon

Kathy Kelly

Norman Morrison

Joseph Mulligan, SJ

Zoharrah Simmons

Alice Walker

John Yungblut

Contents

PART II. BEHIND BARS

Introduction

SINCE THE MANUSCRIPT OF THIS BOOK WAS ESSENTIALLY COMPLETED IN THE spring of 2016, the challenge of breaking the cycle of violence has become a much more present and urgent matter. Breaking the cycle of violence now confronts us not only on the world stage in Syria, Iraq, Afghanistan, and numerous other flashpoints. It may well ask of each of us that we find ways to de-escalate violence in our own neighborhoods. If we believe in human dignity and human rights, we must act accordingly particularly when confronted by people who regard us as the enemy. Until we—all of us—find ways to confront and overcome the cycle of violence within ourselves and among us, little will come of our efforts to create a better world.

Moral Injury

What is "moral injury" and what ties it together with breaking the cycle of violence?

Dr. Jonathan Shay, a psychiatrist working for the Department of Veterans Affairs, was the first person to use the term "moral injury" to describe the reactions of Vietnam veterans to atrocities committed in Vietnam.[1] When men and women in the military believe they did, or saw, or failed to prevent, something that "you know in your heart [is] wrong,"[2] they may experience moral injury. The result in many instances in Vietnam was what Dr. Shay calls a "choking-off of the social and moral world."[3] As frustrations and a sense of betrayal mounted, the number of persons trusted by soldiers shrank to a "small circle of comrades."[4] There was a cutting-off of ties to other people, erosion of a sense of community, drying up of compassion, lack of trust, anger and violence against self or others, and inability to form stable, lasting relationships with other human beings.[5]

Within the military and in prisons, institutions created to use force and violence against perceived enemies, there have arisen new forms of saying No to violence.

---

1   Jonathan Shay, *Achilles in Vietnam: Combat Trauma and the Undoing of Character* (New York: Scribner, 1994) and *Odysseus in America: Combat Trauma and the Trials of Homecoming* (New York: Scribner, 2002).
2   Jonathan Shay, *Achilles in Vietnam*, 4.
3   Ibid., 21.
4   Ibid., 24.
5   A flood of articles and books that use the term "moral injury" has appeared during the months in which we wrote and edited this manuscript. It is our impression that almost all of these publications focus on moral injury as an individual experience. While insisting that moral injury as an individual experience not be neglected, we also insist on the importance of moral injury as something that can be experienced by groups who may also then act together to do something about the experience they have shared.

Ordinary People

We find hope in the lives of certain individuals, and in the emerging movements these men and women typify. As we become more awake to the horrors that we as a society have done or failed to prevent, and when we become aware of what conscience demands of us in the face of recognizable violations of fundamental human rights, we may take heart from the exemplary actions by individuals and groups of individuals described in this book.

Of course there were forerunners in other places and times of those who tell their stories herein. There were the members of a helicopter crew that was directed to observe from above what was happening in My Lai, Vietnam, on March 16, 1968. All three men came from white, working-class families. Glenn Andreotta had dropped out of high school early in his junior year. Door gunner on the aircraft, Larry Colburn, was suspended from high school for two weeks after a run-in with the assistant principal, and decided to join the Army. Hugh Thompson, who commanded the helicopter, came from a military family. His father had spent four years in the army and navy during World War II and "thirty years or more" in the Navy Reserves. Hugh's only sibling, an older brother, spent twenty-two years in the Air Force including two tours of duty in Southeast Asia. Hugh had graduated from high school and a few days afterwards, as was common in working-class families, he began military service. These were the men who, horrified by what they saw going on in My Lai, landed without orders to do so, trained their guns on United States soldiers, and safely evacuated two women, two elderly men, and six children.[6]

As Thompson tried to get some sleep that night, he experienced a growing sense of remorse that he hadn't done more. According to his biographer, over and over in years to come, Thompson prayed, "Had I figured out right away that a massacre was occurring, had I not spent time denying that our soldiers could have done this, had I moved in on first impulse, then more lives could have been saved."[7]

Like the men in that helicopter, the contributors to this book are ordinary people. Among them are:

Brian Willson

Brian says: "I grew up in a working class family in upstate New York. I grew up a redneck." Brian's father was employed as an office worker and salesman who listened

---

6   Trent Angers, *The Forgotten Hero of My Lai: The Hugh Thompson Story* (Lafayette, LA: Acadian House Publishing, 1999), 34–35 (Colburn), 41 (Andreotta), 59, 67 (Thompson), 123–31. Nick Turse, in his deservedly applauded book about the Vietnam War, states that what happened at My Lai "might have remained hidden forever if not for the perseverance of a single Vietnam veteran named Ron Ridenhour," who gathered "testimony from multiple American eyewitnesses." *Kill Anything that Moves: The Real American War in Vietnam* (New York: Henry Holt, 2013), 3–4.

7   Angers, 134.

faithfully to the radio program of Fulton Lewis Jr., carefully listing the names of supposed Communists in case he should ever meet them. Brian himself, when he graduated from high school, wanted to work for the FBI. When his draft call came, Brian volunteered. He entered the Air Force at the age of twenty-five.[8] While in Vietnam, Brian was assigned to visit a Vietnamese village after a bombing raid, a story he tells in Chapter 1 of this book. "I was never to be the same again."[9]

Camilo Mejía

Son of a famous musician in Nicaragua, by the time he was eighteen Camilo and his mother were living in poverty in Miami. Camilo worked in a fast-food restaurant during the day and earned a high school diploma at night. He started attending a community college but ran out of money. "The army offered financial stability and college tuition, two benefits that seemed tough to find anywhere else."[10]

Jeremy Hinzman

Similarly, Jeremy wanted to facilitate his education and also, after 9/11, to defend his country.

> I wanted to be a part of something . . . higher than myself. Something where I could transcend myself. . . . I was in a culture that looked upon the army as a good thing to do and the missions that they carried out were in the name of good or spreading democracy . . . and to me that had more meaning than just working in a work-a-day world.[11]

Rory Fanning

Rory lived with his father in an attic apartment above a garage in a wealthy suburb of Chicago. Kids at school drove BMWs and Range Rovers while Rory "scrounged for change in couch cushions for lunch money."[12]

> [T]he system worked for most of my family and friends. They lived in good homes. They believed they had earned all of what they had and that those who hadn't needed to stop being lazy and blaming others for their dependence on

---

8   Brian Willson, *On Third World Legs* (Chicago: Charles H. Kerr, 1992), 13–16. This was a preliminary account by Brian, assisted by Staughton Lynd.

9   Ibid., 19.

10   Camilo Mejía, *Road from ar Ramadi: The Private Rebellion of Staff Sergeant Camilo Mejía, An Iraq War Memoir* (Chicago: Haymarket Books, 2008), 2nd ed., preface by Chris Hedges, xii–xiii.

11   Immigration and Refugee Board, Jeremy Dean Hinzman et al., claimants, File No: TA4-01429, Toronto, Canada, December 6, 2004, 40–41.

12   Rory Fanning, *Worth Fighting For: An Army Ranger's Journey Out of the Military and Across America* (Chicago: Haymarket Books, 2014), 24.

the government—that, somehow, those who had none of the military, political, or economic power were the ones responsible for all the problems. . . .[13]

Soon after 9/11, he enlisted in the military: if we were attacked, we should defend ourselves, and people like himself should fight it, he thought.[14]

George Skatzes

George says he grew up in a household, not a family. "The way I see it, I was brought into this world, kicked in the ass and left to make my own way as best I could." He would collect pop bottles and milk bottles, search for scrap metal, iron, tin, "anything that would bring a penny or so." He had a paper route. In his late teens and early adult years he broke into parking meters and stole cars. Later, he worked for Quaker Oats. He saved five weeks' paychecks to buy a refrigerator and freezer for his mother.[15]

We met George in an improvised visiting room on Death Row in central Ohio. He seemed unable to pass another human being without attempting to crack a joke. He said to a guard: "It's pretty cold out there. Would you like me to start your car for you?" During the first hours of a prison riot he had devoted himself to carrying wounded guards and prisoners out to the yard where they could get medical assistance.

Todd Ashker

Todd writes that when he was little, his mother worked long hours as a legal secretary, leaving him and his sister alone from 6 a.m. to 7 p.m. Periodically, they were on welfare. His mom did her best to instill values of right and wrong in her children.

> I can't explain what prompted me to begin stealing things I thought my sister and I needed, but I recall the first time was at age six, it was Easter evening and we had nothing for coloring eggs so—I went a block to the corner store and stole a coloring kit. My first arrest was at age eight, for shoplifting some toys.

When he was ten years old, the family moved from Denver to California. Todd was able to participate in various youth sports programs, stealing most of the equipment he needed, but he had to give it up after a year because they could not afford the costs. Between the ages of thirteen and seventeen, he was in and out of juvenile facilities for various property crimes and other minor offenses, "fortunately, never causing physical harm to anyone."[16]

---

13 Ibid., 163.
14 Ibid., 28. *See also*, TomDispatch, "The Wars in Our Schools: An Ex-Army Ranger Finds a New Mission," April 7, 2016, <https://portside.org/print/2016-04-18/wars-our-schools-ex-army-ranger-finds-new-mission>, accessed May 12, 2016.
15 Staughton Lynd, *Lucasville: The Untold Story of a Prison Uprising*, second edition, (Oakland, CA: PM Press, 2011), 39–41.
16 Todd Ashker, "A Prisoner's Story from Pelican Bay's SHU," November 2013, unpublished.

We got to know Todd Ashker as a principal spokesperson for prisoners in the Security Housing Unit at the Pelican Bay State Prison in northern California. He was one among many who were serving indeterminate sentences in solitary confinement, in his case for more than twenty-five years. After helping to lead three hunger strikes in 2011 and 2013, Todd wrote that he felt honored to be part of the collective struggle.[17]

In the Military

Dr. Shay's books are based on the testimonies of countless Vietnam veterans that Dr. Shay encountered in his clinical practice. The testimonies, as indicated below, overwhelmingly assert betrayal of "what's right" by a commander somewhere above the soldier in the chain of command. Among the perceived forms of betrayal (some of which are echoed by Camilo Mejía and others in Chapter 1 of this book) were:

- Bias in assigning the dangerous task of "walking point" (walking at the head of a military unit doing reconnaissance, especially at night);
- Negligence in directing use of existing jungle trails, already known to the enemy, rather than laboriously cutting new but safer trails;
- Providing the troops with rifles, gas masks, and other equipment that did not work;
- Rotating lower-level officers every six months;
- Incidents of death from "friendly fire";
- Sending the informant's closest friend to his death "when the team was sent out on a frivolous mission designed simply to get the men out of the camp."[18]

Of course, the obsessive memories that haunt combat veterans do not sort themselves neatly into separate boxes marked "Post-Traumatic Stress Disorder" and "Moral Injury." (We say more about this in Chapter 1.) Moreover, what is remembered is likely to be a single overpowering narrative.

For example, after two tours as an infantryman in Vietnam, Dave Dillard "came home to a country that he felt didn't understand where he'd been or how the war affected him." Veterans at the VFW told him to forget it, but he couldn't forget. In particular, he could not forget "one long, terrible night in the jungles north of Saigon" during his first tour. Memories of that night would have obliged its narrator to add the following bullets to Dr. Shay's list:

- A radio operator asked Captain Paul Bucha, in command of the 89 members of Delta Company, if he would conduct "reconnaissance by fire": shoot a few rounds to provoke a response from enemies waiting in ambush, who would thereby identify their location. Bucha fired two shots. "The jungle erupted." Surrounded, Delta Company lost 10 men killed and 47 wounded.

---

17 Ibid.
18 Shay, *Achilles in Vietnam*, 11–27.

- Bucha saw the battle as a personal failure. "I must have done something wrong," he says. "By saying that I failed, that allows me to live with the fact that someone died. I don't accept that someone has to die and you did everything right."
- Surviving members of Delta Company lost touch with one another. In 1983, Dillard went by himself to the Veterans Memorial in Washington with a list of dead friends to locate. Then he went in search of survivors, using the internet. By 2001, a Delta Company reunion drew more than 40 men. They were all looking for the same thing: help that drugs and the VA hadn't provided.[19]

Moral injury based on the soldier's perception of such incidents was an important component in what caused many soldiers in the U.S. Army virtually to stop fighting in Vietnam in the early 1970s. Investigative reporter Neil Sheehan wrote:

> [By 1969] it was an Army in which men escaped into marijuana and heroin and other men died because their comrades were "stoned" on these drugs. . . . It was an Army whose units in the field were on the edge of mutiny, whose soldiers rebelled against the senselessness of their sacrifice by assassinating officers and non-coms in "accidental" shootings and "fraggings" with grenades.[20]

Christian Appy quotes an article published in 1971 in the *Armed Forces Journal*: "By every conceivable indicator, our army that now remains in Vietnam is in a state approaching collapse, with individual units avoiding or having refused combat, murdering their officers and noncommissioned officers, drug-ridden and dispirited where not near-mutinous."[21]

Policy makers in Washington evidently assumed that the military's problems in Vietnam arose from the fact that young men in the United States were drafted to fight there. They therefore launched a campaign to substitute a volunteer military for an army recruited by conscription.[22] The campaign was successful, and the policy was changed.

---

19 Brian Mockenhaupt, "The Long Shadow of PTSD," *AARP Bulletin/Real Possibilities*, May 2015, 10–14.

20 Ibid., 28, quoting Neil Sheehan, *A Bright Shining Lie: John Paul Vann and America in Vietnam* (New York: Random House, 1988), 741.

21 Christian G. Appy, *American Reckoning: The Vietnam War and Our National Identity* (New York: Viking, 2015), 214, quoting Col. Robert Heinl, "Collapse of the Armed Forces," *Armed Forces Journal*, June 1971, 35.

22 *See* Tod Ensign, "Who Serves?" in Mary Susannah Robbins, *Peace Not Terror: Leaders of the Antiwar Movement Speak Out Against U.S. Foreign Policy Post 9/11* (Lanham, MD: Lexington Books, 2008), 109–30. The plan to end the draft was supported by antiwar

But the evidence appears to show that this change in policy did not solve the problem of disenchantment and shame among members of the Armed Forces. The problem for the U.S. military in Afghanistan and Iraq, just as in Vietnam, has not been caused by how American soldiers get to the battlefield but by what they are asked to do when they get there. These men and women see incredible evil. They come home with that weighing on them and they do not know how to fit back into society. Referring to himself and a friend, Ben Sledge, a veteran of the wars in Iraq and Afghanistan, writes:

> Readjusting to normal life after deployment didn't happen for us. Instead, we found ourselves overly angry, depressed, violent, and drinking a lot. We couldn't talk to people about war or the cost of it because, well, how do you talk about morally reprehensible things that have left a bruise on your soul?

The gap between citizen and soldier is growing ever wider, he says: since 2001, only 0.45% of our population has served in the Global War on Terror. "Despite the length of the Iraq and Afghan wars, there has been no draft and the burden has been borne by less than a half percent of the population with repeated tours continually deteriorating the mental health of our troops." We don't talk about the moral inequality we are asking our soldiers to bear. We dump the weight of shame and guilt onto their shoulders while we enjoy the benefits of passing the buck, he says. "In order for our soldiers to begin healing it's going to take society owning up to the part they played in sending our troops to war. . . . No one in their right mind wants war. We want peace. And no one wants it more than the soldier."[23]

It seems that even for those who volunteer for military service, what Quakers call an "inner light" or "that of God in every person" causes many volunteers to rebel particularly against the use of violence in a kind of combat that includes fighting an enemy who cannot be clearly identified, or in which it is hard to tell who is a combatant and who is a civilian, or presents situations in which colleagues are being killed but there is nowhere to return fire, or that requires the soldier to take part in a war that lacks moral clarity, or is perceived to be unjustified and futile.

Dr. Shay offers a crucial piece of evidence. His patients who complained bitterly about the incidents described above were themselves *90 percent volunteers!*[24] One is

---

spokespersons Benjamin Spock, Coretta Scott King, Senator George McGovern, and Senator Ernest Gruening, as well as by NAACP head Roy Wilkins. Ibid., 115, 117.

23 Ben Sledge, "The Conversation About War and Our Veterans We Refuse to Have," \<https://medium.com/@benjaminsledge/the-conversation-about-war-and-our-veterans-we-refuse-to-have-a95c26972aee#.gwweqfaiw\>, accessed October 29, 2016. Referring to the statistic that twenty-two veterans take their lives every day, Sledge adds, "I can guarantee you, part of that is because of the citizen/soldier divide."

24 Shay, *Achilles in Vietnam*, 9.

led to wonder whether volunteers were *more* disillusioned than conscripts because volunteers had higher expectations.

The Cycle of Violence

Not only is escape to alcohol and drugs frequent among those who suffer from moral injury; but as Vince Emanuele describes in Chapter 1, "I wanted to release my anger through violence." The suicide rate for veterans has been more than double the suicide rate for civilians.

There is a substantial literature recounting attempts to heal the experience of moral injury among veterans. Individuals may be able to find ways to put the past behind them, and to do constructive things now and in the future. But healing ourselves is not the ultimate goal. It is not just a matter of finding ways to alleviate the suffering of those who have done wrong. Dr. Shay says that war is not inevitable and we must end it: "Those who have been in it hate it with more passion than I am ever likely to match." We must take on "ending the human practice of war."[25]

However, as Pope Francis tells us, "until exclusion and inequality in society and between peoples is reversed, it will be impossible to eliminate violence."[26] International agreements to limit the horrors of war have been developed over many decades, but nations put their own interests ahead of the rights of others. As long as we live in a violent society, more people will become victims and some of the victimizers will suffer moral injury. There is no solution to physical and moral injury as long as people are willing to fight wars.

Accordingly, for the foreseeable future individuals and small groups of service men and women who are confronted with orders perceived to be unlawful and immoral may have to step forward in the knowledge that they may be punished if they say No but with faith in the possibility of a better future.

Behind Bars

Prisoners' experience of moral injury is both very similar to that of soldiers in combat, and very different.

In Chapter 5 the reader will encounter the memories of Lessley Harmon's cellmates, of Glenn Benner, of an unnamed murderer now in his fifties, and of George Skatzes. All have to do with homicides that the informant himself committed or failed to prevent. The torment recounted is indistinguishable from that of many former combat veterans who killed a child, or failed to prevent the death of a comrade, presented in Chapter 1. Read Brian Willson's narrative of the day of infamy he lived

---

25   Shay, *Odysseus in America*, 249–53.
26   Apostolic Exhortation of the Holy Father Francis, *Evangelii Gaudium. The Joy of the Gospel* (Boston: Pauline Books & Media, 2013), 43–59.

through in Vietnam and compare it with Skatzes's anguish about failing to protect hostage officer Robert Vallandingham. Surely, in all these stories, we are listening to a similar morality play. Over and over we hear the tale of moral injury.

Thus moral injury in military service and moral injury in prison have a good deal in common. Ordinary people in violent situations may be driven to affirm their humanity. They may reach out to others in a search for community. They may try to bring into being a better way. They may be willing to swim upstream against powerful currents, at considerable personal risk.

The differences arise mainly from context. In the military, the typical recruit in a volunteer army has little appreciation of the ambiguities he or she will face in combat against an "enemy" that does not wear uniforms and may be any age or sex. Only when contact is made, and shooting to kill begins, does he or she begin the descent into ever-lower circles of hell.

The prisoner in a high security prison, on the other hand, has already been found guilty of a crime that probably involved violence. Predictable assessment of their initial imprisonment and conviction are "I was railroaded" (very often the case) and "I couldn't afford a competent lawyer" (almost always true). Long-term supermax prisoners typically believe, "This is no life!" and that the conditions of their confinement are driven by a thirst for punishment and revenge.

We as a society have failed to provide humane conditions behind bars. We know that prolonged solitary confinement causes mental health disorders, sometimes suicides, and long-term difficulties in relationships with other people. Prisoners know this. They often suffer from the injury they have inflicted on others, but routinely they suffer from the injury inflicted on themselves by those who regard them as incorrigible.

A simple way to think of what combat veterans and long-term prisoners have in common is a desire to protect one another and for fellowship. In Vietnam, soldiers who liked the same music and used the same drugs often gathered in the same "buddy group." One veteran's description of the scene was as follows:

> Everyone stuck together. It was like racism didn't matter. . . . [W]hen you came in from the field, people tended to break down culturally . . . —musically. It was like what part of the country you were from, and it was also how you were going about getting wasted, because that's what we were doing. . . .
> And so you had the heads. You had the juicers. You had the brothers.[27]

Very much in the same way, in high security prisons in the United States inmates tend to gather together in what are perceived as "gangs." At the Southern Ohio

---

27 Richard Moser, *The New Winter Soldiers: GI and Veteran Dissent during the Vietnam Era* (New Brunswick, NJ: Rutgers University Press, 1996), 62.

Correctional Facility (SOCF) during an uprising in 1993, there were Sunni Muslims, the Aryan Brotherhood, and the Gangster Disciples. Beginning a day or two after L block was first occupied, each of these groups had its own "pod" or sleeping area within the cell block, and a governing council made up of representatives of the three groups met frequently.

At their best, as explained in Chapters 5 and 7, prisoners seek to forestall possible hostilities between such groups by an explicit invitation to join in overcoming divisions based on ethnicity and race.

This Book

The chapters of this book present a single argument, each part of which contributes to the whole. Our fundamental premise is that "ordinary" people have a red line, a point beyond which they feel that to continue on a course of action would betray their basic sense of right and wrong.

The soldier concludes this when he or she is ordered to do something unacceptable to conscience. The prisoner may feel that his or her own violent action before incarceration, or during imprisonment, or both, was unforgivable. But what is being done to him or her may also be unacceptable.

This book is divided into two major parts. Part I, In the Military, has four chapters.[28]

Chapter 1 is devoted to moral injury. We glimpse what moral injury looks like, what causes it, its consequences, and some kinds of change that are needed to address it. We listen to the inner workings of conscience as afflicted individuals tell us about their sense of guilt, shame, and blameworthiness for their personal conduct, together with their feelings of remorse and obligation to do or be that which they recognize as good.

In Chapter 2, on international law, we look at attempts to limit war, to protect the innocent, to affirm fundamental human rights.[29] What are those objective internationally recognized standards and expectations that mirror our individual sense of right and wrong? What are "war crimes"? What is a "just war"? What constitutes "torture"? What is "collective punishment"? What kinds of conscientious objection to participation in war are recognized, based on what principles?

---

28 Part I is a revision and combination of two papers by Alice Lynd with the assistance of Staughton Lynd, previously posted on the Historians Against War website. *See* <http://historiansagainstwar.org/resources/militaryservice.pdf>, accessed May 12, 2016.

29 Chapter 2 contains sections from two articles by Alice Lynd with the assistance of Staughton Lynd, "Moral Injury and Conscientious Objection: Saying No to Military Service" (2015), <http://www.historiansagainstwar.org/resources/militaryservice.pdf>, and "International Human Rights Law: Violations by Israel and the Problem of Enforcement" (2014), <http://www.historiansagainstwar.org/resources/InternationalHumanRights.pdf>, accessed May 12, 2016.

While in the military, some men and women instinctively respond to concepts in international law of which they may not even be aware: don't kill civilians; don't use disproportionate or indiscriminate force; collective punishment is unfair and wrong. International law supports "selective" conscientious objection. "Selective" or "particular war" objectors are individuals who object to participation in what they consider to be an unjust or illegal war, or who object to participation in certain "methods or means" of combat (such as destruction of civilian villages and their inhabitants, the practice of torture, or the use of drones). Selective objectors would presumably fight in some other war, especially an attack on their homeland, but not the one in which they are ordered to participate.

Both the United States and Israel recognize conscientious objection based on religious training and belief. Neither the United States nor Israel recognizes "selective" conscientious objectors: they limit recognition of conscientious objectors to those who refuse to participate in all wars. Ironically, the first recognition of conscientious objection in international law was limited to one specific type of service: in 1978, the UN General Assembly affirmed the right to refuse service in military or police forces used to enforce *apartheid*.

Now that the United States relies entirely on voluntary military service, experience in the military may compel the volunteer to reconsider what he or she believes and why. In Chapter 3 we explain the criteria required to be recognized as a conscientious objector under American law, followed by accounts of men whose conscientious objection "crystallized" after they entered the military.[30]

We include a section on Israel because a growing number of Israelis who would willingly defend their country believe that what Israel is doing in the occupied Palestinian territories is morally wrong.[31] In Chapter 4, we describe numerous violations of internationally recognized human rights by Israel, provisions for exemption from military service only for religious reasons, followed by brief descriptions of "refuseniks," ending up with personal accounts that echo those of Americans troubled by moral injury in Chapter 1. Members of the Israeli Defense Forces, like their American counterparts, have experienced the horror of killing a child, or of being ordered to demolish an area where civilians are living, or of carrying out other commands that they

---

30 Sections of this chapter that appeared in Lynd, "Moral Injury," have been omitted in this chapter, particularly pertaining to the history of conscientious objection in the United States, and current procedures to apply for conscientious objector status. *See* <http://www.historiansagainstwar.org/resources/militaryservice.pdf>.

31 Chapter 4 is a composite of sections from Lynd, "International Human Rights Law," and Lynd, "Moral Injury." Extensive sections of Lynd, "International Human Rights Law" have been omitted, including detailed material concerning the occupation of, and collective punishment in, the West Bank (including East Jerusalem), Gaza, and the Golan Heights since 1967; Oslo II, Areas A, B, and C, the Separation Barrier, and the Gaza Buffer Zone. *See* <http://www.historiansagainstwar.org/resources/InternationalHumanRights.pdf> and <http://www.historiansagainstwar.org/resources/militaryservice.pdf>.

believe to be immoral. Israeli refuseniks are outspoken, take risks and punishments, and are publicly recognized to an extent that has not yet occurred in the United States.

Part II of this book explores violence and nonviolence as experienced by people being held behind bars. Unlike the matter of "moral injury" among combat veterans, there are few scholarly or governmental publications on this subject. Accordingly, Part II is based for the most part on our twenty years of inquiry, advocacy, and accompaniment among prisoners in Ohio, Illinois, and California.

However, while the concept of "moral injury" has not been recognized in the literature about prisoners, there is an important point of contact between studies of men and women in the military and studies of prisoners. Moral injury has been recognized as a specific variant of post-traumatic stress disorder (PTSD) among combat veterans. Whereas moral injury arises from action or inaction in the past that cannot now be altered, most veterans suffering from PTSD are fearful of what may happen to them in the present or future. For example, a veteran with PTSD who dines at a restaurant may insist on sitting with a wall at his back and clear vision of the front door.

There is a startling resemblance between symptoms associated with this more general form of PTSD and the experience of prisoners held in solitary confinement for long periods of time. As explained at the outset of this Introduction, Dr. Shay, who first used the term "moral injury," perceived among many combat veterans a shrinking of the individual's "social and moral horizon" and a reduction in the number of persons that the veteran trusted. How extraordinary, then, that Professor Craig Haney, principal expert witness for plaintiffs at the Pelican Bay State Prison in California, described in his Report to the Court in a class action lawsuit the psychological state of men who had been confined alone for more than ten years as "social death."[32] A more detailed description of his findings is presented at the beginning of Part Two.

Just as the diagnosis of the traumatized veteran converges with that of the isolated prisoner, so too, we shall argue, does their path to recovery. It is that path of nonviolent resistance which gives this book its subtitle.

Chapter 5 describes moral injury among individual prisoners we have known, ending with a portrait of George Skatzes. Skatzes was a spokesperson for prisoners at SOCF, a maximum security prison in Lucasville, Ohio, who in April 1993 took part in an eleven-day occupation of a major cell block. George felt strongly that an uprising like that one should never be repeated. He expressed profound moral injury that the prisoners in rebellion had needlessly killed a hostage officer.

Chapter 6 turns to our efforts to assist prisoners required to stay in their cells, usually alone and usually for an indefinite period, twenty-two or more hours per

---

32   "Expert Report of Craig Haney," Ph.D., J.D. , *Todd Ashker, et al. v. Edmund G. Brown, Jr., Governor, et al.,* Case No. 4:09 CV 05796 CW (United States District Court, Northern District of California, Oakland Division), <https://ccrjustice.org/sites/default/files/attach/2015/07/Redacted_Haney%20Expert%20Report.pdf>, accessed May 12, 2016.

day.[33] The American Friends Service Committee asked us to monitor conditions of confinement at Ohio's supermaximum security prison, the Ohio State Penitentiary (OSP), being built in Youngstown, Ohio, near our home. Many of the prisoners convicted after the negotiated surrender at Lucasville were transferred to the Ohio State Penitentiary. We soon found ourselves both monitoring the harsh conditions of confinement at the OSP and investigating the facts of the Lucasville disturbance. The findings of our monitoring became the skeleton for a class action lawsuit that made its way to a successful unanimous ruling by the United States Supreme Court.

Chapter 6 then proceeds to describe in detail the struggle of prisoners at the Menard Correctional Center in Illinois, who opted in both 2014 and 2015 to protest conditions similar to those in other supermaximum security facilities by means of nonviolent hunger strikes.

Chapter 7 tells the story of the largest and most successful hunger strikes in U.S. history. Thousands of prisoners in the Pelican Bay, California, Security Housing Unit and other high security prisons in the state went without food for several weeks in July 2011 and then again in September 2011, and in even larger numbers for close to sixty days in the summer of 2013. Early on, we received a letter from Todd Ashker, a prisoner at Pelican Bay who had heard of the Ohio class action and wondered what help it might be to similarly situated prisoners in California. We offer extracts from Todd's letters over a period beginning before the first hunger strike as a window into the minds of the hunger strikers. The chapter ends with the text of an Agreement to End Hostilities among leaders of Hispanic, African American, and Caucasian prisoner organizations, and extracts from a similar manifesto by "youth in the streets, schools and lock-ups throughout California."

Finally, in Chapter 8 we characterize the strategy of the California hunger strikers as a combination of nonviolent direct action and federal litigation. We review this combination of tactics in the light of past successes and defeats in the civil rights and labor movements.

Acknowledgments

The authors wish to thank the following:

---

33 *See*, Department of Justice, "Report and Recommendations Concerning the Use of Restrictive Housing," Executive Summary, defining "restrictive housing" as any type of detention that involves removal from the general population, placement in a room or cell alone or with another inmate, typically for twenty-two hours or more per day. <https://www.justice.gov/dag/file/815561/download>, accessed May 12, 2016. *See also*, "United Nations Standard Minimum Rules for the Treatment of Prisoners (the Nelson Mandela Rules)," UN-Doc A/Res/70/175, December 17, 2015: "solitary confinement shall refer to the confinement of prisoners for 22 hours or more a day without meaningful human contact. Prolonged solitary confinement shall refer to solitary confinement for a time period in excess of 15 consecutive days." <http://www.penalreform.org/wp-content/uploads/1957/06/ENG.pdf>, accessed May 12, 2016.

Carl Mirra, himself a former Marine and conscientious objector, and Luke Stewart for providing some of the personal accounts;

Monica Benderman, who offers military counseling and support near Fort Stewart, Georgia;

Kerry Berland and David Finke, old friends and colleagues from CADRE (Chicago Area Draft Resisters) in Vietnam War days whose assistance was invaluable in producing material that appears in Chapter 1;

Lynn Newsom of Quaker House near Fort Bragg in North Carolina who introduced to Alice the concept of "moral injury";

Rory Fanning, who met the late Pat Tillman in basic training for the U.S. Army Rangers, became a conscientious objector, and endured mean-spirited retaliation while performing alternative service in Afghanistan;

Brian Willson and other veterans for sharing memories of their extraordinary protests against war and violence;

Todd Ashker, and other prisoners held in solitary confinement for years in Ohio, Illinois, and California.

Carl Mirra has granted permission to reprint material copyrighted by himself. Brian Willson and PM Press have granted permission to reprint material from *Blood on the Tracks*.[34]

The cover image by Lincoln Cushing shows soldiers conducting a nonviolent sit-down while imprisoned at the Presidio stockade in San Francisco in October 1968. The "Presidio 27" demanded investigation of the killing of a fellow prisoner who was charged with being absent without leave and shot when he was allegedly trying to escape, improvement of stockade conditions, and an end to racist harassment of African American prisoners, as well as declaring their opposition to the war in Vietnam. Firemen were summoned and directed to turn their hoses on the protesting soldiers, but refused. The soldiers were charged with mutiny and threatened with execution. Once the sentences were made public, the outcry was such that none of the accused served more than eighteen months.[35]

---

34   S. Brian Willson, *Blood on the Tracks: The Life and Times of S. Brian Willson, A Psychohistorical Memoir* (Oakland, CA: PM Press, 2011).

35   "Presidio 27, Historical Essay by the Friendly Fire Collective," <http://www.foundsf.org/index.php?title=Presidio_27>, accessed August 6, 2016.

PART I.
IN THE MILITARY

Chapter 1.
Moral Injury and the Making of a Conscientious Objector

The Nature of Moral Injury

LONG BEFORE ANYONE BEGAN TO RECOGNIZE MORAL INJURY, SERVICE MEMBERS were confronted with moral and ethical challenges in war: "They may act in ways that transgress deeply held moral beliefs or they may experience conflict about the unethical behaviors of others. Warriors may also bear witness to intense human suffering and cruelty that shakes their core beliefs about humanity. . . ."[1]

There can be no better way to grasp the meaning of "moral injury" than to examine the experience in Vietnam that turned the life of Brian Willson upside down.

Brian Willson enlisted in the Air Force officer program.[2] While serving in Vietnam he was asked to accompany a Vietnamese lieutenant, nicknamed Bao, to visit freshly bombed sites, to perform a quick estimate of the pilots' success at hitting their specified targets, and to conduct damage assessments.

As they approached a site in the Mekong Delta, Willson saw a water buffalo, a third of its skull gone and a three-foot gash in its belly, but still alive.

My first thought was that I was witnessing an egregious, horrendous mistake. The "target" was no more than a small fishing and rice farming community. The "village" was smaller than a baseball playing field. . . . The pilots who bombed this small hamlet . . . would have been able to see the inhabitants, mostly women with children taking care of various farming and domestic chores. . . . The buildings were virtually flattened by explosions or destroyed by fire. I didn't see one person standing. Most were ripped apart from bomb shrapnel and machine gun wounds, many blackened by napalm beyond recognition; the majority were obviously children.

. . . I couldn't fathom what I was seeing, smelling, thinking. I took a few faltering steps to my left, only to find my way blocked by the body of a young woman lying at my feet. She had been clutching three small, partially

1   B.T. Litz et al., "Moral injury and moral repair in war veterans: A preliminary model and intervention strategy," *Clinical Psychology Review* (2009), 695–706, (hereafter, "Litz et al.") <https://msrc.fsu.edu/system/files/Litz%20et%20al%202009%20Moral%20injury%20and%20moral%20repair%20in%20war%20veterans--%20a%20preliminary%20model%20and%20intervention%20strategy.pdf>, 696, accessed May 12, 2016.

2   S. Brian Willson, *Blood on the Tracks: The Life and Times of S. Brian Willson, A Psychohistorical Memoir* (Oakland, CA: PM Press, 2011), 26.

blackened children when she apparently collapsed. I bent down for a closer look and stared, aghast, at the woman's open eyes. The children were motionless, blackened blood drying on their bullet and shrapnel-riddled bodies. Napalm had melted much of the woman's face, including her eyelids, but as I focused on her face, it seemed that her eyes were staring at me.

She was not alive. But at the moment her eyes met mine, it felt like a lightning bolt jolted through my entire being. . . .

I was startled when Bao . . . asked why I was crying. . . . "She is my family," I said, or something to that effect. . . . I felt, in my body, that she and I were one.

But Bao just smirked, and said something about how satisfied he was with the bombing success in killing communists. I did not reply. I had nothing to say. From that moment on, nothing would ever be the same for me. . . .

I could not talk about this experience for twelve years, and the thought of it still creates tremors in my body. I often find myself crying at the thought of it, and at times feel a rage that nearly chokes me. . . . Buried deeper inside me, however, was an even more radical epiphany. . . . *She is my family.* It would take me many years to understand the real meaning of this experience—that we are all one—a lesson that continues to deepen and expand as I grow older.[3]

We can see in Brian's writings over a period of years how that experience did "deepen and expand."

In his first narrative of the day, published in 1992, Brian wrote: "We rode together in stone silence the hour or so back to Binh Thuy."[4]

In a much fuller account, published in 2011, Brian recalled a sequence of events that significantly added to what he had written earlier:

I was experiencing such a shock that it did not occur to me to seek medical help for those who still might be alive in the village. We just walked away from the moaning of those still alive. They did not count as human beings. Though I was crying inside, I did nothing. In our return drive to Binh Thuy, we passed directly by the Army's 29th Evacuation Hospital next to Binh Thuy and I did not even think of stopping to report the critical need for medical attention in that village.[5]

In a third version of that jeep trip, which Brian sent to us in 2015, he confesses:

---

3   Willson, *Blood on the Tracks*, 47–49.
4   S. Brian Willson, *On Third World Legs* (Chicago: Charles H. Kerr, 1992), 19.
5   Willson, *Blood on the Tracks*, 48.

[O]n the drive back to Binh Thuy . . . as we pass the US Army's 29th Evacuation Hospital just east of the base, I burst out in tears. "Shouldn't we stop and seek emergency medical assistance to aid those still alive in that village?" Bao vigorously shakes his head. . . . He is adamant. I argue emotionally that we should stop . . . and I do not stop the jeep.[6]

Thus, we see how this experience "continued to deepen and expand." Brian Willson is haunted by remorse, not only by what he witnessed, but also by what he did not do or failed to prevent. Adding to the horror of what he saw and a desire to separate himself from such actions, his memory evolves into self-condemnation for his failure to prevent further loss of life. It is a profound deepening of moral injury.

Dr. Jonathan Shay used the term "moral injury" to describe the reactions of Vietnam veterans, like Brian Willson, to atrocities commanded or condoned by their superiors.[7] Dr. Shay begins his first book on the subject with a chapter called "Betrayal of 'What's Right'." He writes: "We begin in the moral world of the soldier—what his culture understands to be right—and betrayal of that moral order by a commander." He describes "violations of what American soldiers understood to be right by holders of responsibility and trust." In one instance, a reconnaissance patrol became aware that three small boats were being unloaded at night on the shore of a bay. The "word came down" that they were unloading weapons. "And we opened up on them . . . constant firepower" into those boats. But daylight came "and we found out we killed a lot of fishermen and kids." The colonel told them not to worry about it; "you know in your heart it's wrong, but . . . here's your superiors telling you that it was okay." This veteran concluded: "The lieutenants got medals . . . medals for killing civilians."[8]

In recent years, the definition of moral injury has focused less on the betrayal of trust by higher military authority and more on acts by oneself or others that violate the person's fundamental sense of right and wrong.[9]

---

6   S. Brian Willson, extract from "My Personal Viet Nam Experiences and Afterword" (unpublished, June 10, 2015). For essays by Brian Willson, *see* his blog, <http://www.brianwillson.com/>, accessed May 12, 2016. *See also*, Wikipedia, <https://en.wikipedia.org/wiki/Brian_Willson>, accessed May 12, 2016.

7   Beth Schwinn, "Moral Injury Poses Hidden Risks for Service Members," Defense Centers of Excellence for Psychological Health and Traumatic Brain Injury, March 11, 2015, ascribing a first use of the term to psychiatrist Jonathan Shay, then with the Department of Veterans Affairs. <http://www.dcoe.mil/blog/15-03-11/Moral_Injury_Poses_Hidden_Risks_for_Service_Members.aspx>, accessed May 13, 2016.

8   Jonathan Shay, *Achilles in Vietnam: Combat Trauma and the Undoing of Character* (New York: Macmillan Publishing Company, 1994), 3–4.

9   There is recognition that moral injury is not limited to men and women in the military and veterans. *See* Joseph M. Palmer, edited by James H. Mukoyama, Jr., "Moral Injury and the Role of Your Church: A Guide for Clergy and Lay Ministries," *Military Outreach USA* (2014), iv (hereafter, "Palmer, 'Moral Injury'"), <http://media.wix.com/

In order to maintain their fighting capacity, the Armed Forces of the United States are trying to grapple with moral injury. A publication by the United States Navy and Marine Corps comments that during the Vietnam War,

> combat stress must surely have contributed to the in-theater substance abuse, misconduct, and psychological disability after returning to civilian life that have come to characterize that war and its veterans. A significant number of Service members deployed to Operation Iraqi Freedom or Operation Enduring Freedom and exposed to combat or other operational stressors experience persistent, life-altering stress problems during and after deployment, even though most were not recognized as stress casualties in theater. Some postdeployment stress problems may be delayed in onset, surfacing many months after returning from a war zone.[10]

"Everyone is at risk and no one is immune," the document continues.

> Studies of the causes of combat-related posttraumatic stress disorder (PTSD), for example, have shown again and again that the degree and frequency of exposure to combat and other intense stressors are a much more powerful determinant of outcome than maturity level, early life experience, or personality style.[11]

The U.S. Navy and Marine Corps use the term "inner conflict." "Inner conflict" is one of four "combat operational stress" (COS) injuries. "Stress arises due to moral damage from carrying out or bearing witness to acts or failures to act that violate deeply held belief systems."[12] Those deeply held beliefs may or may not be religious.

---

ugd/9c76c8_749e804bbcda4fc39e8a635fd35d7a23.pdf>, accessed May 13, 2016: "It is not uncommon for those in the field of law enforcement, firefighting or nursing to suffer from moral injury. In the case of an individual, a woman who had an abortion at an early age may suffer from moral injury in her later years when reflecting on her prior decision."

10   U.S. Navy NTTP 1-15M and U.S. Marine Corps, MCRP 6-11C, "Combat and Operational Stress Control," Marine Corps Combat Development Command 2010 (Edition December 2010), 1-4–1-5 (hereafter, "Marine Corps COS"). <http://www.med.navy.mil/sites/nmcsd/nccosc/coscConference/Documents/COSC%20MRCP%20NTTP%20Doctrine.pdf>, accessed May 13, 2016.

11   Marine Corps COS, 1-5.

12   Marine Corps COS, 1-11. *See*, William P. Nash and Brett T. Litz, "Moral Injury: A Mechanism for War-Related Psychological Trauma in Military Family Members," *Clin Child Fam Psychol Rev* (2013) 16:365-375, DOI 10.1007/s10567-013-0146-y (hereafter, "Nash and Litz"), published online, July 13, 2013, 368 <https://www.law.upenn.edu/live/files/4754-nash-and-litz-moral-injury-in-military-familiespdf>, accessed May 13, 2016: "Although defined in words similar to moral injury, the term 'inner conflict' is sometimes preferred for training of service members in the Marine Corps because the potential synonym, moral injury, is perceived by some to be pejorative." (Citation omitted.)

Participation in the military requires a transformation from a "civilian code" to a "warrior code," sacrificing one's unwillingness to kill to being willing to kill when ordered.[13] A publication for active service members warns:

> As a service member, you may encounter inner conflicts, ethical or moral challenges during deployments, special missions, or in the course of one's duty. You may be required to act in ways that go against your moral beliefs or witness behaviors by others that make you feel uncomfortable. . . . It is the betrayal of what you may feel is morally right.[14]

An article published by the United States Department of Veterans Affairs explains that moral injuries

> may stem from direct participation in acts of combat, such as killing or harming others, or indirect acts, such as witnessing death or dying, failing to prevent immoral acts of others, or giving or receiving orders that are perceived as gross moral violations. The act may have been carried out by an individual or a group, through a decision made individually or as a response to orders given by leaders.[15]

Killing or harming others, witnessing death or dying, handling human remains, and being unable to help ill or wounded women and children were common experiences among soldiers and Marines in Iraq and Afghanistan.

> Service members deployed to Iraq or Afghanistan have been exposed to high levels of violence and its aftermath. In 2003, 52% of soldiers and Marines surveyed reported shooting or directing fire at the enemy, and 32% reported

---

13 Palmer, "Moral Injury," 3.

14 Real Warriors, "Understanding Moral Injury," <http://www.realwarriors.net/active/treatment/moralinjury.php>, accessed May 13, 2016. The Real Warriors Campaign, launched in 2009 by the Defense Centers of Excellence for Psychological Health and Traumatic Brain Injury, is an integral part of the Defense Department's overall effort to encourage service members, veterans and military families to cope with invisible wounds. <http://www.realwarriors.net/aboutus>, accessed May 13, 2016. *See also*, Shira Maguen and Brett Litz, "Moral Injury in Veterans of War," *PTSD Research Quarterly*, Vol. 23, No. 1 (2012), ISSN: 1050-1835 (hereafter, "Maguen and Litz (2012)"), 1, <http://www.ptsd.va.gov/professional/newsletters/research-quarterly/v23n1.pdf>, accessed May 13, 2016: "An act of serious transgression that leads to serious inner conflict because the experience is at odds with core ethical and moral beliefs is called *moral injury*."

15 Shira Maguen and Brett Litz, "Moral Injury in the Context of War," PTSD: National Center for PTSD (last updated January 20, 2015), (hereafter, "Maguen and Litz (2015)"), (footnote omitted), <http://www.ptsd.va.gov/professional/co-occurring/moral_injury_at_war.asp>, accessed May 13, 2016.

being directly responsible for the death of an enemy combatant [citation omitted]. Additionally, 65% of those surveyed reported seeing dead bodies or human remains, 31% reported handling or uncovering human remains, and 60% reported having seen ill/wounded women and children who they were unable to help. . . .[16]

According to a doctor who works for the VA Medical Center in Richmond, Virginia, one fifth of soldiers kill civilians by mistake.[17] Other studies indicate that during the Gulf War, 11% of veterans reported killing during their deployment, and 40% of soldiers returning from Operation Iraqi Freedom reported killing or being responsible for killing during their deployment.[18]

"When moral injury occurs, a soldier may be convinced what he or she did is unforgivable. . . . It is the presence of inner conflict and personal guilt that cannot be forgiven."[19] An army chaplain describes moral injury as "soul damage."[20]

What Causes Moral Injury?

There are various theories as to what causes moral injury. One VA doctor published an article called "Guilt and Moral Injury in Veterans: What We Know and What We Don't."[21] Much research still needs to be done on causes and treatment.

Moral injury overlaps with, but is not the same as, post-traumatic stress disorder (PTSD). A person may experience PTSD if he or she has been the target of others' attempts to kill or injure, or has survived when others did not. But having been a killer, or having failed to prevent death and injury, may result in moral injury.

The same person may suffer from both PTSD and moral injury. Camilo Mejía describes them both as he experienced them. He attributes his fear and apprehension to unspoken assumptions about the outside world: that bombs don't explode on

---

16   Litz et al., 696, citing Hoge et al., "Combat duty in Iraq and Afghanistan, mental health problems, and barriers to care," *The New England Journal of Medicine*, 351:13-22 (July 1, 2004), DOI: 10.1056/NEJMoa040603, <http://www.nejm.org/doi/full/10.1056/NEJMoa040603#t=articleTop>, accessed May 13, 2016.

17   Brian L. Meyer, "Guilt and Moral Injury in Veterans: What We Know and What We Don't," May 13, 2014, 14. <http://sites.utexas.edu/jdtr/files/2014/05/Session-12_Guilt-and-Moral-Injury-in-Veterans_Brian-Meyer.pdf>, accessed May 13, 2016.

18   Maquen and Litz (2012), 4, summarizing articles by Maguen, Litz and other authors in 2011.

19   Rhonda Quillin, "Army Values Keep Moral Injury at Bay," *Army: The Magazine of the Association of the United States Army*, April 20, 2015, <http://www.armymagazine.org/2015/04/20/army-values-keep-moral-injury-at-bay/>, accessed May 13, 2016.

20   "Moral Injury: Unseen Wounds," www.army.mil: The Official Home Page of the United States Army, December 11, 2014, quoting Chaplain Col. John Read at Fort Gordon, GA. <http://www.army.mil/article/139776/Moral_Injury__Unseen_wounds/>, accessed May 13, 2016.

21   Meyer, "Guilt and Moral Injury."

the road; that a dead cat is not an improvised explosive device; that kids don't throw grenades at people even if those people are outsiders occupying their country; that mortar rounds don't fall from the sky as he walks to the toilet or to the shower or to the mess hall; and that those appointed to positions of power are supposed to protect life, not destroy it.

> PTSD appeared in my life when the world no longer was a safe place; when I realized I did not trust the roads anymore; when children became a mortal threat; when every beat of my heart pumped fear into my body, reminding me that my life was expendable and could be over at any moment; when death became real, and present, and graphic, and refused to leave my side, and forced me into isolation.

His life changed after he came back from Iraq. He became withdrawn from society so as to avoid the fear and anxiety he experienced from interacting with the outside world.

> When I go to a public place, such as a bookstore, I always prefer to sit with my back to the wall, and in a place that allows me to see what's going on around me. I like to be in clear sight of all the exits. And I always identify places that could provide cover and concealment from possible attacks.

Moral injury is different, Mejía says. PTSD resulted from a violation of trust between himself and the world outside himself. But moral injury violated his internal world. As he observed a young man through the sight of his rifle, a voice inside himself told him not to squeeze the trigger.

> [C]onscience is the most secret place where we can see the unwritten law of morality. . . . When I opened fire that day, I violated that law and desecrated the most sacred sanctuary of my being. As I observed that young man through the sight of my rifle, I was staring at a point of no return, the very Rubicon of my life, and I crossed it.
>
> My moral injury is the pain I inflicted upon the very core of my being when I took something I could never give back.[22]

There is strong support among professionals for the following analysis. PTSD is based more on fear and a sense of constant threat or helplessness, while moral injury is based more on guilt, shame, anger or outrage.[23] A person with PTSD has lost his

---

22 Camilo E. Mejía, "Healing Moral Injury: A Lifelong Journey," *Fellowship: A Magazine of Peacemaking*, Winter 2011, <http://forusa.org/fellowship/2011/winter/healing-moral-injury/11606>, accessed May 13, 2016.

23 Maguen and Litz (2012), 2–3; Litz et al., 698. *See also*, Schwinn, "Moral Injury," and Meyer, "Guilt and Moral Injury," 26.

sense of safety; a person with moral injury has lost his ability to trust.[24] This is a "loss of trust in previously deeply held beliefs about one's own or others' ability to keep our shared moral covenant,"[25] or about the acts of peers and leaders who betray their expectations in grievous ways.[26]

Two years after returning from combat tours in Iraq and Afghanistan, a Marine staff sergeant, Felipe Tremillo, was

> still haunted by images of the women and children he saw suffer from the violence and destruction of war in Afghanistan. "Terrible things happened to the people we are supposed to be helping," he said. "We'd do raids, going in people's homes and people would get hurt." . . .
>
> American soldiers had to act that way, Tremillo recognizes, "in order to stay safe." But the moral compromise, the willful casting aside of his own values, broke something inside him, changing him into someone he hardly recognizes, or admires.[27]

Steve Dundas was a U.S. Navy chaplain who went to Iraq in 2007. Dundas returned home broken. "Seeing the devastation of Iraqi cities and towns, some of it caused by us, some by the insurgents and the civil war that we brought about, hit me to the core. . . . I felt lied to by our senior leadership. And I felt those lies cost too many thousands of American lives and far too much destruction." His faith in God and in his country were shattered.[28]

According to a retired navy psychiatrist, patients who experience moral injury are likely to be highly moral.[29] It is people who have strong moral beliefs who are more likely to experience moral injury: "anguish, guilt, and shame are signs of an intact conscience and self."[30]

For Jacob George, a veteran of three tours in Afghanistan, the post-traumatic horror he experienced was not a disorder, but a natural human response to the inhumanity of war.[31] While serving in Afghanistan as a U.S. Army sergeant, Jacob George said,

---

24 Meyer, ibid.

25 Nash and Litz, 4.

26 Maguen and Litz (2015).

27 David Wood, "Healing: Can We Treat Moral Wounds?" *Huffington Post*, March 20, 2014, <http://projects.huffingtonpost.com/moral-injury/healing>, accessed May 13, 2016.

28 David Wood, "The Grunts: Damned If They Kill, Damned If They Don't," *Huffington Post*, March 18, 2014, <http://projects.huffingtonpost.com/moral-injury/the-grunts>, accessed May 13, 2019. If one reads nothing else about moral injury, this is the article to read.

29 Schwinn, "Moral Injury," quoting Dr. William Nash.

30 Litz et al., 701.

31 Abby Zimet, "Soldier's Heart: Jacob George's Sorrowful Ride Till the End," *Common Dreams*, September 29, 2014, <http://www.commondreams.org/further/2014/09/29/soldiers-heart-jacob-georges-sorrowful-ride-till-end>, accessed May 13, 2016. *See,*

There were lots of incidents that bothered me. The interrogation of people at Bagram . . . people are stored all around Afghanistan, micro-prisons, no one knows where they are at or why they are being held; the interrogation of children, arms tied behind their backs on a flight line with helicopters blowing sand and pushing them into the wire behind them . . . but one incident stands out. We were in Khost. Two Apache gunships winchestered a building without knowing who was in it. My job was to carry two bags of body parts out of the building to figure out who it was. We had no idea if they were civilians or insurgents. . . . [We] never determined who the arms and legs belonged to. Total negligence. We had no idea who was in there, more than likely women and children.[32]

U.S. Army Specialist Brock McIntosh recalled attacking targets without knowing whether the enemy was present: "I was confused about what we did. We didn't know if we took out any enemy. We destroyed a building; destroyed irrigation canals; shot up a village and shot at houses and the report said we did an awesome job."[33]

A U.S. Marine by the name of Nick Rudolph described the following as "the worst, best experience" of his life. During a gun battle in Afghanistan, Nick spotted somebody darting around the corner of a wall firing a rifle at him and other Marines. "He sees the shooter is a child, maybe 13. With only a split second to decide, he squeezes the trigger and ends the boy's life." Nick has lived with the story for more than three years. "He was just a kid. But I'm sorry, I'm trying not to get shot and I don't want any of my brothers getting hurt, so when you are put in that kind of situation . . . it's shitty that you have to, like . . . shoot him. You know it's wrong. But . . . you have no choice." The boy's death haunts him, mired in the swamp of moral confusion and contradiction so familiar to returning veterans of the wars in Iraq and Afghanistan.[34]

Brandon Bryant was a drone pilot sitting at the controls of a "cockpit" in a special Air Force unit in New Mexico. "When Bryan pressed a button in New Mexico, someone died on the other side of the world." Bryant remembers an incident

when a Predator drone was circling in a figure-eight pattern in the sky above Afghanistan, more than 10,000 kilometers (6,250 miles) away. There

---

Maguen and Litz (2012), 1: "even in optimal operational contexts, some combat and operational experiences can inevitably transgress deeply held beliefs that undergird a service member's humanity."

32   Jacob George, interview by Carl Mirra, December 16, 2010, in Carl Mirra, "Insurgents, accidental guerrillas and valley-ism: an oral history of oppositional US soldiers' attitudes toward the enemy in Afghanistan," *Cambridge Review of International Affairs*, Vol. 26, No. 2 (2013), 465, <http://dx.doi.org/10.1080/09557571.2013.784577>, access denied May 13, 2016.

33   Brock McIntosh, interview by Carl Mirra, December 16, 2010, Mirra, "Insurgents," 465.

34   Wood, "Grunts."

was a flat-roofed house made of mud, with a shed used to hold goats in the crosshairs, as Bryant recalls. When he received the order to fire, he pressed a button with his left hand and marked the roof with a laser. The pilot sitting next to him pressed the trigger on a joystick [control column], causing the drone to launch a Hellfire missile. . . .

With seven seconds left to go, there was no one to be seen on the ground. Bryant could still have diverted the missile at that point. Then it was down to three seconds. . . . Suddenly a child walked around the corner. . . .

Bryant saw a flash on the screen: the explosion. Parts of the building collapsed. The child had disappeared. Bryant had a sick feeling in his stomach.

"Did we just kill a kid?" he asked the man sitting next to him.

"Yeah, I guess that was a kid," the pilot replied.

"Was that a kid?" they wrote into a chat window on the monitor.

Then someone they didn't know answered, someone sitting in a military command center somewhere in the world who had observed their attack. "No, that was a dog," the person wrote.

They reviewed the scene on video. A dog on two legs?[35]

What Are the Consequences of Moral Injury?

In the words of Camilo Mejía, moral injury "is a pain that redefined my life, and that not only transformed who I was, but continues to transform me." It is not something "like a backpack that I can strap to my body and drop at any time, but something that shapes an important part of who I am as a human being."

> While I was in Iraq, when people in charge exercised poor judgment, others got badly hurt or killed. As a result, I developed a sense of suspicion of people in positions of authority and control. Today that suspicion applies to everyone from physicians to bus drivers. . . .[36]

---

35   Nicola Abé, translated from German by Christopher Sultan "Dreams in Infrared: The Woes of an American Drone Operator," *SpiegelOnLine2012*, December 14, 2012, <http://www.spiegel.de/international/world/pain-continues-after-war-for-american-drone-pilot-a-872726-druck.html>, accessed May 13, 2016. *See also*, Andrea Germanos, "I resign because I refuse to serve as an empire chaplain," *Common Dreams*, May 13, 2016: less than a month after army chaplain John Antal was deployed to the Kandahar Airbase in Afghanistan, a grandmother who was gathering okra in a field was killed by a U.S. drone strike; months later Chaplain Antal watched the testimony of a thirteen-year-old boy who said his grandmother was blown to bits by two hellfire missiles on the day in question, and asked his American audience, "Why?" <https://portside.org/print/2016-05-14/i-resign-because-i-refuse-serve-empire-chaplain>, accessed May 14, 2016.

36   Mejía, "Healing Moral Injury."

"Moral Injury has a slow burn quality that often takes time to manifest and to be detected."[37] In Brian Willson's case, it took twelve years before he could talk about the incident that changed his life. When individual service members and units experience unanticipated moral choices and demands, they may have a delayed impact.

> [M]ost service members are able to assimilate most of what they do and see in war because of training and preparation, the warrior culture, their role, the exigencies of various missions, rules of engagement and other context demands, the messages and behavior of peers and leaders, and the acceptance (and recognition of sacrifices) by families and the culture at large. However, once redeployed and separated from the military culture and context (e.g., with family or after retirement), some service members may have difficulty accommodating various morally conflicting experiences.[38]

"[A]n individual with moral injury may begin to view him or herself as immoral, irredeemable, and un-reparable or believe that he or she lives in an immoral world."[39]

"If the service members feel remorse about various behaviors, they will experience guilt; if they blame themselves because of perceived personal inadequacy and flaw, they will experience shame." Such individuals may become "convinced and confident that not only their actions, but *they* are unforgiveable."[40] They fail to forgive themselves and they expect to be judged and rejected. Then they withdraw from relationships and isolate themselves, feeling helpless and hopeless. Focusing on their own internal distress, they may have less empathy for others.[41]

People with post-traumatic stress disorder and moral injury experience some of the same things: anger, depression, anxiety, insomnia, nightmares, reckless behavior and self-medication with alcohol or drugs. They recall and re-experience painful thoughts and images. Their emotional intensity may be uncontrollable and inappropriate. They may avoid situations or people that trigger memories. Close relationships with family and friends, especially those involving intimacy, suffer and deteriorate when normal emotional responses become numb. They may respond that God is not good or there is no God.[42]

But people with moral injury also experience sorrow, grief, regret, shame. Negative consequences of moral injury include distrust of others, isolation, fatalism,

---

37   Rhonda Quillin, "The Importance of Unit Climate in Effecting Moral Injury," Command and General Staff College Foundation, Inc., 2014 Ethics Symposium Archive, 4. [No longer online.]

38   Litz et al., 697.

39   Ibid., 698.

40   Ibid., 700.

41   Ibid., 700, 701; and Army, "Moral Injury: Unseen Wounds."

42   Meyer, "Guilt and Moral Injury," 15, 24, 27; and Marine Corps COS, A-3.

self-condemnation, self-destructive and self-harming behaviors, spiritual damage and loss of faith.[43]

A former U.S. Marine, Stephen Canty, explained:

> "We spent two deployments where you couldn't trust a single person except the guys next to you." Back in civilian society now, . . . "we have trouble trusting people." . . .
>
> "You just can't communicate the knowledge of war to somebody else. It's something that you know or don't know, and once you know it you can't un-know it and you have to deal with that knowledge."[44]

While serving as a drone pilot, Brandon Bryant observed people in Afghanistan for weeks. He felt that he got to know them. "They were good daddies." He wanted to do something that saved lives rather than take them away. He wrote in his diary, "On the battlefield there are no sides, just bloodshed. Total war. Every horror witnessed. I wish my eyes would rot." When he came home, he couldn't sleep. He began talking back to his superior officers. He broke up with his girlfriend after she asked him about the burden he carries. He told her about it. But it was a hardship that neither he nor she could cope with or share. He could not "just switch and go back to normal life."[45]

According to people who work with veterans at the Soul Repair Center of Brite Divinity School, there is "no basic un-training for combat veterans." Return to civilian life can be even more difficult than serving in war and can last a lifetime: "Who are we? How do we come to grips with what we have seen or done? Can we trust ourselves to do what is right?" While in combat,

> [e]motional numbing allows the person to put aside feelings and do whatever it takes to survive or help others survive. . . . Later such numbing may include a sense of not really being a person, feelings of not fitting in, believing that no one can understand, . . . and not being able to feel emotions in situations calling for intimacy, tenderness, sexuality or grief. . . .

Or, said another way, "We come home to a nation that either ignores us or blindly praises us for our service, yet how can we accept such thanks when we feel ashamed, not just of what we did, but of who we are?"[46]

---

43   Meyer, ibid.; and Marine Corps COS, ibid.

44   David Wood, "The Recruits—When Right and Wrong Are Hard to Tell Apart," *Huffington Post*, March 19, 2014, <http://projects.huffingtonpost.com/moral-injury/the-recruits>, accessed May 14, 2016.

45   Abé, "Dreams in Infrared."

46   Soul Repair Center at Brite Divinity School, "Moral Injury Meeting: A Twelve-Step Program toward Recovery from Moral Injury for Veterans and Their Families and

Many veterans isolate themselves, not knowing how to respond when thanked for their service or asked about their wartime experiences:

Unable to explain, even to a wife or girlfriend, the joy and horror of combat. That *yes, I killed a child,* or *yes, soldiers I was responsible for got killed and it was my fault.* Or, *yes, I saw a person I loved get blown apart.* From there it can be an easy slide into self-medication with drugs or alcohol, or overwork. Thoughts of suicide can beckon.[47]

When Vince Emanuele returned from his second tour as a Marine in Iraq, he was badly addicted to drugs, alcohol, and violence. "The act of killing someone is not simply traumatic and brutal," he says, "it's also invigorating and powerful."

If someone didn't say "thank you" at the supermarket, I thought about the various ways in which I could torture them. When someone at the local gas station wouldn't hold the door open for the next patron, I fantasized about killing them. Their lack of discipline and manners made me physically ill. Sometimes, when I drove around town, I'd find myself dreaming about a confrontation with someone, *anyone.* I wanted to show them what *war* was all about. I wanted to release my anger through violence, often imagining the most gruesome scenarios. Really, I wanted them to feel the same anxiety and anger that I felt during those days. My thinking was shallow: Why should they go through life unscathed by *war?*

Of course, all of this had a tremendously negative impact on my life. . . . Each day is a struggle. The more I try and put the war behind me, the more the dog of war bites at my heels as I run away from the grief. One day, my mother asked me to stop smoking in her and my father's garage. I picked up a garbage can, threw it at the wall and threatened to kill her. Two hours later I was sobbing, head in hands, trying to explain to my friend what happened. He didn't know what to say. How could he?[48]

Friends," no date, 5, 10, <http://brite.edu/wp-content/uploads/2013/07/12Step-Moral-Injury-Meeting-Book.pdf>, accessed May 14, 2016.

47 Wood, "Grunts."

48 Vince Emanuele, "All of My Friends Are Dying," *TeleSur TV,* November 5, 2014, <http://www.telesurtv.net/english/opinion/All-of-My-Friends-are-Dying-20141105-0014.html>, accessed May 14, 2016. Vince Emanuele was one of the veterans who joined the Standing Rock Sioux Tribe's "peace and prayer" demonstration against the North Dakota oil pipeline. "'A lot of people here are willing to sacrifice their body, willing to give their life,' said Vincent Emanuele, thirty-two, a former Marine who served in Iraq and has spoken out extensively against what he called a futile war. 'You might as well die for something that means something.'"Jack Healy, "As North Dakota Pipeline Is Blocked, Veterans at Standing Rock Cheer," *New York Times,* December 5, 2016, <http://www.nytimes.com/2016/12/05/us/veterans-north-dakota-standing-rock.html?_r=0>, accessed December 19, 2016.

"We habitually let other people determine how we act, what we value, who we are," says the Soul Repair Center: "When I hit people, I am announcing I'm powerless and I don't know how to get along with people." "If I want control, I will blame someone else. I want others to change first."[49]

Suicide is the ultimate self-punishment.[50] There appears to be a link between suicide and guilt for having killed, or failing to prevent death or injury. A significant percentage of suicidal veterans killed women and children while emotionally out of control due to fear or rage. Killing results in "more easily being able to turn the weapon of destruction onto oneself." In theory at least, a suicidal person feels that he or she does not belong with other people, is a burden on others or society, and has the ability to overcome the fear and pain of suicide.[51]

The suicide rate for veterans has been more than double the suicide rate for civilians. "Records from 48 states show the annual suicide rate among veterans is about 30 for every 100,000 of population, compared to a civilian rate of about 14 per 100,000." Of suicides nationally between 2005 and 2011, 49,000, nearly one in five, were veterans.[52]

Military spouses and children may also be vulnerable to moral injury. Military spouses and children can experience moral injury directly when they hear stories or see images of death and carnage, especially of women and children, and indirectly when the military parent withdraws or resorts to violence or self-destructive behavior. Children may seriously act out at home or in school. They may blame themselves for changes in their parents' behavior, or divorce, or the death of a family member. "To the extent members of families are interdependent, moral injuries resulting from betrayals of trust within the family can be transmitted and retransmitted between family members like waves generated by the fall of a rock in a small pond."[53]

---

49   Soul Repair Center, "Twelve-Step Program," 11.

50   Nash and Litz, 372.

51   Maguen and Litz (2012), 2, 4.

52   Jeff Hargarten, Forrest Burnson, Bonnie Campo, and Chase Cook, *Center for Public Integrity*, August 30, 2013, updated May 19, 2014, <http://www.publicintegrity.org/2013/08/30/13292/suicide-rate-veterans-far-exceeds-civilian-population>, accessed May 14, 2016. "Based on the 2012 data, VA estimated the number of Veteran deaths by suicide averaged 22 per day. The current analysis indicates that in 2014, an average of 20 Veterans a day died from suicide." Since 2001, the rate of suicide among male Veterans who used VA services increased 11%, while rate of suicide increased 35% among male Veterans who do not use VA services; the rate of suicide among female Veterans who use VA services increased 4.6% while the rate of suicide increased 98% among female Veterans who do not use VA services." Press release, Department of Veterans Affairs, Office of Public and Intergovernmental Affairs, "VA Conducts Nations' Largest Analysis of Veteran Suicide," July 7, 2016, <http://www.va.gov/opa/pressrel/pressrelease.cfm?id=2801>, accessed October 28, 2016.

53   Nash and Litz, 371.

What Is Needed?

The Department of Defense does not formally recognize moral injury, but the Pentagon is funding a program to explore ways to adapt PTSD therapies for Marines suffering from moral injury. It is unknown whether evidence-based treatments for PTSD can sufficiently reduce war-related moral injury.[54] "New forms of therapy for moral injury are being explored, and moral injury as a concept is increasingly being discussed in military treatment facilities."[55]

A battalion chaplain in Iraq at the end of a twelve-month combat tour gathered the troops together for a kind of ritual of forgiveness: "He asked the soldiers to jot down everything they were sorry for, ashamed of, angry about or regretted. The papers went into a makeshift stone baptismal font, and as the soldiers stood silently in a circle, the papers burned to ash. . . . The idea was to leave all the most troubling things behind in Iraq."[56]

It is clearly the intent of the Armed Forces to return troops to active duty. The Naval Medical Center in San Diego has a residential program called Overcoming Adversity and Stress Injury Support (OASIS). The mission statement in its Patient Handbook explicitly states one of its goals is to "facilitate the return of troops to full duty with improved self esteem, resilience, and capacity for relationships."[57]

At an Armed Forces Public Health Conference, methods and goals of treatment for moral injury were listed as

- Rationally assessing own or others culpability
- Making or seeking amends
- Compassionate forgiveness of self and others[58]

There appears to be general agreement that self-forgiveness and forgiveness of others is central to healing from moral injuries. But little is known about what treatments best promote forgiveness.[59]

54   Maguen and Litz (2015).

55   Svanderwerff, "Navy Medicine Perspective: Moral Injury," *Navy Medicine Live, The Official Blog of the U.S. Navy and Marine Corps Health Care*, April 2, 2015, <http:// navymedicine.navylive.dodlive.mil/archives/8437>, accessed May 14, 2015.

56   Wood, "Healing."

57   Naval Medical Center San Diego, "Patient Handbook," updated July 26, 2013, *Oasis Program—Overcoming Adversity and Stress Injury Support*, <http://www.med.navy. mil/sites/nmcsd/Patients/Documents/oasis/OASIS%20Patient%20Handbook%20 JUL2013.docx>, accessed May 14, 2016.

58   William P. Nash, Richard J. Westphal, and Brett Litz, "Trauma, Loss, and Moral Injury: Different Approaches for Prevention and Treatment," Armed Forces Public Health Conference (March 23, 2011), 10, <http://www.pdhealth.mil/education/2011_ Presentations/AFPCH%2011%20Trauma,%20Loss,%20and%20Moral%20Injury.pdf>, accessed June 5, 2015, no longer online. *See also*, Litz et al., 704, re making amends.

59   Nash and Litz, 371; Litz et al., 702.

Because of shame, guilt and anger, and the expectation of being judged or shunned, it is likely that the person experiencing moral injury has not wanted to talk about it. Yet talking, re-experiencing moral injury memories, may be a necessary first step.[60] It is important for the individual to be able to express remorse and to reach his or her own conclusions about the causes of the events. The person's judgments and beliefs about the transgressions may be quite appropriate and accurate.[61] While guilt and shame can help a person to see his or her own culpability, according to a military chaplain, these emotions can have adverse effects when the person experiencing them is not also connected with a stable source of compassion.[62]

Camilo Mejía came to believe that "the transformative power of moral injury cannot be found in the pursuit of our own moral balance as an end goal, but in the journey of repairing the damage we have done onto others." Due to his experience in Iraq, he added, "I no longer view the suffering of others as alien to my own experience. I view hunger, disease, and the brutality of war and occupation as global-scale issues, not as issues of individual nations." And, repairing the damage "within ourselves will require a life-long commitment to atone for the wrongs we have committed against others."[63]

The question remains whether anything other than rejection of warfare and taking action in affirmation of life can truly bring about healing. Jacob George spoke of the limitations of the Department of Veterans Affairs. The VA "isn't designed to address the depths of the wounds we have." The VA doesn't "really look at the soul and how the soul has been injured in war." He told his therapist that he had thrown back his medals at a demonstration, and that act had released something inside of him. "[T]he VA could never endorse something like that," his therapist responded. "The VA couldn't say, 'Hey, look, you need to organize a protest. You need to march to the Pentagon with 100,000 veterans.'" George replied: "Do you hear what you're saying? You're telling me that you can't offer me the actual healing rituals and ceremonies that I need, that an entire generation of people needs in order to heal their soul."[64] Jacob George committed suicide on September 17, 2014.[65]

As a combat veteran who had been twice deployed to Iraq, Vince Emanuele had viewed his life as "worthless, easily discardable. Suicide was always an option.

60   Nash and Litz, 372, and Litz et al., 702.

61   Litz et al., 702–3.

62   Bautistas por le Paz, "What Your Church Can Do about Moral Injury of War," Introduction by Zachary Moon.

63   Mejía, "Healing Moral Injury."

64   Truthdig, "Beloved War Veteran Commits Suicide," September 19, 2014, <http://www.truthdig.com/avbooth/item/beloved_young_war_veteran_kills_self_after_obamas_war_announcement_20140919>, accessed May 14, 2016.

65   Geoff Millard, "Jacob George, Hillbilly Storyteller, Survives 3 Tours in Afghanistan But Not His Road Back Home," *Huffington Post*, October 23, 2014, updated December 23, 2014, <http://www.huffingtonpost.com/geoff-millard/jacob-george-hillbilly-st_b_6030246.html>, accessed May 14, 2016.

Homicide was always a fantasy." In 2006 he became involved with the antiwar movement and linked up with Iraq Veterans Against the War. Unlike when he was in the Marine Corps, he felt comfortable in the antiwar community. "[M]any of us simply needed a new mission, a mission dedicated to peace and justice, not war and destruction." But, he discovered, activism was not enough. His activist friends were not immune to suicide.

> In the veteran community, suicide is often joked about. . . . Often, the only way to engage with *death* is to obscure the darkness with a fog of *humor*. . . . It's the only way to deal with extreme levels of violence and death. Dark humor, as it's often called, helps us deal with the emptiness of death. But the jokes only function as a topical ointment. At home, alone, or with loved ones, we're reminded of this emptiness. It's an emptiness that will not go away.
>
> . . . Victims of US aggression, unlike US veterans and their families . . . live . . . in a constant war-zone. While veterans like myself hope to catch a decent night's sleep, Iraqis and Afghans are lucky to have a bed to sleep in. . . . Sure, veterans have it bad. But those we occupied have it much worse. This dynamic must be recognized and confronted in a serious fashion if we ever hope to bridge the gap between justice and absurdity.
>
> Meanwhile, my friends continue to die—my Iraqi friends, my Afghan friends, my Syrian friends, my Libyan friends, my Pakistani friends, my Palestinian friends, my Somalian friends, my veteran friends.[66]

The Making of a Conscientious Objector

Jeremy Hinzman, during Basic Training

Jeremy Hinzman volunteered for four years in the army, and he chose to be in the infantry. He earned an Expert Infantryman's Badge, and was assigned to a parachute regiment.[67]

Hinzman described basic training as the collective shedding of self. During basic training (January–May 2001) trainees would march around yelling, "Trained to Kill, Kill We Will." When they began rifle marksmanship training, during the first week they shot at black circles: "Then the second week the black circles have shoulders. The third week they have torsos . . ." It became a reflex, a target.[68]

The purpose of a Parachute Airborne Regiment was to seize airfields, drop behind enemy lines: "Wipe out whatever's on the airfield that's preventing you from

---

66   Emanuele, "All of My Friends Are Dying."

67   Immigration and Refugee Board, Jeremy Dean Hinzman et al., claimants, File No: TA4-01429, Toronto, Canada, December 6, 2004, 43–44, 57, 63.

68   Ibid., 52, 69, 70.

carrying out your mission. Set up a secure landing zone for allied aircraft."[69] More specifically, he explained:

> If there's hindrances or enemy on the airfield you deal with that. If you need to establish a landing strip you have to find level ground. If you need to blow up stuff that's in the way or that's obstructing you or other people from landing then you take care of that. . . . [Y]our sole function in the infantry is to eliminate the enemy that you encounter . . . [with] any means at your disposal.[70]

When asked what caused him to apply for conscientious objector status in 2002, Hinzman responded that it was a gradual unfolding of events, through training, and witnessing what was happening in the world at the time. "I came to the conclusion that I couldn't kill. That all violence does is perpetuate more violence." When asked what impact the birth of his son had on his decision, Hinzman replied that he "didn't ever want to have the possibility of killing babies."[71]

Geoffrey Millard, Briefing on the Way to Iraq

Geoffrey Millard described a briefing when he first arrived in Kuwait. The gist of the briefing was that "[a]ll these fucking hajis are out to kill you. You can't trust any of these fucking hajis." Then the colonel asked a simple question:

> "What do you do if one of these fucking haji kids is in the middle of the road and your convoy is going straight at this fucking kid?" And somebody yelled, "Stop." And he says, "No. You just fucking killed your entire unit because they ambushed you with this little fucking haji kid." And so he says, "What do you do when you've got this little haji kid in the middle of the road and your convoy is speeding at him?" And someone else says, "Turn down another road." And he says, "Wrong. No fucking time."
> So someone else begrudgingly says, "Run him over." And he says, "Exactly." "One of these little fucking haji kids is in your way, you don't put your entire unit's life on the line. You run the little fucking haji over." He yelled, "Hoo-rah." We responded with a "Hoo-rah." The briefing was over. That's what we were left with.[72]

---

69 Ibid., 67.
70 Ibid., 68–69.
71 Ibid., 76, 100.
72 Geoffrey Millard, in Mary Susannah Robbins, ed., *Peace Not Terror: Leaders of the Antiwar Movement Speak Out Against U.S. Foreign Policy Post 9/11* (Lanham, MD: Lexington Books, 2008), Testimony on War Crimes, Iraq Veterans Against the War, Preliminary Report, "Citizens' Hearing on the Legality of U.S. Actions in Iraq: The Case of Lt. Ehren Watada," Tacoma, WA, January 20–21, 2007, 199.

The word "haji," Millard explained, was traditionally a term of respect for someone who had completed the *Hajj*, the pilgrimage to Mecca, one of the Pillars of Islam. Yet American service members use it to racially dehumanize the Iraqi people. "Because no one can possibly see a little kid in the road and run them over. No one can possibly look through their sight post and see a human being and still pull the trigger. So we're forced to dehumanize. And at this point it's being used as racial dehumanization."[73]

Until he heard the colonel make the remark about hajis, Millard thought such comments were made by the guys on the ground just trying to make it through every day. What he realized at that moment was that "it comes from the top and works its way down. That was a division level staff, the second-highest level of command in Iraq, . . . and it was pushed down directly to our units. . . ."[74]

Geoffrey Millard, in Iraq

Geoffrey Millard is an example of someone who witnessed betrayals of what he felt was morally right and became an "Iraqi war refuser." Millard was a staff sergeant for thirteen months in Iraq, filing paperwork in a rear operation center. In 2007, as a member of Iraq Veterans Against the War, he testified at a Citizens' Hearing on the Legality of U.S. Actions in Iraq.[75]

The turning point for him was an incident at a traffic control point in Iraq where young soldiers, who were very scared and nervous, would point heavy machine guns at civilian vehicles. Iraqis, he said, were not accustomed to sudden roadblocks. They drove very quickly and would stop very quickly.

> And on one particular day . . . as the vehicle sped towards this traffic control point, an eighteen-year-old kid . . . a Private First Class . . . made the split-second decision that that vehicle was a threat. He pressed the butterfly trigger on his .50-caliber machine gun and put more than 200 rounds into that vehicle. He then stood there and watched as the results of his decision were extracted from that vehicle: A mother, a father, and two children: boy age four, girl age three.[76]

At the briefing that evening, the colonel said to the entire division level staff: "If these fucking hajis [would] learn to drive, this shit wouldn't happen."[77]

At a certain point, Millard refused to return to his unit. "I told my unit that I would not be coming back and that I resigned from the U.S. military."[78]

---

73   Ibid., 199–200.
74   Ibid., 200.
75   Ibid., 196–201.
76   Ibid., 198.
77   Ibid., 199.
78   Ibid., 196.

Camilo Mejía, in and after Iraq

Camilo Mejía served as a staff sergeant in Iraq from April to September 2003.[79] At the main base in al Assad, there was a concrete structure, enclosed in concertina wire, where they held prisoners and used sleep deprivation to get them ready for interrogation:

> The prisoners—called enemy combatants—were barefoot, hooded and bound with plastic ties. We were told you're here to run this camp. We were instructed to keep the enemy combatants on sleep deprivation. . . . The way we did that was to yell at them, tell them constantly to get up and down. But sometimes yelling didn't work because they were so tired. Someone would then hit the wall with a huge sledge hammer. . . . The prisoners were hooded, so when they hit the wall with a sledge hammer it sounded like a huge explosion. It scared the hell out of the prisoners. When that didn't work, they produced a 9 millimeter pistol and put it to their head and cocked it. There was no bullet in it, but they made it seem like they were going to get shot in the head. The person you were doing it to would cry and scream. . . . They would let prisoners sleep for thirty seconds then wake them up to destroy their sense of time and space. . . .[80]

A lieutenant explained: "When you let them sleep thirty to forty-five seconds, after they've been awake for so long, you just totally fuck them up psychologically. Right now these hajjis, who slept for just forty-five seconds, don't know if they slept for a day, an hour, or five fucking minutes."[81]

The first time Mejía fired at a human being who died was in ar Ramadi. "[N]othing prepares you for it. You don't know what it does to you when you fire a rifle at a human being." His platoon was responding to a political protest that had turned violent:[82]

> The protesters started throwing grenades at the mayor's office, and my squad had been sent to the rooftop to occupy defensive positions. Our platoon leader relayed to us the order to shoot anyone who threw anything that looked like a grenade. . . . A young Iraqi emerged from one corner of the street, all by himself, and carrying something in his right hand. The object turned out to be a grenade, and just before he threw it we all opened fire on

---

79　Carl Mirra, *Soldiers and Citizens: An Oral History of Operation Iraqi Freedom from the Battlefield to the Pentagon* (New York: Palgrave Macmillan, 2008), 58.

80　Ibid., 62.

81　Camilo Mejía, *Road from ar Ramadi: The Private Rebellion of Staff Sergeant Camilo Mejía, An Iraq War Memoir* (Chicago: Haymarket Books, 2008), 53; 1st ed. New York: New Press, 2007.

82　Mirra, *Soldiers*, 63.

him. The grenade exploded far from everyone and the young man was shot to death. . . . It is impossible to say exactly when I fired my weapon, I just know that I fired it. This incident stayed on my mind for many weeks. The image of the young man, killed by a rain of fire, is still fresh in my memory. Many times I have told myself that maybe the bullets from my rifle only touched his leg [or] maybe his shoulder, that maybe I missed him completely. . . . [T]he thing that troubles me the most, although this action was ordered and justified by the rules of engagement, is that I know this man we killed had no chance of hurting us, he was too far away.[83]

In May 2003, twenty minutes after their return from a firefight, Mejía's squad was ordered to go out again and set up a traffic control point in the vicinity of the fight.[84] When they had gone about two miles down the road that divided ar Ramadi north and south, they saw an object the size of a shoe box in the road. Then a blast engulfed the front of one of their vehicles, and bullets were hitting the concrete all around them. Mejía began firing in the general direction of the attackers. They made it back to their base with no injuries.[85]

During a briefing upon their return, Mejía was asked why his squad did not stay and fight. "I had a feeling we were going to get ambushed, so I . . . told them to return fire and keep moving back to base," Mejía responded. The briefing continued: "What we want to know . . . is why you gave the order to leave the scene instead of fighting." "I thought the SOP [standard operating procedure] for a moving ambush was to return fire and keep moving," Mejía replied. "You sent the wrong message to the enemy," said the commander.[86] "By getting away . . . you let them know that we are afraid. It was a victory for them," added the First Sergeant.[87]

Now we were dealing with a command that was asking us to expose ourselves unnecessarily to serious danger in order to "send the right message." They knew damn well that we had acted according to regulations, just as we knew that it was our asses on the line while they were safe back at the base. I left the command post with my two team leaders, wondering who the real enemy was in Iraq. . . .[88]

While in Iraq, his thoughts "had more to do with surviving than with questioning the war." Going home on leave gave him the opportunity to listen to his conscience.

---

83 Camilo Mejía, Application for Conscientious Objector Status, 41–42. A lengthier description by Mejía of this event appears in Mirra, *Soldiers*, 63.

84 Mejía, *ar Ramadi*, 62, 66.

85 Ibid., 70–71.

86 Ibid., 73–74.

87 Ibid., 76.

88 Ibid., 76.

People wanted to know about his experience in war. Answering them took him back to the horrors of combat, firefights, ambushes: "the time I saw that young Iraqi being dragged by his shoulders through a pool of his own blood, the time that other man was decapitated by machine gun fire, the time my friend shot a child through the chest."[89]

He learned about conscientious objection, but he kept thinking, "How could I be a CO after I did all these things in Iraq?"[90]

> I have held a rifle to a man's face, a man on the ground and in front of his mother, children, and wife, and not knowing why I did it. I have walked by the headless body of an innocent man right after our machine guns decapitated him. I have seen a soldier broken down inside because he killed a child. I have seen an old man on his knees, crying, with his arms raised to the sky, perhaps asking God why we were taking the lifeless body of his son. . . .[91]

It took Mejía a while to realize that there is no more compelling argument against war than war itself. "It is not what you have done, but what you are willing or unwilling to do after experiencing these things."[92] He came to a decision. "I was done with violence; I was done with war. I didn't want to hurt a human being again in my life."[93]

After the end of his leave, in October 2003, Mejía was found to be AWOL (absent without leave). In March 2004 he declared himself a conscientious objector and applied for conscientious objector status. In May 2004, he was convicted of desertion by a military tribunal. He was sentenced to a year in military prison, was stripped in rank to private, and was issued a bad conduct discharge. Amnesty International declared him to be a prisoner of conscience, having concluded that he was a "genuine conscientious objector whose objection to war evolved in response to witnessing human rights violations in Iraq." He was released from prison on February 15, 2005.[94]

> My sense is that a lot of people in the military feel that their duties to the military and their duty to their conscience are in complete disagreement. . . . [T]hey might be afraid to act on their conscience because they could go to jail or be called cowards. But you really can't be free unless you follow your heart. I have no regret for taking a stand against this war and against killing. There is no greater freedom than the freedom to follow your conscience.[95]

---

89   Mejía, CO application, 39.
90   Mirra, *Soldiers*, 65.
91   Mejía, CO application, 44–45.
92   Mirra, *Soldiers*, 65.
93   Ibid., 66.
94   Ibid., 58. The month in which he went AWOL was corrected by Camilo Mejía, e-mail, February 22, 2015: "I was not officially considered AWOL until after the end of my leave, which was October 15, 2003."
95   Mirra, *Soldiers*, 66.

Chapter 2.
International Law

WHERE DO OUR MORAL BELIEFS, OUR SENSE OF WHAT IS RIGHT AND WRONG, COME from? For some people it is their religious training and belief. For others, it is a comparable sense of what is moral and ethical.

Rory Fanning, who declared himself to be a conscientious objector while serving in Afghanistan, wrote that he wished he had known more about international law while trying to escape the clutches of the military:

> The urge to resist war starts as a feeling or an emotion. When you are surrounded by aggressive soldiers who reject your developing thoughts on the morality of what you are doing, it is extremely difficult to begin to present and articulate an argument detailing why you need to leave. . . . The law (international or otherwise) is what I needed to understand. I needed to see that there was authority in what I was trying to tell my chain of command beyond simple Bible passages. It is so easy to doubt yourself in such a situation. . . .[1]

In international law there are treaties, agreements, "just war" principles, and United Nations advisory memoranda, that set forth the principles and guidelines that have been developed primarily during the twentieth century in response to World Wars I and II and the Holocaust.

International recognition of conscientious objection to war has developed over a period of many years. However, because there is no consensus among nations, conscientious objectors are governed by the law of the country in which they live and must find a way to stand up for emerging international values in that context. At present, international law defines "conscientious objection" more broadly than do many nations including the United States and Israel.

International law recognizes "selective" as well as absolute conscientious objection. Conscientious objection to military service has recently been defined in United Nations guidelines as an objection to military service

> which "derives from principles and reasons of conscience, including profound convictions, arising from religious, moral, ethical, humanitarian or similar motives." Such an objection is not confined to **absolute conscientious objectors** [pacifists], that is those who object to all use of armed force or participation in all wars. It also encompasses those who believe that "the

---

1   E-mail from Rory Fanning to Alice Lynd, February 18, 2015.

use of force is justified in some circumstances but not in others, and that therefore it is necessary to object in those other cases" [**partial** or **selective objection** to military service]. A conscientious objection may develop over time, and thus volunteers may at some stage also raise claims based on conscientious objection, whether absolute or partial.[2]

And,

The right to conscientious objection applies to absolute, partial, or selective objectors, volunteers as well as conscripts before and after joining the armed forces; during peace time and during armed conflict. It includes objection to military service based on moral, ethical, humanitarian or similar motives.[3]

Crimes Against Peace, War Crimes, and Crimes Against Humanity

International law has developed along parallel and interlocking lines. The Hague Conventions, the Kellogg-Briand Pact, the Charter of the United Nations, the London Treaty that established the Nuremberg Principles, the Geneva Conventions and its later Protocols, and the Rome Statute of the International Criminal Court, renounced war or were intended to limit the means and methods used in self-defense.

The Universal Declaration of Human Rights, the International Covenant on Civil and Political Rights, the Convention Against Torture and the Istanbul Protocol, and the International Committee of the Red Cross, declared certain human rights as absolute: the right to life, the prohibition against torture and cruel, inhuman, or degrading treatment or punishment, and the right to freedom of thought, conscience, and religion.[4]

---

2   United Nations High Commissioner for Refugees, *Guidelines on International Protection No. 10*, "Claims to Refugee Status related to Military Service within the context of Article 1A(2) of the 1951 Convention and/or the 1967 Protocol relating to the Status of Refugees (hereafter, "UNHCR *Guidelines*"), ¶ 3 (emphasis and brackets in original), <http://www.refworld.org/pdfid/529ee33b4.pdf>, accessed November 3, 2016, citing UN Commission on Human Rights, Resolution 1998/77, "*Conscientious Objection to Military Service*," E/CN.4/RES/1998/77, April 22, 1998, <http://www.refworld.org/docid/3b00f0be10.html>; and UN *Conscientious Objection to Military Service*, E/CN.4/sub.2/1983/30/Rev. 1, 1985, ¶ 21, <http://www.refworld.org/pdfid/5107cd132.pdf>, accessed May 15, 2016.

3   UNHCR *Guidelines*, ¶ 11 and sources cited therein; *see*, ibid., n.27, "a number of countries do make provision for selective or partial conscientious objectors."

4   *See*, Office of the High Commissioner for Human Rights, "Note to the Chair of the Counter-Terrorism Committee: A Human Rights Perspective On Counter-Terrorist Measures," (September 23, 2002), <http://www.un.org/en/sc/ctc/docs/rights/2002_09_23_ctcchair_note.pdf>, accessed May 15, 2016.

Of particular relevance to the person who would fight under some circumstances (selective conscientious objector) are the "just war" principles, limiting warfare to military and not civilian targets; and using no more force than is militarily necessary.

The Hague Conventions

During the latter part of the nineteenth century and early twentieth century, conferences were convened at The Hague in the Netherlands to declare what were understood to be "the Laws and Customs of War on Land" according to already existing customary international law.[5]

The Hague Conventions of 1899 and 1907 and Regulations concerning the Laws and Customs of War on Land were attempts to define limits as to what warring parties were required to do or not do, for instance, to protect prisoners of war, civilians and others not engaged in the conflict. Examples are: forbidding the killing or wounding of an enemy who has laid down his arms or has surrendered; requiring prisoners of war to be treated humanely; prohibiting the use of materials calculated to cause unnecessary suffering such as poison (or chemical weapons); prohibiting attacks on undefended towns, villages, and homes; sparing hospitals, historic monuments or buildings dedicated to religion, art, or science, if they are not being used at the time for military purposes; and not punishing a population for acts of individuals for which they are not responsible (collective punishment).[6]

Where actions such as those prohibited by the Hague Conventions and Regulations are taking place, there will be conscientious objectors who refuse to participate.

Kellogg-Briand Pact

The "General Treaty for Renunciation of War as an Instrument of National Policy," better known as the "Kellogg-Briand Pact," was signed by fifteen parties (including Germany, Italy, Japan, France, Great Britain and the United States) on August 27,

---

5   International Committee of the Red Cross (hereafter, "ICRC"), "Convention (IV) respecting the Laws and Customs of War on Land and its annex: Regulations concerning the Laws and Customs of War on Land," The Hague, October 18, 1907, citing the Conference of Brussels in 1874, the First Hague Peace Conference of 1899, and the Second International Peace Conference in 1907. "The provisions of the two Conventions on land warfare, like most of the substantive provisions of the Hague Conventions of 1899 and 1907, are considered as embodying rules of customary international law. As such they are also binding on States which are not formally parties to them." In 1946, the Nüremberg International Military Tribunal said that rules of land warfare expressed in the Hague Convention of 1907 "undoubtedly represented an advance over existing International Law at the time of their adoption" and by 1939 (when Germany invaded Poland) were regarded as being declaratory of the laws and customs of war. These rules were partly reaffirmed and developed in the Geneva Conventions of 1949 and additional Protocols adopted in 1977. <http://www.icrc.org/ihl/INTRO/195>, accessed May 15, 2016.

6   Ibid., Regulations, Articles 4, 23, 25, 27, and 50.

1928 and ratified by forty-five countries as of July 25, 1929. The parties declared that "the time has come when a frank renunciation of war as an instrument of national policy should be made"; and they agreed that all changes in the relations between nations "should be sought only by pacific means. . . ."[7]

Charter of the United Nations

On June 25, 1945, at the end of World War II, after Germany had surrendered (shortly before the United States dropped two atomic bombs and Japan surrendered to the Allies), the Charter of the United Nations affirmed in Article 2(3) and (4) that: "All Members shall settle their international disputes by peaceful means in such a manner that international peace and security, and justice, are not endangered"; and "All Members shall refrain in their international relations from the threat or use of force against the territorial integrity or political independence of any state, or in any other manner inconsistent with the Purposes of the United Nations."[8]

However, Article 51 of the UN Charter provided for self-defense: "Nothing in the present Charter shall impair the inherent right of individual or collective self-defence if an armed attack occurs against a Member of the United Nations, until the Security Council has taken measures necessary to maintain international peace and security. . . ."[9] Since the UN Charter came into effect, nations that have resorted to the use of force have typically invoked self-defense or the right of collective defense.

Typically, conscientious objectors would fight to defend their homeland, but object to fighting a war of "collective self-defense" where the homeland is not under attack.

Treaty of London and Charter of the International Military Tribunal (Nuremberg Principles)

On August 8, 1945, two days after an atomic bomb fell on Hiroshima, one day before a second atomic bomb landed on Nagasaki, and a week before Japan surrendered, the Treaty of London was signed.[10] It provided for the establishment of an International

---

7   League of Nations Treaty Series Vol. XCIV (1929), No. 2137, 59, 63, <https://treaties. un.org/doc/Publication/UNTS/LON/Volume%2094/v94.pdf>, and <http://www.yale. edu/lawweb/avalon/imt/kbpact.htm>, accessed May 15, 2016. In addition to binding the nations that signed it, the Kellogg-Briand Pact was one of the legal bases establishing that the threat or use of military force and territorial acquisitions resulting from it, are unlawful. "Notably, the pact served as the legal basis for the creation of the notion of crime against peace. It was for committing this crime that the Nuremberg Tribunal and Tokyo Tribunal sentenced a number of people responsible for starting World War II." <http:// en.wikipedia.org/wiki/Kellogg%E2%80%93Briand_Pact>, accessed May 15, 2016.

8   Charter of the United Nations, June 26, 1945, <http://www.un.org/en/sections/un-charter/un-charter-full-text/index.html>, accessed May 15, 2016.

9   Ibid.

10   Agreement for the Prosecution and Punishment of the Major War Criminals of the European Axis, and Charter of the International Military Tribunal, London, August 8, 1945:

Military Tribunal "for the just and prompt trial and punishment of the major war criminals of the European Axis."[11] Individuals can be held responsible for:

(a) "Crimes against peace": namely, planning, preparation, initiation or waging of a war of aggression, or a war in violation of international treaties, agreements or assurances, or participation in a common plan or conspiracy for the accomplishment of any of the foregoing;

(b) "War crimes": namely, violations of the laws or customs of war. Such violations shall include, but not be limited to, murder, ill-treatment or deportation to slave labour or for any other purpose of civilian population of or in occupied territory, murder or ill-treatment of prisoners of war or persons on the seas, killing of hostages, plunder of public or private property, wanton destruction of cities, towns or villages, or devastation not justified by military necessity;

(c) "Crimes against humanity": namely, murder, extermination, enslavement, deportation, and other inhumane acts committed against any civilian population, before or during the war, or persecutions on

---

In the course of World War II the Allied Governments issued several declarations concerning the punishment of war criminals. On 7 October 1942 it was announced that a United Nations War Crimes Commission would be set up for the investigation of war crimes. It was not, however, until 20 October 1943, that the actual establishment of the Commission took place. In the Moscow Declaration of 30 October 1943, the three main Allied Powers (United Kingdom, United States, USSR) issued a joint statement that the German war criminals should be judged and punished in the countries in which their crimes were committed, but that, "the major criminals, whose offences have no particular geographical localization," would be punished "by the joint decision of the Governments of the Allies."

The International Military Tribunal for the Far East (Tokyo 1948) was established by a special proclamation of General MacArthur as the Supreme Commander in the Far East for the Allied Powers.

<https://www.icrc.org/applic/ihl/ihl.nsf/Treaty.xsp?action=openDocument&documentId=87B0BB4A50A64DEAC12563CD002D6AAE>, accessed May 15, 2016.

11 Agreement for the Prosecution and Punishment of the Major War Criminals of the European Axis, and Charter of the International Military Tribunal, London, August 8, 1945. Article 1 states:

In pursuance of the Agreement signed on 8 August 1945, by the Government of the United Kingdom of Great Britain and Northern Ireland, the Government of the United States of America, the Provisional Government of the French Republic and the Government of the Union of Soviet Socialist Republics, there shall be established an International Military Tribunal (hereinafter called "the Tribunal") for the just and prompt trial and punishment of the major war criminals of the European Axis.

<https://www.icrc.org/applic/ihl/ihl.nsf/9ac284404d38ed2bc1256311002afd89/65642c46c05fbc85c12563cd00519ba4>, accessed May 15, 2016.

political, racial or religious grounds in execution of or in connection with any crime within the jurisdiction of the Tribunal, whether or not in violation of the domestic law of the country where perpetrated.[12]

An individual may be held personally responsible for a crime of aggression only if he or she was in a position of authority, but an individual does bear responsibility for engaging in war crimes or crimes against humanity.[13]

In 1956, the Department of the Army of the United States incorporated the Nuremberg principles into the Army Field Manual, assigning personal responsibility and liability for punishment to "any person . . . who commits an act which constitutes a crime under international law."[14]

During the early 1960's, after intervention by the United States in the Dominican Republic and the beginning of the Vietnam War, David Mitchell asked the courts to decide

whether a draftee, ordered to report for induction in the Armed Forces of the United States may lawfully refuse to obey the order upon the grounds that the Government is engaged in the commission of crimes against peace, war crimes, and crimes against humanity as defined by international law recognized by the Charter and Judgment of the Nuremberg Tribunal and affirmed by the United Nations General Assembly; and, therefore, that obedience to the Order would render him guilty of complicity in these crimes.

The Supreme Court of the United States refused to apply international law to judge the validity of the Vietnam War, and Mitchell went to prison.[15]

---

12   Charter of the International Military Tribunal, annexed to the Agreement for the Prosecution and Punishment of the Major War Criminals of the European Axis, 8 August 1945, affirmed by the UN General Assembly Resolution 95(1), 11 December 1946, Art. 6, <https://www.icrc.org/applic/ihl/ihl.nsf/ART/350-530014?OpenDocument>, accessed May 15, 2016.

13   "UNHCR *Guidelines*," ¶¶ 23, 27, <http://www.refworld.org/pdfid/529ee33b4.pdf>, accessed November 3, 2016. "The fact that the Defendant acted pursuant to order of his Government or of a superior shall not free him from responsibility, but may be considered in mitigation of punishment if the Tribunal determines that justice so requires." Charter of the International Military Tribunal, Art. 8, <https://www.icrc.org/applic/ihl/ihl.nsf/ART/350-530016?OpenDocument>, accessed May 15, 2016.

14   Department of the Army, Field Manual No. 27-10, *The Law of Land Warfare*, July 18, 1956 [unchanged as of July 15, 1976], Chapter 8, Section II, ¶ 498, Crimes Under International Law, and ¶ 499, War Crimes, <http://www.globalsecurity.org/military/library/policy/army/fm/27-10/index.html>, accessed May 15, 2016.

15   David Mitchell, "What Is Criminal," in *We Won't Go: Personal Accounts of War Objectors*, collected by Alice Lynd (Boston: Beacon Press, 1968), 100, 103. *See below,* page 65, note 5, *Mitchell v. United States*, 386 U.S. 972 (1967), Douglas, J., dissenting.

Universal Declaration of Human Rights

In December 1948, thirteen months after the United Nations General Assembly passed a resolution calling for the establishment of a Jewish State, and seven months after the United States recognized the State of Israel, the United Nations General Assembly adopted the Universal Declaration of Human Rights.[16]

The preamble to the Universal Declaration declares that "the peoples of the United Nations have in the [UN] Charter reaffirmed their faith in fundamental human rights, in the dignity and worth of the human person and in the equal rights of men and women. . . ."

Among the articles that follow, the Declaration calls for human beings to "act towards one another in a spirit of brotherhood."

- Everyone is entitled to human rights and freedoms without distinction based on race, color, sex, language, religion, political or other opinion, national or social origin, property, birth or other status.
- No one shall be subjected to torture or to cruel, inhuman or degrading treatment or punishment.
- No one shall be subjected to arbitrary arrest, detention or exile.
- No one shall be arbitrarily deprived of his property.
- Everyone has the right to seek and to enjoy in other countries asylum from persecution.

And,

- "Everyone has the right to freedom of thought, conscience and religion," including "freedom to change his religion or belief, and freedom . . . to manifest his religion or belief in teaching, practice, worship and observance."[17]

Geneva Conventions and Protocols

"In time of war," the International Committee of the Red Cross says, "certain humanitarian rules must be observed, even with regard to the enemy."

> The Geneva Conventions are founded on the idea of respect for the individual and his [or her] dignity. Persons not directly taking part in hostilities and those put out of action through sickness, injury, captivity or any other cause must be respected and protected against the effects of war; those who suffer must be aided and cared for without discrimination.

---

16 Declaration of the Establishment of the State of Israel, May 14, 1948, <http://www.mfa.gov.il/MFA/ForeignPolicy/Peace/Guide/Pages/Declaration%20of%20Establishment%20of%State%20of%Israel.aspx>; Universal Declaration of Human Rights, <http://www.un.org/en/universal-declaration-human-rights/index.html>, accessed May 15, 2016.

17 Ibid., Preamble, Articles 1, 2, 5, 9, 14(1), 17(2), and 18, <http://www.un.org/en/universal-declaration-human-rights/index.html>, accessed May 15, 2016. *See below*, discussion of Article 18, right to freedom of thought, conscience and religion, in relation to conscientious objection.

The Additional Protocols extend this protection to any person affected by an armed conflict. They furthermore stipulate that the parties to the conflict and individual combatants must not attack the civilian population or civilian objects and must conduct their military operations in conformity with the recognized rules of international humanitarian law.[18]

The International Committee of the Red Cross (ICRC) played a major role in the formulation of the Geneva Conventions. "[I]n 1863, the ICRC persuaded governments to adopt the first Geneva Convention. This treaty obliged armies to care for wounded soldiers, whatever side they were on. . . ."[19] During World War I, the ICRC "intervened over the use of arms that caused extreme suffering—in 1918 it called on belligerents to renounce the use of mustard gas." "The ICRC persuaded governments to adopt a new Geneva Convention in 1929 to provide greater protection for prisoners of war."[20] During World War II the ICRC "tried to work to assist and protect victims on all sides." But lacking a specific legal basis, it "was unable to take decisive action" "on behalf of victims of the Holocaust and other persecuted groups."[21]

In 1949, at the ICRC's initiative, states agreed on the revision of the existing three Geneva Conventions (covering wounded and sick on the battlefield, victims of war at sea, prisoners of war) and the addition of a fourth: to protect civilians living under enemy control. The Conventions provide the ICRC's main mandate in situations of armed conflict.[22]

The Fourth Geneva Convention, adopted in 1949, has certain provisions that apply to occupied territories:

---

18   International Committee of the Red Cross, "Summary of the Geneva Conventions of 12 August 1949 and Their Additional Protocols," August 2005, second edition November 2012, 2–3, https://www.icrc.org/eng/assets/files/publications/icrc-002-0368. pdf, accessed May 15, 2016. A footnote after the word "his" states: "Throughout this text, pronouns and adjectives in the masculine gender apply equally to men and women, unless otherwise specified."

19   ICRC, "History of the ICRC," 29-10-2010 Overview (hereafter, "ICRC, Overview"), <https://www.icrc.org/eng/who-we-are/history/overview-section-history-icrc.htm>.

20   Ibid. *See also*, Protocol for the Prohibition of the Use of Asphyxiating, Poisonous or Other Gases, and of Bacteriological Methods of Warfare, Geneva, June 17, 1925: "the use in war of asphyxiating, poisonous or other gases, and of all analogous liquids materials or devices, has been justly condemned by the general opinion of the civilized world; . . . this prohibition shall be universally accepted as a part of International Law, binding alike the conscience and the practice of nations. . . ." <https://www.icrc.org/applic/ihl/ihl.nsf/ Article.xsp?action=openDocument&documentId=58A096110540867AC12563CD005 187B9>, accessed May 15, 2016.

21   ICRC, "Overview."

22   Ibid.

- Article 32 prohibits torture.
- Article 33 says that individuals should be held responsible for violating the rights of protected persons, and it prohibits collective punishment.
- Article 49 prohibits forcible transfers or deportations of people from occupied territory to the territory of the Occupying Power or any other country.
- Article 76 says that persons who are detained or convicted in an occupied territory must serve their sentences within the occupied territory.
- Article 147 lists as "grave breaches": wilful killing, torture, or inhuman treatment, wilful causing of great suffering or serious injury to body or health, unlawful deportation or transfer of a protected person, wilfully depriving a protected person of a fair trial or unlawful confinement, and extensive destruction or taking of property not justified by military necessity.[23]

Thus, by the end of the 1940s, these human rights had been codified into internationally recognized human rights law. Article 1 of all four Geneva Conventions calls on the signers "to respect and to ensure respect for" the Convention "in all circumstances." Parties to the Conventions should not be content merely to apply the provisions themselves, "but should do everything in their power to ensure that the humanitarian principles underlying the Conventions are applied universally."[24]

In 1977, protocols to the Geneva Conventions reaffirmed the customary rule that the civilian population and individual civilians should be protected against dangers arising from military operations under all circumstances, even in self-defense. Indiscriminate attacks are prohibited. These include using methods or means of combat that strike military objectives and civilians or civilian property without distinction, and attacks that would be excessive when comparing the harm to civilians compared to the anticipated military advantage. In conducting military operations at sea or in the air, each party to the conflict is required to take all reasonable precautions to avoid losses of civilian lives and damage to civilian property.[25]

---

23 Fourth Geneva Convention Relative to the Protection of Civilian Persons in Time of War, August 12, 1949. The text was drafted by the International Committee of the Red Cross and adopted with only slight changes. <http://www.icrc.org/ihl/INTRO/380>, accessed May 16, 2016. *See also*, International Committee of the Red Cross, "How 'grave breaches' are defined in the Geneva Conventions and Additional Protocols" and links to the full text of each of the four Geneva Conventions and Additional Protocols, <https://www.icrc.org/eng/resources/documents/misc/5zmgf9.htm>, accessed May 16, 2016.

24 Jean S. Pictet, gen. ed., "Commentary, IV Geneva Convention Relative to the Protection of Civilian Persons in Time of War," International Committee of the Red Cross, Geneva, 1958, 16. <http://www.loc.gov/rr/frd/Military_Law/pdf/GC_1949-IV.pdf>, accessed May 16, 2016.

25 For precise provisions and commentary, *see* "Protocol Additional to the Geneva Conventions of 12 August 1949, and relating to the Protection of Victims of International Armed Conflicts (Protocol I), 8 June 1977," <http://www.icrc.org/ihl/WebART/470-750065> re protection of the civilian population; and <http://www.icrc.org/applic/ihl/ihl.nsf/9ac284404d38ed2bc1256311002afd89/50fb5579fb098faac12563cd0051dd7c> re precautions in attack, accessed May 16, 2016.

International Covenant on Civil and Political Rights

The International Covenant on Civil and Political Rights went into effect in 1976. It says,

- "No one shall be subjected to torture or to cruel, inhuman or degrading treatment or punishment";
- "No one shall be subjected to arbitrary arrest or detention";
- "All persons deprived of their liberty shall be treated with humanity and with respect for the inherent dignity of the human person"; and
- "Everyone shall have the right to freedom of thought, conscience and religion. . . ."[26]

Convention Against Torture

In 1984, the Convention Against Torture (CAT) defined "torture" and "other cruel, inhuman or degrading treatment."[27]

Torture, according to the CAT, consists of severe physical or mental pain or suffering, intentionally inflicted for purposes such as obtaining information or a confession, punishment, intimidation, coercion, or discrimination, inflicted or instigated by a person acting in an official capacity.[28] There are no exceptions.[29] An order from a superior officer or public authority does not justify torture.[30] The prohibition against

---

26 International Covenant on Civil and Political Rights (ICCPR), Articles 7, 9, 10(1), and 18(1), adopted December 16, 1966, entered into force March 23, 1976), <http://www. ohchr.org/EN/ProfessionalInterest/Pages/CCPR.aspx>, accessed May 23, 2016.

27 Convention Against Torture and Other Cruel, Inhuman or Degrading Treatment or Punishment, adopted December 10, 1984, entered into force June 26, 1987, <http:// www.ohchr.org/EN/ProfessionalInterest/Pages/CAT.aspx>, accessed May 16, 2016.

28 According to the Convention Against Torture (CAT), Article 1.1,

> the term "torture" means any act by which severe pain or suffering, whether physical or mental, is intentionally inflicted on a person for such purposes as obtaining from him or a third person information or a confession, punishing him for an act he or a third person has committed or is suspected of having committed, or intimidating or coercing him or a third person, or for any reason based on discrimination of any kind, when such pain or suffering is inflicted by or at the instigation of or with the consent or acquiescence of a public official or other person acting in an official capacity. It does not include pain or suffering arising only from, inherent in or incidental to lawful sanctions.

> *See also*, International Committee of the Red Cross (ICRC) policy on torture and cruel, inhuman or degrading treatment inflicted on persons deprived of their liberty, "Policy adopted by the Assembly Council of the ICRC on 9 June 2011," 2 n.1, <http://www.icrc. org/eng/assets/files/publications/icrc-002-4088.pdf>, accessed May 16, 2016.

29 CAT, Article 2.2, "No exceptional circumstances whatsoever, whether a state of war or a threat of war, internal political instability or any other public emergency, may be invoked as a justification of torture."

30 CAT, Article 2.3, "An order from a superior officer or a public authority may not be invoked as a justification of torture."

torture is absolute, even in the face of threat of terrorist acts, war or threat of war, internal political instability or any other public emergency.[31]

Other cruel, inhuman, and degrading treatment or punishment which does not amount to torture, when committed or instigated or consented to by a person in an official capacity,[32] is known as "ill-treatment"[33] or "CIDT." According to the International Committee of the Red Cross, cruel, inhuman, or degrading treatment consists of acts that cause serious mental pain or suffering that any reasonable person would feel to be a serious outrage upon individual dignity. Ill-treatment "has the potential to destroy the social ties that underpin a community or a society," and is a "flagrant violation" of international human rights law.[34]

In practice, according to the UN Committee Against Torture, the difference between ill-treatment and torture is often not clear; "conditions that give rise to ill-treatment frequently facilitate torture and therefore the measures required to prevent torture must be applied to prevent ill-treatment."[35]

> The main distinction between torture and CIDT is the intent. It is not the intensity of pain or suffering that distinguishes torture from CIDT, but the purpose of the ill-treatment and the powerlessness of the victim in a situation of detention or similar direct control. In other words, a law enforcement official is entitled to use force that causes light or even severe pain or suffering in order to effect the arrest of a person suspected of having committed a criminal offense. But when the person has been arrested, handcuffed, detained, or otherwise brought under the direct control of the official, no further use of force or infliction of pain is permitted. Even non-severe pain or suffering, if inflicted in a humiliating manner, might amount to degrading treatment. If severe pain or suffering is inflicted on a detainee for any of the purposes listed in Article 1 CAT, this not only amounts to cruel and inhuman treatment, but also constitutes torture.[36]

---

31 Committee Against Torture, General Comment No. 2, "Implementation of article 2 by States Parties," November 23, 2007, ¶ 5, <http://www2.ohchr.org/english/bodies/cat/docs/CAT.C.GC.2.CRP.1.Rev.4_en.pdf>, accessed May 16, 2016; *see*, CAT, Article 17, providing for the establishment of the Committee Against Torture.

32 CAT, Article 16: ". . . other acts of cruel, inhuman or degrading treatment or punishment which do not amount to torture as defined in article 1, when such acts are committed by or at the instigation of or with the consent or acquiescence of a public official or other person acting in an official capacity."

33 Committee Against Torture, General Comment No. 2, ¶ 3.

34 ICRC Policy, June 9, 2011, 2. The ICRC regards "cruel" and "inhuman" as meaning the same thing; likewise, "humiliating" and "degrading" mean the same thing. Ibid. n.1.

35 Committee Against Torture, General Comment No. 2, ¶ 3.

36 Manfred Nowak, "What Practices Constitute Torture? US and UN Standards," *Human Rights Quarterly* 28 (2006), 809–41, DOI: 10.1353/hrq.2006.0050, 836–37, <http://faculty.maxwell.syr.edu/hpschmitz/PSC354/PSC354Readings/NowakTorture.pdf>, accessed May 22, 2016.

It was not until 2004 that the United Nations High Commissioner for Human Rights issued the Istanbul Protocol Manual on the Effective Investigation and Documentation of Torture and Other Cruel, Inhuman or Degrading Treatment or Punishment. It lists many methods of torture, including burns with cigarettes, electric shocks; conditions of detention such as overcrowding or solitary confinement; exposure to extremes of temperature; restriction of sleep, food, water, toilet facilities, medical care; deprivation of privacy; humiliation; threats to harm the detainee or family; and psychological techniques that break down the individual.[37]

The Convention Against Torture specifies that "Each State Party shall take effective legislative, administrative, judicial or other measures to prevent acts of torture in any territory under its jurisdiction."[38]

The United States of America was one of the nations that signed and later ratified the Convention Against Torture, subject to several reservations.[39] However, in 2003, legal counsel for the Justice Department took the position that torture was "excruciating pain equivalent to losing organs and systems" and that waterboarding did not meet the generally recognized definition of torture. Those opinions were rescinded in 2009.[40]

---

37   Office of the United Nations High Commissioner for Human Rights, Istanbul Protocol Manual on the Effective Investigation and Documentation of Torture and Other Cruel, Inhuman or Degrading Treatment or Punishment, Professional Training Series No. 8/Rev.1, New York and Geneva, 2004, ¶ 145, <http://www.ohchr.org/Documents/Publications/training8Rev1en.pdf>, accessed May 16, 2016.

38   CAT, Article 2.1.

39   The United States signed the Convention Against Torture on April 18, 1988, and the Senate ratified it on October 21, 1994. With reference to Article 1 of the Convention Against Torture,

> the United States understands that, in order to constitute torture, an act must be specifically intended to inflict severe physical or mental pain or suffering and that mental pain or suffering refers to prolonged mental harm caused by or resulting from (1) the intentional infliction or threatened infliction of severe physical pain or suffering; (2) the administration or application, or threatened administration or application, of mind altering substances or other procedures calculated to disrupt profoundly the senses or the personality; (3) the threat of imminent death; or (4) the threat that another person will imminently be subjected to death, severe physical pain or suffering, or the administration or application of mind altering substances or other procedures calculated to disrupt profoundly the senses or personality.

United Nations Treaty Collection, Chapter IV, Human Rights, 9. Convention against Torture and Other Cruel, Inhuman or Degrading Treatment or Punishment. <https://treaties.un.org/pages/ViewDetails.aspx?src=TREATY&mtdsg_no=IV-9&chapter=4&lang=en>, accessed May 16, 2016.

40   *See*, Withdrawal of Office of Legal Counsel CIA Interrogation Opinions, April 15, 2009, Memorandum for the attorney General, signed by David J. Barron, Acting Assistant Attorney General, and memoranda cited therein. <https://fas.org/irp/agency/doj/olc/withdraw-0409.pdf>, accessed May 16, 2016.

International Criminal Court

The International Criminal Court was established by the Rome Statute of the International Criminal Court.[41] Crimes within the jurisdiction of the Court are the crime of genocide, crimes against humanity, war crimes, and the crime of aggression. A lengthy list of war crimes includes:

- Extensive destruction and appropriation of property, not justified by military necessity;
- Taking of hostages;
- Intentionally launching an attack in the knowledge that such attack will cause incidental loss of life or injury to civilians or damage to civilian property or widespread, long-term and severe damage to the natural environment which would be clearly excessive in relation to the direct overall military advantage anticipated;
- Intentionally directing attacks against the civilian population as such or against individual civilians not taking direct part in hostilities;
- Attacking or bombarding, by whatever means, towns, villages, dwellings or buildings which are undefended and which are not military objectives;
- Killing or wounding a combatant who, having laid down his arms or having no longer means of defence, has surrendered at discretion;
- Intentionally directing attacks against buildings dedicated to religion, education, art, science or charitable purposes, historic monuments, hospitals and places where the sick and wounded are collected, provided they are not military objectives;
- Intentionally directing attacks against buildings, material, medical units and transport, and personnel using the distinctive emblems of the Geneva Conventions in conformity with international law;
- Intentionally using starvation of civilians as a method of warfare by depriving them of objects indispensable to their survival, including wilfully impeding relief supplies as provided for under the Geneva Conventions. . . .[42]

The United States signed the Rome Statute on December 31, 2000, but has not ratified it. On May 6, 2002, the U.S. formally notified the UN that it did not intend to become a party to the Rome Statute.[43]

---

41 Rome Statute of the International Criminal Court, adopted by treaty 1998, went into force on July 1, 2002, <https://www.icc-cpi.int/NR/rdonlyres/EA9AEFF7-5752-4F84-BE94-0A655EB30E16/0/Rome_Statute_English.pdf>, accessed May 16, 2016.

42 Rome Statute of the International Criminal Court, Article 8, War crimes, July 17, 1998, <http://www.icrc.org/applic/ihl/ihl.nsf/Article.xsp?action=openDocument&documentId=E4C44E2F1347B99D412566900046EACB>, accessed May 16, 2016.

43 American Red Cross, "International Criminal Court (ICC)", <http://www.redcross.org/images/MEDIA_CustomProductCatalog/m3640111_IHL_ICC.pdf>, accessed May 16, 2016. *See*, "A Stronger Court for War Crimes," editorial, *New York Times*, November 3, 2016, <http://www.nytimes.com/2016/11/03/opinion/a-stronger-court-for-crimes-against-humanity.html?_r=0>, accessed November 3, 2016:

Customary International Humanitarian Law: Distinction and Proportionality

In 2005, the International Committee of the Red Cross published a study on the rules of customary international humanitarian law, "applicable in both international and non-international armed conflicts." These rules make two main points: civilians must be protected, and the collateral damage caused by military action must not be excessive. Stated another way, there are two concepts, "distinction" between civilian and military targets, and "proportionality," weighing the damage to civilians against the gaining of military advantage.

As one reads these rules, one may be reminded of carpet bombing of cities during World War II, sending unguided missiles into enemy territory with no control over where they will land, laying of land mines with no way of anticipating who will cause them to explode, or shooting to kill a boy with a rock in his hand. Specifically, some of these rules of customary international humanitarian law state:

- Rule 11. Indiscriminate attacks are prohibited.
- Rule 12. Indiscriminate attacks are those:
  (a) which are not directed at a specific military objective;
  (b) which employ a method or means of combat which cannot be directed at a specific military objective; or
  (c) which employ a method or means of combat the effects of which can-not be limited as required by international humanitarian law; and consequently, in each such case, are of a nature to strike military objectives and civilians or civilian objects without distinction.
- Rule 14. Proportionality in Attack. Launching an attack which may be expected to cause incidental loss of civilian life, injury to civilians, damage

---

Since it began operations in 2002, the International Criminal Court has secured just four convictions, fueling the perception that it has been largely ineffectual as a tribunal of last resort for the world's worst criminals. Making matters worse, Gambia, Burundi and South Africa have announced their intention to leave the court, which some African leaders see as a vestige of colonialism because it has so far tried cases only from their continent.

. . . The autocratic leaders of Gambia and Burundi fear not a resurgence of colonialism but being held accountable for their abuses. In South Africa, President Jacob Zuma is motivated by domestic and regional politics at a time when his integrity and leadership have rightly come under scrutiny. The International Criminal Court has focused much of its resources on Africa not out of racism, but at the request of victims' groups and often governments that recognized they were not equipped to handle complex prosecutions.

Many of the world's major powers, including China, Russia, and the United States did not join the International Criminal Court, which means that in most cases their citizens are not subject to its jurisdiction without the Security Council's approval. Somini Sengupta, "As 3 African Nations Vow to Exit, International Court Faces Its Own Trial," *New York Times*, October 26, 2016, <http://www.nytimes.com/2016/10/27/world/africa/africa-international-criminal-court.html>, accessed December 25, 2016.

to civilian objects, or a combination thereof, which would be excessive in relation to the concrete and direct military advantage anticipated, is prohibited.

- Rule 15. Precautions in Attack. In the conduct of military operations, constant care must be taken to spare the civilian population, civilians and civilian objects. All feasible precautions must be taken to avoid, and in any event to minimize, incidental loss of civilian life, injury to civilians and damage to civilian objects.

- Rule 17. Choice of Means and Methods of Warfare. Each party to the conflict must take all feasible precautions in the choice of means and methods of warfare with a view to avoiding, and in any event to minimizing, incidental loss of civilian life, injury to civilians and damage to civilian objects.

- Rule 19. Control during the Execution of Attacks. Each party to the conflict must do everything feasible to cancel or suspend an attack if it becomes apparent that the target is not a military objective or that the attack may be expected to cause incidental loss of civilian life, injury to civilians, damage to civilian objects, or a combination thereof, which would be excessive in relation to the concrete and direct military advantage anticipated.

- Rule 21. Target Selection. When a choice is possible between several military objectives for obtaining a similar military advantage, the objective to be selected must be . . . the attack . . . which may be expected to cause the least danger to civilian lives and to civilian objects.

- Rule 23. Location of Military Objectives outside Densely Populated Areas. Each party to the conflict must, to the extent feasible, avoid locating military objectives within or near densely populated areas.[44]

A large number of military manuals lay down the principle of proportionality in attack. Among those listed by the ICRC are Israel's Manual of the Laws of War,[45] and half a dozen U.S. military handbooks.

When determining what is "excessive," military advantage is weighed against suffering by civilians. Thus, the ICRC quotes the U.S. Naval Handbook concerning first the scope and means of attack and then whether the expected damage to civilians is excessive considering the expected military advantage:

44　"ICRC Customary IHL," <https://www.icrc.org/customary-ihl/eng/docs/v1_rul>, accessed May 16, 2016.

45　Israel, "Laws of War in the Battlefield," Manual, Military Advocate General Headquarters, Military School, 1998, 40, "The commander is required to refrain from an attack that is expected to inflict harm on the civilian population that is disproportionate to the expected military gain." Quoted in "ICRC Customary IHL" under Rule 14, Military Manuals, Israel, <https://www.icrc.org/customary-ihl/eng/print/v2_rul_rule14>. *See below*, Chapter 4, Proportionality and the Dahiya Doctrine.

The principle of proportionality is directly linked to the principle of distinction. While distinction is concerned with focusing the scope and means of attack so as to cause the least amount of damage to protected persons and property, proportionality is concerned with weighing the military advantage one expects to gain against the unavoidable and incidental loss to civilians and civilian property that will result from the attack. The principle of proportionality requires the commander to conduct a balancing test to determine if the incidental injury, including death to civilians and damage to civilian objects, is excessive in relation to the concrete and direct military advantage expected to be gained. . . .[46]

Violations of any of these principles of international law are not recognized by either the United States or Israel as grounds for an individual to refuse to participate in military service. They are regarded as political rather than religious grounds.

"Just War" Principles

As we have seen, under international law there are constraints on the use of force, and limits on the means and methods of warfare. Latin words are used to refer to the use of force, "*jus ad bellum*," and the way in which war is conducted, "*jus in bello.*"[47] These "just war" principles may be compared with the Nuremberg principles. Crimes against peace, such as waging an aggressive war, would come under constraints on the use of force. War crimes have to do with conduct during war, such as devastation not justified by military necessity. Crimes against humanity include inhumane acts committed against any civilian population.

Catholic "just war" principles are a religious counterpart, based not on international law but on moral principles of the Christian ethic. As under international law, Catholic just war draws the "distinction" between civilian and military targets (otherwise known as the principle of "discrimination" or "noncombatant immunity"), and affirms the principle of "proportionality" (the use of no more force than is militarily necessary). The Catholic Bishops have supported "conscientious objection

---

46 United States, The Commander's Handbook on the Law of Naval Operations, NWP 1-14M/MCWP 5-12.1/COMDTPUB P5800.7, issued by the Department of the Navy, Office of the Chief of Naval Operations and Headquarters, US Marine Corps, and Department of Homeland Security, US Coast Guard, July 2007, § 5.3.3, quoted in "ICRC Customary IHL, <https://www.icrc.org/customary-ihl/eng/print/v2_rul_rule14>, accessed May 16, 2016.

47 ICRC, "IHL and other legal regimes—jus ad bellum and jus in bello," Overview, 29-10-2010, <https://www.icrc.org/eng/war-and-law/ihl-other-legal-regmies/jus-in-bello-jus-ad-bellum/overview-jus-ad-bellum-jus-in-bello.htm>, accessed November 3, 2016. "The clear distinction between jus in bello and jus ad bellum is comparatively recent. The terms did not become common in debates and writings about the law of war until a decade after World War II." A third term, "*jus contra bellum*," refers to law on the prevention of war.

in general and selective conscientious objection to participation in a particular war, either because of the ends being pursued or the means being used."[48]

However, the Church fathers have increasingly recognized the impossibility of abiding by the just war principles given the nature of modern warfare. The United States National Conference of Catholic Bishops, in consultation with European bishops' conferences, issued a Pastoral Letter on War and Peace in 1983,[49] and a follow-up statement in 1993.[50]

In 1983, the focus was on avoiding nuclear war and concluded that nuclear deterrence was not adequate as a long-term basis for peace.[51]

[A]n attack on military targets or militarily significant industrial targets could involve "indirect" (i.e., unintended) but massive civilian casualties. . . . This problem is unavoidable because of the way modern military facilities and production centers are so thoroughly interspersed with civilian living and working areas. . . . [E]ven with attacks limited to "military" targets, the number of deaths in a substantial exchange would be almost indistinguishable from what might occur if civilian centers had been deliberately and directly struck. . . .

The location of industrial or militarily significant economic targets within heavily populated areas or in those areas affected by radioactive fallout could well involve such massive civilian casualties that, in our judgment, such a strike would be deemed morally disproportionate, even though not intentionally indiscriminate.[52]

In 1982, Pope John Paul II spoke about peace near the city of Coventry, a city devastated by war.[53] The following year, the Catholic Bishops wrote:

[I]t is not only nuclear war that must be prevented, but war itself. Therefore, with Pope John Paul II we declare:

---

48 "The Challenge of Peace: God's Promise and Our Response," A Pastoral Letter on War and Peace by the National Conference of Catholic Bishops, May 3, 1983, ¶¶ 233(b) <http://www.usccb.org/upload/challenge-peace-gods-promise-our-response-1983.pdf>, accessed November 3, 2016.

49 Catholic Bishops (1983).

50 "The Harvest of Justice Is Sown in Peace," A Reflection of the National Conference of Catholic Bishops on the Tenth Anniversary of The Challenge of Peace, November 17, 1993, <http://www.usccb.org/beliefs-and-teachings/what-we-believe/catholic-social-teaching/the-harvest-of-justice-is-sown-in-peace.cfm>, accessed May 17, 2016.

51 Catholic Bishops (1983), ¶ 186.

52 Catholic Bishops (1983), ¶¶ 180, 182.

53 "Holy Mass of Pentecost Homily of John Paul II," Solemnity of Pentecost, Coventry (May 30, 1982), <http://www.thepapalvisit.org.uk/Visit-Background/A-Retrospective-of-the-1982-Visit/Coventry-Airport/Holy-Mass-Of-Pentecost-homily-of-John-Paul-II-Solemnity-of-Pentecost-Coventry-30-May-1982>, accessed May 17, 2016.

> Today, the scale and the horror of modern warfare—whether nuclear or not—makes it totally unacceptable as a means of settling differences between nations. War should belong to the tragic past, to history, it should find no place on humanity's agenda for the future.

> Reason and experience tell us that a continuing upward spiral, even in conventional arms, coupled with an unbridled increase in armed forces, instead of securing true peace will almost certainly be provocative of war.[54]

In 1993, the Catholic Bishops reiterated: "Strategies calling for use of overwhelming and decisive force can raise issues of proportionality and discrimination. . . . Fifty years after Coventry, Dresden, Hamburg, Hiroshima and Nagasaki, ways must be found to apply standards of proportionality and noncombatant immunity in a meaningful way to air warfare."[55]

"We believe there is no 'just war,'" declared participants of a Nonviolence and Just Peace gathering in Rome convened by Pax Christi International, the Pontifical Council for Justice and Peace, and other international Catholic organizations in 2016.

> Too often the "just war theory" has been used to endorse rather than prevent or limit war. Suggesting that a "just war" is possible also undermines the moral imperative to develop tools and capacities for nonviolent transformation of conflict. . . . [W]e call on the Church we love to . . . no longer use or teach "just war theory" [and] to continue advocating for the abolition of war and nuclear weapons. . . .[56]

Conscientious Objection under International Law

Basis for Conscientious Objection in International Declarations
There is no international agreement that explicitly recognizes the right to conscientious objection to military service. Rather, a right to refuse military service is derived from the right to freedom of thought, conscience and religion.[57]

---

54   Catholic Bishops (1983), ¶ 219, and endnote 94 referring to John Paul II. "Homily at Bagington Airport," Coventry, 2.

55   Catholic Bishops (1993), B, 2.

56   Nonviolence and Just Peace gathering, Rome, April 11–13, 2016, "An appeal to the Catholic Church to recommit to the centrality of Gospel nonviolence," <http://www.paxchristi.net/news/appeal-catholic-church-recommit-centrality-gospel-nonviolence/5855#sthash.RkIk6WZX.F6O4hdzS.dpbs>, accessed May 17, 2016.

57   United Nations Human Rights Office of the High Commissioner, "Conscientious Objection to Military Service," United Nations Publication HR/PUB/12/1, New York and Geneva, 2012, ISBN 978-92-1-154196-0, e-ISBN 978-92-1-055405-3 (hereafter, "OHCHR (2012)"), 7 <http://www.ohchr.org/Documents/Publications/ConscientiousObjection_en.pdf>, accessed May 17, 2016.

The Universal Declaration of Human Rights and the Covenant on Civil and Political Rights both say, with slight variations in wording, that everyone has the right to freedom of thought, conscience and religion including freedom to change their religion or belief, and freedom to manifest their religion, either alone or in community with others, in public or private, in worship, observance, practice and teaching.[58] Thus, a claim of conscientious objection by someone who has volunteered to serve in the armed forces should be granted if based on a change of religion or belief. What is critical is that the objection be grounded in conscience. The obligation to use lethal force may seriously conflict with the freedom of conscience and the right to manifest one's religion or belief.[59]

Article 4 of the Covenant on Civil and Political Rights does not permit any exceptions, even in a time of public emergency that threatens the life of the nation.[60]

> It is precisely in time of armed conflict, when the community interests in question are most likely to be under greatest threat, that the right to conscientious objection is most in need of protection, most likely to be invoked and most likely to fail to be respected in practice.[61]

Conscientious Objection to Enforcing Apartheid

Less than three years after the International Covenant on Civil and Political Rights went into force, when racial segregation known as "apartheid" in South

---

58   Article 18, paragraph 1, of the Universal Declaration of Human Rights says:
   Everyone has the right to freedom of thought, conscience and religion; this right includes freedom to change his religion or belief, and freedom, either alone or in community with others and in public or private, to manifest his religion or belief in teaching, practice, worship and observance.
   <http://www.un.org/en/universal-declaration-human-rights/index.html>, accessed May 17, 2016.Article 18(1) of the International Covenant on Civil and Political Rights says:
   Everyone shall have the right to freedom of thought, conscience and religion. This right shall include freedom to have or to adopt a religion or belief of his choice, and freedom, either individually or in community with others and in public or private, to manifest his religion or belief in worship, observance, practice and teaching.
   <http://www.ohchr.org/en/professionalinterest/pages/ccpr.aspx>, accessed May 17, 2016.
59   UN General Assembly, Human Rights Council, *Analytical report on conscientious objection to military service: Report of the United Nations High Commissioner for Human Rights,* June 3, 2013, A/HRC/23/22 (hereafter, "HRC (2013)"), ¶¶ 12-13, and sources cited therein, <http://www.refworld.org/docid/51b5c73c4.html>, accessed May 17, 2016.
60   It appears that there are no circumstances where the right to conscientious objection to military service could be set aside. HRC (2013), ¶ 11; *see also,* International Covenant on Civil and Political Rights, Art. 4(2), <http://www.ohchr.org/EN/ProfessionalInterest/Pages/CCPR.aspx>, accessed May 23, 2016.
61   HRC (2013), ¶ 10, citing an opinion by three Committee members in *Jeong et al. v. Republic of Korea,* Communications Nos. 1642-1742/2007, views adopted on March 24, 2011.

Africa had been government policy for decades,[62] the General Assembly of the United Nations passed a resolution recognizing what amounted to selective conscientious objection. The resolution recognized the right of all persons to refuse service in military or police forces which are used to enforce apartheid, and called on UN member states to grant asylum (or safe transit to another country) to individuals who were compelled to leave their country "solely because of a conscientious objection to assisting in the enforcement of *apartheid* through service in military or police forces." Member states were urged to grant such persons all the rights and benefits accorded to refugees, and UN bodies including the United Nations High Commissioner for Refugees, specialized agencies and nongovernmental organizations, were called on to provide all necessary assistance to such persons.[63]

International Norms and Standards Pertaining to Conscientious Objectors

Resolutions of the UN Commission on Human Rights, and its successor, the Human Rights Council, are not legally binding, and there is some disagreement as to whether there is a right to conscientious objection to military service.[64] Therefore, each country decides whether, or to what extent, to recognize conscientious objection.

---

62   Authors of the 1985 Report to the UN Sub-Commission on Prevention of Discrimination and Protection of Minorities point out that apartheid is a racially prejudiced policy, but no government would agree that its use of armed forces is illegal:

> Objection to military service always implies some degree of conflict of values between the authorities and the person who objects. . . . No Government is likely to agree that the way in which it uses its armed forces is illegal, under national or international law. Even in South Africa, the existing government (which is based on a racial minority) [as of 1985 when this was written] does not accept that its military actions run counter to international law. While therefore an objector may consider himself entitled, by reference to international law, to oppose military service in the South African armed forces, this right is not accepted under the national law of South Africa as at present enforced.

> Asbjørn Eide and Chama Mubanga-Chipoya, "Conscientious Objection to Military Service," a report prepared by members of the Sub-Commission on Prevention of Discrimination and Protection of Minorities (United Nations: New York, 1985), E/CN.4/Sub.2/1983/30/Rev.1 (hereafter, "UN Sub-Commission Report (1985)"), ¶¶ 33–34, <http://www.refworld.org/pdfid/5107cd132.pdf>, accessed May 17, 2016.

63   UN General Assembly Resolution 33/165, "Status of persons refusing service in military or police forces used to enforce *apartheid*," December 20, 1978 (footnotes omitted), <http://www.un.org/documents/ga/res/33/ares33r165.pdf>, accessed May 18, 2016.

64   OHCHR (2012), 18. In 2002 sixteen member states notified the Commission on Human Rights that they did "not recognize the universal applicability of conscientious objection to military service." OHCHR (2012), 17 and 17 n.24: "The letter (E/CN.4/2002/188) was submitted by the Permanent Representative of Singapore and co-signed by: Bangladesh, Botswana, China, Egypt, Eritrea, Iran (Islamic Republic of), Iraq,

Nevertheless, the Commission on Human Rights and the Human Rights Council issued a series of human rights resolutions defining international norms and standards calling on nations not only to recognize conscientious objectors but also to offer them alternative service; not to punish them more than once for continuing refusal to perform military service; and to grant asylum to refugees who had a legitimate fear of persecution.[65] The nation granting asylum evaluates the grounds for asylum.[66]

Asylum for refugees

A claim of persecution related to military service obligations must be linked to one or more of five grounds stated in the 1951 Convention Relating to the Status of Refugees. A "refugee," as defined in the Convention is a person who is unable or unwilling to return to his own country because of a "well-founded fear of being persecuted for reasons of race, religion, nationality, membership of a particular social group or political opinion, is outside the country of his nationality and is unable or, owing to such fear, is unwilling to avail himself of the protection of [his own] country. . . ."[67]

Claims for refugee status need to distinguish between "prosecution" and "persecution." Fear of prosecution and punishment for desertion or draft evasion does not constitute a well-founded fear of persecution. Desertion is invariably considered a criminal offence. A person is clearly not a refugee if his or her only reason for desertion or draft evasion is dislike of military service or fear of combat.[68]

In 2014, in order to provide guidelines on international protection of individuals who seek refugee status related to military service, the United Nations High Commissioner for Refugees addressed the question whether a nation's law on military service adequately provides for conscientious objectors, either by exempting them from military service, or by providing appropriate alternative service. If inconsistent with international standards, conscription may amount to persecution.[69]

Lebanon, Myanmar, Rwanda, Singapore, the Sudan, Syrian Arab Republic, Thailand, United Republic of Tanzania and VietNam." *See also*, HRC (2013), ¶ 15, and ¶ 15 n.13.

65   UN Commission on Human Rights, *Conscientious objection to military service*, Commission on Human Rights resolution 1998/77, April 22, 1998, E/CN.4/RES/1998/77, ¶¶ 1, 4, 5 and 7, <http://www.refworld.org/docid/3b00f0be10.html>, accessed May 18, 2016.

66   UN Sub-Commission Report (1985), ¶ 137, "since the granting of asylum appears to remain within the sovereign power of a State, extradition proceedings may be defeated by the receiving State granting political asylum to the objector or draft evader." <http://www.refworld.org/pdfid/5107cd132.pdf>, accessed May 18, 2016.

67   1951 Convention Relating to the Status of Refugees, Art. 1A(2), (July 28, 1951), <http://www.unhcr.org/3b66c2aa10.html>, accessed May 18, 2016.

68   OHCHR (2012), 74-75, <http://www.ohchr.org/Documents/Publications/Conscientious Objection_en.pdf>, accessed May 18, 2016.

69   UNHCR Guidelines, ¶ 17, <http://www.refworld.org/pdfid/529ee33b4.pdf>, accessed November 3, 2016.

Jeremy Hinzman—Canada

At a Canadian Immigration and Refugee Board hearing in the case of Jeremy Hinzman in 2004, the Presiding Member determined that "evidence with respect to the legality of the U.S. incursion into Iraq would not be admitted into evidence because it was not relevant" to the claims of Jeremy Hinzman and his family.[70] The main issues were:

- "Is Jeremy Hinzman a Convention refugee by reason of a well-founded fear of persecution by the government of the United States and its military for reasons of political opinion, religion, or membership in a particular social group, namely conscientious objectors to military service in the U.S. Army in Iraq"; and,

- "[I]s Jeremy Hinzman a person in need of protection in that his removal to the United States of America would subject him personally to a risk of cruel and unusual treatment or punishment by the government of the United States and its military and we could include risk to life there as well . . . ."[71]

Jeremy Hinzman was denied refugee status in Canada.[72]

Andre Lawrence Shepherd—European Union

Andre Lawrence Shepherd was a maintenance mechanic for Apache helicopters who served in Iraq from September 2004 to February 2005 when his unit returned to its base in Germany. When his unit was redeployed to Iraq in 2007, he had come to view the war in Iraq as contrary to international law and the UN Charter when considering the systematic indiscriminate and disproportionate use of weapons without regard to the civilian population. In his view, the helicopters could not have been deployed if he and other maintenance mechanics did not make them combat-ready.[73]

---

70 Immigration and Refugee Board, Jeremy Dean Hinzman et al., claimants, File No: TA4-01429, Toronto, Canada, December 6, 2004, 10; *but see* 23–25, certain articles might be relevant to how the United States ended up in Iraq, but legal opinions dealing with the legality of the war were not admitted; and *see* 33, exhibits that are not admitted are still "part of the record so if it went up to Federal Court and my ruling was challenged about the relevance of the legality of the war that court would have something to look at. . . ."

71 Hinzman hearing transcript, 5–6 (reworded, among "substantive issues" in decision dated March 16, 2005, <http://www.irb-cisr.gc.ca/Eng/BoaCom/decisions/Documents/hinzman_e.pdf>, accessed December 23, 2016.) *See also*, hearing transcript, 13, evidence includes why he left, whom he fears, and why he fears returning to the United States; and 31, the test for Convention refugee is a future-looking test.

72 Hinzman stated in a speech in Toronto, on September 24, 2011, that his claims had been denied at every step in the court process, but that a court in 2010 decided that his case should be reevaluated on humanitarian and compassionate grounds.

73 [Preliminary] *Opinion of Advocate General Sharpston: Andre Lawrence Shepherd v. Bundesrepublik Deutschland*, C472/13, European Union: Court of Justice of the European Union, November 11, 2014, ¶¶ 2–4, <http://www.refworld.org/docid/546233b44.html>; *see also*, Judgment of the Court (Second Chamber), Court of Justice of the European Union in Case C-472/13, February 26, 2015, ¶¶ 14–16, <http://curia.europa.

He did not apply for conscientious objector status because he did not completely reject the use of war and force, and he did not think that a conscientious objector application would have protected him from further deployment in Iraq. He deserted on April 11, 2007, thereby putting himself at risk of prosecution for desertion. In August 2008, he applied for asylum in Germany.[74]

According to the advocate general in the Shepherd case, the minimum standards for qualification and status as refugees who need protection must be interpreted as meaning:

- The situation is covered even if the applicant for refugee status would participate only indirectly in the commission of war crimes, if it is reasonably likely that he would provide indispensable support to the preparation or execution of those crimes;
- Even if war crimes have not already been committed, the situation is covered if it is highly likely that such crimes will be committed;
- The national authorities in the applicant's country of origin determine whether it is credible that the alleged war crimes would be committed, based on all the relevant facts and circumstances. . . .[75]

The Court of Justice of the European Union subsequently ruled that all military personnel, including logistical and support staff such as a helicopter maintenance mechanic, should be able to apply for refugee status even though the refuser did not personally participate in combat. However, a person who refused to perform military service could not qualify for refugee status without having first tried unsuccessfully to use whatever procedures were available to claim conscientious objector status.[76]

---

eu/juris/document/document.jsf?text=&docid=162544&pageIndex=0&doclang=EN& mode=req&dir=&occ=first&part=1&cid=625846>, accessed May 18, 2016.

74   *Shepherd*, AG Opinion, ¶¶ 4, 58.

75   In her preliminary opinion, *Shepherd*, AG Opinion, ¶ 84, the Advocate General stated that national authorities must consider these among other issues: whether there is a direct link between the acts of the person concerned and the reasonable likelihood that war crimes might be committed, because his actions comprise a necessary element of those crimes and without his contribution or all the contributions made by individuals in his situation, the war crimes or acts would not be possible; whether there are objective grounds for considering that the person concerned could be involved in committing war crimes; whether a dishonorable discharge from the army and a prison sentence is discriminatory because the applicant is a member of a particular social group, whether there are similarly situated social groups in the country that are comparable to that to which the applicant claims to belong, whether the applicant's group is likely to be subject to different treatment, and if so whether any apparent difference in treatment could be justified; and, whether prosecution or punishment for desertion is disproportionate, that is, whether such acts go beyond what is necessary for the State to exercise its legitimate right to maintain an armed force.

76   *Shepherd*, Court Judgment, ¶¶ 45–46, 57. Anyone seriously interested in asylum issues for military deserters in countries within the European Union should look at the

Although theoretically possible, it is predictable that few, if any, conscientious objectors will be able to achieve refugee status and be granted asylum in Canada or in any of the member states of the European Union.

Conclusion

In the following chapters on the United States and Israel, we encounter numerous violations of international law such as the use of disproportionate force, collective punishment, prolonged detention without trial, and torture; and in the chapters on prisoners, prolonged solitary confinement, and excessive use of force when men are already in restraints.

Moral injury is about an individual's conscience. Fundamental human rights are about humanity's conscience. We need both.

---

preliminary Opinion and the Judgment of the Court of Justice of the European Union in the Shepherd case.

Chapter 3.
United States

THE UNITED STATES INITIALLY EXEMPTED SOME MEN FROM MILITARY SERVICE IN time of war based on religious affiliation. That tradition persists in U.S. law. Supreme Court decisions and military regulations continue to recognize objection to military service only if it is based on "religious training and belief," and only if the individual objects to "participation in war in any form." Over the years, the definition of "religious training and belief" has become more inclusive, but the requirement that the individual object to "participation in war in any form" has not expanded.

No one has been drafted to serve in the U.S. military since 1973. As a result, the central issue for American conscientious objectors who are already in the military is whether their objections to participation in war "crystallized" after they volunteered and were inducted.

The situation of such volunteers is very different from that of objectors who grew up as pacifists because their objections emerge in response to their experience while in the military. Some of these individuals develop an objection to participation in any war. Some find themselves objecting to the war in which they have been ordered or expect to be ordered to participate, or wars of a certain character such as wars of aggression or nuclear war, and they do not qualify for recognition as conscientious objectors.

Conscientious Objection: Statutory Provisions and Legal Interpretations

Section 6(j) of the Military Selective Service Act provides that no person shall "be subject to combatant training and service in the armed forces of the United States who, by reason of religious training and belief, is conscientiously opposed to participation in war in any form. . . . [T]he term 'religious training and belief' does not include essentially political, sociological, or philosophical views, or a merely personal moral code."[1]

The Supreme Court explains the requirements for recognition as a conscientious objector:

> In order to qualify for classification as a conscientious objector, a registrant must satisfy three basic tests. He must show that he is conscientiously opposed to war in any form. . . . He must show that this opposition is based

---

1   Military Selective Service Act (MSSA), 50 U.S.C. App. 456(j), as amended Aug. 10, 2012, <https://www.law.cornell.edu/uscode/html/uscode50a/usc_sec_50a_00000456 ----000-.html>, or <http://law.justia.com/codes/us/2010/title50/app/militarys/sec456/>, accessed May 20, 2016.

upon religious training and belief, as the term has been construed in our decisions. . . . And he must show that this objection is sincere. . . . [2]

Religious Training and Belief

In *Welsh v. United States*, the Supreme Court defined "religious training and belief" as it is now understood.

> What is necessary . . . for a registrant's conscientious objection to all war to be "religious" within the meaning of § 6(j) is that this opposition to war stems from the registrant's moral, ethical, or religious beliefs about what is right and wrong and that these beliefs be held with the strength of traditional religious convictions. . . . If an individual deeply and sincerely holds beliefs that are purely ethical or moral in source and content, but that nevertheless impose upon him a duty of conscience to refrain from participating in any war at any time, those beliefs certainly occupy in the life of that individual "a place parallel to that filled by . . . God" in traditionally religious persons. Because his beliefs function as a religion in his life, such an individual is as much entitled to a "religious" conscientious objector exemption under § 6(j) as is someone who derives his conscientious opposition to war from traditional religious convictions.[3]

The Court concluded that Section 6(j) "exempts from military service all those whose consciences, spurred by deeply held moral, ethical, or religious beliefs, would give them no rest or peace if they allowed themselves to become a part of an instrument of war."[4]

---

2   *Clay v. United States*, 403 U.S. 698, 700 (1971), citing *Gillette v. United States*, 401 U.S. 437 (1971); *United States v. Seeger*, 380 U.S. 163 (1965); *Welsh v. United States*, 398 U.S. 333 (1970); and *Witmer v. United States*, 348 U.S. 375 (1955). <https://supreme.justia.com/cases/federal/us/403/698/>, or <https://www.law.cornell.edu/supremecourt/text/403/698#writing-type-17-per_curiam>, accessed May 21, 2016. Cassius Clay, known as the World Heavyweight Boxing Champion, Muhammad Ali, was convicted in 1967 and sentenced to five years in prison and a $10,000 fine for refusing to be inducted into the armed forces. That was the maximum sentence under the Military Selective Service Act of 1948, 50 U.S.C. Appendix Sec. 462(a), <http://trac.syr.edu/laws/50/50AUSC00462.html>, accessed May 20, 2016. The Supreme Court reversed the conviction.

3   *Welsh*, 398 U.S. at 339-40. <https://www.law.cornell.edu/supremecourt/text/398/333>, accessed May 20, 2016.

4   *Welsh*, 398 U.S. at 344. Remarkably, the Court stated, 398 U.S. at 342,

> We certainly do not think that § 6(j)'s exclusion of those persons with "essentially political, sociological, or philosophical views or a merely personal moral code" should be read to exclude those who hold strong beliefs about our domestic and foreign affairs or even those whose conscientious objection to participation in all wars is founded to a substantial extent upon considerations of public policy.

Although *Welsh* broadened what could be recognized as religious, objections based upon international law are not recognized as "religious."

Participation in War in Any Form

An applicant for conscientious objector status must declare an unwillingness to participate in war in any form. This has been interpreted to mean opposition to all war, not a particular war.

In the 1960s, David Mitchell did not report for induction, claiming that the "waging of a war of aggression" is a "crime against peace," imposing "individual responsibility" under the judgments of the Nuremberg Tribunal. In 1967, the Supreme Court of the United States denied Mitchell's request to hear his case. But Justice William O. Douglas dissented. Justice Douglas said that Mitchell raised a number of "extremely sensitive and delicate questions" that he thought should be answered.[5]

Later that same year, in the case of three draftees (known as the "Fort Hood Three") who were ordered to go to Vietnam, Supreme Court Justices Stewart and Douglas dissented when the Supreme Court refused to hear their case. Two of the questions presented were whether the executive branch constitutionally could order the soldiers to participate in military activity in Vietnam when no war had been declared by Congress, and of what relevance were treaty obligations (including renunciation of war in the Kellogg-Briand Pact). "We cannot make these problems go away simply by refusing to hear the case of three obscure Army privates," Douglas wrote.[6]

Four years later, the Supreme Court of the United States did consider conscientious objection to a particular war, rather than objection to war itself. The case concerned two men. One did not report for induction. The other applied for separation from the army as a conscientious objector after he had completed basic training and received orders for duty in Vietnam. Both men regarded the war in Vietnam as "unjust" and believed that their deeply held religious views required them not to participate in an unjust war. In *Gillette v. United States*, the Supreme Court said that the words "conscientiously opposed to participation in war in any form"

> can bear but one meaning; that conscientious scruples relating to war and military service must amount to conscientious opposition to participating personally in any war and all war. *See Welsh v. United States.* . . . [C]onscientious scruples must implicate "war in any form," and an objection involving a particular war, rather than all war, would plainly not be covered by § 6(j).[7]

---

5   *Mitchell v. United States*, 386 U.S. 972 (1967), Douglas, J., dissenting, <https://bulk.resource.org/courts.gov/c/US/386/386.US.972.1012.html>, accessed May 20, 2016.

6   *Mora v. McNamara*, 389 U.S. 934 (1967), Stewart, J., joined by Douglas, J., dissenting; and Douglas, J., joined by Stewart, J., dissenting. <https://www.law.cornell.edu/supremecourt/text/389/934#writing-type-16-STEWARTDOUGLAS>, accessed May 20, 2016. *See also*, Dennis Mora, James Johnson, and David Samas, "The Fort Hood Three," in *We Won't Go: Personal Accounts of War Objectors*, collected by Alice Lynd (Boston: Beacon Press, 1968), 181–202.

7   *Gillette v. United States*, 401 U.S. 437, 443 (1971). <http://caselaw.findlaw.com/us-supreme-court/401/437.html>, accessed May 20, 2016.

The Court held that

> Congress intended to exempt persons who oppose participating in all war—
> and that persons who object solely to participation in a particular war are
> not within the purview of the exempting section, even though the latter
> objection may have such roots in a claimant's conscience and personality
> that it is "religious" in character.[8]

A conscientious objector may use force under some circumstances, but under no
circumstances may choose what war, or in what aspect of war, he or she will serve. The
Supreme Court said in *Gillette*, "Willingness to use force in self-defense, in defense of
home and family, or in defense against immediate acts of aggressive violence toward
other persons in the community, has not been regarded as inconsistent with a claim
of conscientious objection to war as such."[9]

The Army Regulation on Conscientious Objection says, "A conscientious objector
is not necessarily a pacifist. An applicant may be willing to use force to protect himself
or herself or his or her family and still be a conscientious objector. However, if he or she
is willing to defend the United States, he or she cannot choose when and where."[10] The
issue is whether a person is willing to be a combatant in war: "A person who desires to
choose the war in which he or she will participate is not a conscientious objector under
the regulation. His or her objection must be to all wars rather than a specific war."[11]

Sincerity
The ultimate question in conscientious objector cases is the sincerity of the applicant
in objecting, on religious grounds, to participation in war in any form.[12]

---

8 *Gillette*, 401 U.S. at 447. *See also*, *Gillette*, 401 U.S. at 460: "[W]e conclude that it is
   supportable for Congress to have decided that the objector to all war—to all killing in
   war—has a claim that is distinct enough and intense enough to justify special status,
   while the objector to a particular war does not."
9 *Gillette*, 401 U.S. at 448, citing cases by U.S. Courts of Appeal.
10 Army Regulation 600-43, Conscientious Objection, 21 Aug. 2006, effective 21 Sept.
   2006 (hereafter, "AR 600-43"), Appendix D-4, d (emphasis added), <https://fas.org/irp/
   doddir/army/ar600-43.pdf>, accessed December 19, 2016.
11 Ibid., AR 600-43, Glossary, Section II, Terms, "War in any form." The definition
   continues: "However, a belief in a theocratic or spiritual war between the powers of good
   and evil does not constitute a willingness to participate in 'war' within the meaning of
   this regulation." Similarly, *see*, Department of Defense, "Instruction," DoDI 1300.06,
   May 31, 2007, 3.5.2: "A belief in a theocratic or spiritual war between the powers of good
   and evil does not constitute a willingness to participate in 'war' within the meaning of
   this Instruction." <http://fas.org/irp/doddir/dod/i1300_06.pdf>, accessed May 21, 2016.
   See also, *Sicurella v. United States*, 348 U.S. 385, 389–91 (1955), <https://supreme.justia.
   com/cases/federal/us/348/385/case.html>, accessed June 3, 2016.
12 *Witmer v. United States*, 348 U.S. 375, 381 (1955). <http://caselaw.findlaw.com/us-
   supreme-court/348/375.html>, accessed May 21, 2016. Witmer first claimed exemption

The Army Regulation uses the same language as the Supreme Court: "A conscientious objector is one whose conscience . . . allows him or her no rest or inner peace if he or she is required to fulfill the present military obligation."[13]

Volunteers for Military Service May Become Conscientious Objectors

The central issue for American conscientious objectors who are already in the military is whether their objections to participation in war "crystallized" after they volunteered and were inducted. Some of these individuals develop an objection to participation in any war and they may qualify for recognition as conscientious objectors. Some find themselves objecting to the war in which they have been ordered or expect to be ordered to participate, or wars of a certain character such as wars of aggression or nuclear war, and they do not qualify for recognition as conscientious objectors.

Criteria
The criteria for granting or denying conscientious objector status are the same whether or not the person has entered into military service.[14]

> Army regulation defines conscientious objection as "[a] firm, fixed and sincere objection to participation in war in any form or the bearing of arms, because of religious training and belief" and defines religious training and belief to include "deeply held moral or ethical belief[s]" even if the applicant himself characterizes them as non-religious. . . . Religious training and belief does not encompass "a belief that rests solely upon consideration of policy, pragmatism, expediency, or political views." . . . Further, "[a] person who desires to choose the war in which he or she will participate is not a

---

as a farmer and as a conscientious objector, asserting that the ministerial classification did not apply to him; but after his claim for exemption as a farmer had been denied he claimed he was a full-time minister. 348 U.S. at 381–82. "This is not merely a case of a registrant's claiming three separate classifications; it goes to his sincerity and honesty in claiming conscientious objection to participation in war. It would not be mere suspicion or speculation for the Board to conclude, after denying Witmer's now abandoned claims of farmer and minister, that he was insincere in his claim of conscientious objection." 348 U.S. at 383.

13   AR 600-43, Appendix D-4, b.

14   *Gillette*, 401 U.S. at 442: "Department of Defense Directive No. 1300.6 . . . prescribes that post-induction claims to conscientious objector status shall be honored, if valid, by the various branches of the armed forces. Section 6(j) of the Act, as construed by the courts, is incorporated by the various service regulations issued pursuant to the Directive, and thus the standards for measuring claims of in service objectors . . . are the same as the statutory tests applicable in a preinduction situation." *See also*, Department of Defense, "Instruction," DoDI 1300.06, May 31, 2007.

conscientious objector under the regulation. His or her objection must be to all wars rather than a specific war."[15]

Late Crystallization of Belief

When a person enters military service and then applies for discharge or reassignment to noncombatant duty because of conscientious belief, the question is whether he or she has undergone a real change or development of belief since entry into military service.

> Applicants who held their beliefs before entry into military service, but failed to make these beliefs known, cannot be discharged or reassigned to noncombatant duty. However, those who have undergone a real change or development of belief since entry into military service . . . may be discharged or reassigned to noncombatant duty, as proper. The investigating officer must attempt to determine if the person has undergone a sudden, easily identifiable experience or exposure to new beliefs, or if old beliefs have matured gradually and taken on new meanings in his or her life and, if so, when, where, and under what circumstances or influences.[16]

---

15 *Watson v. Geren*, 569 F.3d 115, 130 (2d Cir. 2009) (en banc review denied, 587 F.3d 156 (2d Cir. 2009), citing Army Reg. 600-43, Glossary, Section II, Terms, *Gillette*, *Welsh*, *Witmer*, and DoDI 1300.06, Glossary, Section II, Terms. <http://www.casemakerlegal. com/docView.aspx?DocId=793187&Index=D%3a%5cdtsearch%5cIndex%5c01Test% 5cALL%5fCITED%5fCASE&HitCount=5&hits=2771+278d+278e+278f+2790+&is FirstPass=&categoryAlias=Case%20Law&fCount=2&cf=0&dt=CASE&jurisdictions. allFederal=False&jurisdictions.allStates=False&searchType=BROWSE&bReqSt=FED *&dataT=CASE>, accessed May 21, 2016.

16 AR 600-43, Appendix D-4, e. The application procedure is summarized by a district court judge in *Kanai v. Geren*, 671 F.Supp. 713, 716 n.2 (D.Md. 2009); reversed on other grounds, *Kanai v. McHugh*, 638 F.3d 251 (4th Cir. 2011):

> An application for CO status is a multi-stage process. First, the applicant submits a formal application and any supporting materials to his immediate commanding officer. Army Reg. 600-43, ¶ 2-1(a). The application is then submitted to an interviewing chaplain, who submits a detailed report to the commander, commenting on the nature and basis of the claim, opinion on the source of the beliefs, sincerity and depth of conviction, and appropriate comments on demeanor and lifestyle. Army Reg. 600-43, ¶ 2-3. The application is next forwarded to a military mental health physician, who evaluates whether the applicant is suffering from any mental disease or defect. Army Reg. 600-43, ¶ 2-3(b). If the applicant is able to cooperate intelligently in the administrative proceedings, an Investigating Officer ("IO") from outside the applicant's chain of command is appointed to review the evidence, hold a hearing, and write a report. Army Reg. 600-43, ¶ 2-4, 2-5. The IO's report and the entire case file is then forwarded through command channels for review and recommendation. Army Reg. 600-43, ¶ 2-6. An applicant has the opportunity to comment or rebut these additional recommendations. Eventually, the entire package is forwarded to the DACORB [Department of the Army Conscientious

Agustin Aguayo volunteered to serve in the United States Army in November 2002. He signed up for eight years in the army with four years of active duty. In his enlistment agreement, Aguayo answered "no" to the following question: "Are you now or have you ever been a conscientious objector? (That is, do you have, or have you ever had, a firm, fixed, and sincere objection to participation in war in any form or to the bearing of arms because of religious belief or training?)"[17]

Aguayo entered the service as a healthcare specialist in January 2003. In February 2004, shortly before he was deployed to Iraq, he applied for a discharge from the army on the basis of conscientious objection. The captain who investigated Aguayo's application recommended that the discharge be granted: "it seemed clear to me that PFC Aguayo is absolutely sincere in his stated beliefs," that "Aguayo's opposition to war grew during basic training and solidified during live fire exercises," and that "he is internally incapable of participating in any form of war without being in a constant state of personal moral dilemma." Yet his application was repeatedly denied at higher levels in the chain of command.[18]

Aguayo insisted unsuccessfully that "the 'crystallization' of conscientious objector beliefs, like the process of religious conversion, is not always the result of prolonged study and can instead be dramatic and quick, as when it is precipitated by a life crisis," in his case, his experience in weapons training.[19]

Assignment to Noncombatant Service

A member of the military who applies for conscientious objector status should be immediately assigned to noncombatant tasks until his request is ruled on. He or she may be offered and may accept noncombatant service for the duration of his or her enlistment.

The Department of Defense recognizes the same two classifications of conscientious objector as the Military Selective Service Act, designated as 1-O and 1-A-O:

> *Class 1-O Conscientious Objector.* A member who, by reason of conscientious objection, sincerely objects to participation in military service of any kind in war in any form.
> *Class 1-A-O Conscientious Objector.* A member who, by reason of conscientious objection, sincerely objects to participation as a combatant in war in

---

Objector Board], which makes the final determination on all applications for discharge on the basis of conscientious objection. Army Reg. 600-43, ¶ 2-8(a). Criteria and procedures are spelled out in detail in Department of Defense Instruction 1300.06.

17 *Aguayo v. Harvey*, 476 F.3d 971, 973 (D.C. Cir. 2007). An applicant who would have qualified for CO status before entering the military is generally not eligible for CO status once in the service. *Aguayo*, 476 at 973 citing 32 C.F.R. § 75.4(a).

18 *Aguayo*, 476 F.3d at 973–74.

19 *Aguayo*, 476 F.3d at 981.

any form, but whose convictions are such as to permit military service in a non-combatant status.[20]

Army Regulation 600-43 sets forth the policy, criteria, and procedures applicable to conscientious objectors in military service. Conscientious objectors who enlist as 1-A-O noncombatants for the medical career management field are assigned to modified basic training (MBT), which excludes training in the study, use, or handling of arms or weapons; but they may be assigned hazardous duties.[21] A person who has applied for conscientious objector status after enlisting may be deployed with his or her unit.[22]

Jeremy Hinzman applied for noncombatant status.[23] If he were a combat medic with an infantry platoon, he would be in harm's way with bullets whizzing over his head, and he was fully willing to do that. His "sole concern was with taking other lives."[24] When asked whether he would draw a distinction between offensive and defensive operations, he said Yes:

> [I]f somebody broke the lines in our camp and started shooting . . . like anybody else . . . I would [be] obligated to the other soldiers that I'm with to take some sort of action, but that's a lot different than planning out a raid or an ambush that's rehearsed oftentimes weeks beforehand and then carrying it out. It's an instantaneous reaction versus a very well orchestrated plan or attack.[25]

Hinzman was aware of the Army Regulation that does not require a conscientious objector to be a pacifist and, he insisted, a conscientious objector retains the right to self-defense.[26]

Within three days after he applied for conscientious objector status, Jeremy Hinzman was reassigned to noncombatant duties, first as a gate guard checking

---

20 DoDI 1300.06, 3.1.1 and 3.1.2.
21 AR 600-43, 1-6.
22 AR 600-43, 2-10, c(1).
23 Justice Douglas, dissenting, in *Ehlert v. United States*, 402 U.S. 99, 113 (1971), warned (and Jeremy Hinzman experienced):
>   In a choice between civilian and military factfinders dealing in an area of conscience, clearly the former are to be preferred.
>   Moreover, proof of a conscientious objector's claim will usually be much more difficult after induction than before. Military exigencies may take him far from his neighborhood, the only place where he can find the friends and associates who know him. His chances of having a fair hearing are therefore lessened when the hearing on his claim is relegated to in service procedures.
24 Immigration and Refugee Board, Jeremy Dean Hinzman et al., claimants, File No: TA4-01429, Toronto, Canada, December 6, 2004, hearing transcript, 101.
25 Ibid., 103–4.
26 Ibid., 110.

people's identification and license plates. After a couple of months he was assigned to work in the kitchen and dining facility of his battalion; and during his entire deployment in Afghanistan, he worked fourteen or fifteen hours a day doing menial kitchen tasks.[27]

Rory Fanning's experience as a noncombatant was not so benign. Twelve hours after he formally declared his intention to file the papers necessary to be recognized as a conscientious objector, he was deployed to Afghanistan for a second time. "[T]hey sent me to 'walk with the donkeys' in a supply role in a combat zone. I would also be the gofer for my first sergeant, who was now referring to me as 'bitch' and 'vile piece of shit' for betraying the Ranger Creed."[28] During the twenty-one-hour plane ride and two-hour helicopter trip, Rory Fanning remembers no one speaking to him. He was scared. In high mountain terrain, he was sent out to chop wood.[29]

> Occasionally I was sent off with the donkey train to gather more supplies at the bottom of the mountain. At nights I slept outside, often in the snow and the mud, by myself with a single blanket. I soon caught a high fever. There was no room for me in the rooms we were told to sleep in. . . . In the beginning I was overwhelmed. . . . I couldn't imagine getting home safely at that point. You need support when you are halfway around the world in a combat zone—this is what famously bonds soldiers together. Being rejected in such an environment has a strong effect. . . .[30]

If he made it home, Rory Fanning thought, he could never say a word about it. He was afraid that the connection with his family would be damaged from the shame. He would have to hide part of himself because he didn't think his family would ever understand.[31]

During the Korean War, Staughton Lynd applied for and was granted 1-A-O classification as a medic who would not carry a weapon. During basic training the question was asked, "If there were a seriously wounded soldier and a lightly wounded soldier on the battlefield, who would you help first?" Staughton thought he knew enough about the Hippocratic Oath to answer that question. To his astonishment, the correct answer was "the lightly wounded soldier, because he can get back into combat sooner." That was when Staughton realized that he had made a major mistake to enter military service at all.

---

27   Ibid., 93, 105–7.
28   Rory Fanning, *Worth Fighting For: An Army Ranger's Journey Out of the Military and Across America* (Chicago: Haymarket Books, 2014), 99.
29   Ibid., 100–101.
30   Ibid., 101–2.
31   Ibid., 103.

Veterans for Peace

In the United States, the strongest opposition to war and militarism has come from veterans acting in networks of individuals and small groups. Once again, we turn to Brian Willson.

After Brian Willson's traumatic experience at the village bombed during the Vietnam War, and while he was still stationed in Vietnam, the librarian at the Air Force base library noticed the books that Lieutenant Willson was checking out and invited him to have dinner with her family.

> After dinner the family sang some songs, one of which they translated into English specially for me. . . . The song was dedicated to a North American hero to the Vietnamese people, Norman R. Morrison. Four of the lines went something like this:
> *The flame which burned you will clear and lighten life*
> *And many new generations of people will find the horizon,*
> *Then a day will come when the American people*
> *Will rise, one after another, for life.*

Brian knew that a man older than himself, named Norman Morrison, had burned himself to death at the Pentagon in November 1965 to protest the Vietnam War. He and Norman had graduated from the same high school in western New York State and Norman, Brian recalls, was the first Eagle Scout he knew personally! When Brian Willson, before coming to Vietnam, first learned of Norman Morrison's self-immolation, he concluded that Norman "had cracked, and shamed himself." In Vietnam, at the hospitable home of the Air Force base librarian and her family, Lieutenant Willson broke into tears. "I finally understood Norman's deep anguish about the war."[32]

Brian returned to the United States and was honorably discharged. In 1986, he and three others undertook a fast on the steps of Congress to protest U.S. aid to the "contras" in Nicaragua.[33] One of the others was Duncan Murphy, who had served as an ambulance driver in World War II and who took part in the liberation of the Bergen-Belsen concentration camp. The second was Charlie Liteky. Liteky had been a Catholic chaplain in Vietnam and had been awarded the Congressional Medal of Honor for rescuing more than twenty wounded soldiers while under intense enemy fire. Finally there was George Mizo, a highly decorated Vietnam veteran who had been seriously wounded when most of his unit was wiped out in an ambush.

The fast failed to change U.S. policy but, after it ended, Brian and his friends helped to form a group known as the Veterans Peace Action Team. In March 1987

---

32   Willson, *On Third World Legs*, 19–20, and *Blood on the Tracks*, 69.
33   The paragraphs that follow are based on Willson, *Blood on the Tracks*, Chapters 14–22.

several members of the group began, unarmed and undefended, a seventy-mile walk along a dangerous rural road in northern Nicaragua. We (the Lynds) have traveled that road and remember the white crosses along the roadside at points where the U.S.-supported "contras" had killed Nicaraguan civilians. Symbolically, the American veterans accompanied the Nicaraguan campesinos who were obliged to use the road. All of the participants survived the walk unscathed.

Finally, Brian and his growing assemblage of fellow veterans and peace activists decided to engage in nonviolent direct action to obstruct the flow of U.S. arms to repressive governments in Central America. Brian, Duncan Murphy and David Duncombe, a veteran of World War II and the Korean War who was then serving as a university chaplain, decided to fast for forty days. During that time they would position themselves on the train tracks over which a train passed every day carrying munitions to a point on the California coast from which they were shipped to El Salvador and other countries where governments sought to suppress popular uprisings. The project was called Nuremberg Actions, thinking of the document promulgated by the victorious Allies of World War II that prohibited war crimes, crimes against peace, and crimes against humanity, and led to trials of German leaders in Nuremberg, Germany.

The project began on September 1, 1987. Brian informs us that the men knew that the speed limit for trains at that location was five miles per hour, and they also knew that base protocol and regulations specifically required demonstrators to be arrested before movement of any trains if demonstrators were on the tracks. But as a train approached the three men on the tracks, it did not stop. It accelerated.[34] Duncan and Duncombe managed to evade the train. Brian did not. It was immediately apparent that both of his feet were cut off and his head was split open. Miraculously, he survived.[35] He now stands tall on prosthetic legs. He continues to be a peace activist and a writer. According to Wikipedia:

[H]e has documented U.S. policy in nearly two dozen countries. Since 1986, Willson has studied on-site policies in a number of countries, among them

---

34 E-mail from Brian Willson to Alice Lynd, March 4, 2016: "[T]he Posted train speed limit was 5 mph and the Navy base protocol, and its regulations, specifically required arrests before movement of any trains if demonstrators were noted on the tracks." Brian adds, "[T]he train crew that day was ordered to NOT stop despite protocol and regulations. . . . [T]he FBI determined that the train was accelerating to 16–17 mph at time of impact. . . ."

35 Willson, *Blood on the Tracks*, 214, and caption to photograph between pages 232 and 233: "My visibly indented skull shows a hole where a piece of my skull the size of a lemon was completely dislodged and thrust into my right frontal lobe, destroying it. My outer left ear had been sliced off but was sewn back on and restored to near its original state. Other injuries included a broken right shoulder, cracked ribs, broken right wrist, two broken elbows, damaged right kidney, extensive abrasions on arms and shoulders, and multiple cuts inside my mouth."

Nicaragua, El Salvador, Honduras, Panama, Brazil, Argentina, Mexico, Colombia, Ecuador, Cuba, Haiti, Iraq, Israel (and Palestinian territories), Japan, and Korea, both North and South. Documenting the pattern of policies that he says "violate U.S. Constitutional and international laws prohibiting aggression and war crimes," Willson has been an educator and activist, teaching about the dangers of these policies. He has participated in lengthy fasts, actions of nonviolent civil disobedience, and tax refusal along with voluntary simplicity.[36]

Torture by the United States

We who wish to affirm human rights and to break the cycle of violence have serious tasks ahead of us. At this writing many men have been detained at Guantánamo for years, some without charges.

As mentioned in the chapter on international law, the United States ratified the Convention Against Torture with several reservations. Those reservations do not, however, relieve the United States from its responsibility for what we do to detainees at Guantánamo. Article 2.2 of the Convention Against Torture states: "No exceptional circumstances whatsoever, whether a state of war or a threat of war, internal political instability or any other public emergency, may be invoked as a justification of torture."[37]

In 2014, the Senate Select Committee on Intelligence released a report on the Central Intelligence Agency's Detention and Interrogation Program.[38] Its findings show that the CIA practiced many of the methods of torture listed in paragraph 145 of the Istanbul Protocol Manual on the Effective Investigation and Documentation of Torture and Other Cruel, Inhuman or Degrading Treatment or Punishment.[39]

- The CIA applied its enhanced interrogation techniques with significant repetition for days or weeks at a time. Interrogation techniques such as slaps and "wallings" (slamming detainees against a wall), frequently concurrent with sleep deprivation and nudity. . . . At times, detainees were walked around naked or were shackled with their hands above their heads

36 Wikipedia, <https://en.wikipedia.org/wiki/Brian_Willson>, accessed May 21, 2016. For essays by Brian Willson, *see* his blog, <http://www.brianwillson.com/>.

37 Convention Against Torture, Article 2.2. <http://www.ohchr.org/EN/Professional Interest/Pages/CAT.aspx>, accessed May 21, 2016.

38 Senate Select Committee on Intelligence, *Committee Study of the CIA's Detention and Interrogation Program*, Findings and Conclusions, approved December 13, 2012, updated for release April 3, 2014, Declassification Revisions December 3, 2014, 3–4, <http://www.feinstein.senate.gov/public/index.cfm/files/serve?File_id=a992171e-fd27-47bb-8917-5ebe98c72764&SK=04753BC866283C0F5913D7E1A24FA851>, accessed May 21, 2016.

39 Istanbul Protocol Manual, ¶ 145. <http://www.ohchr.org/Documents/Publications/training8Rev1en.pdf>, accessed May 16, 2016.

for extended periods of time. Other times, detainees were subjected to what was described as a "rough takedown," in which approximately five CIA officers would scream at a detainee, drag him outside of his cell, cut his clothes off, and secure him with Mylar tape. The detainee would then be hooded and dragged up and down a long corridor while being slapped and punched. The Istanbul Protocol Manual prohibits blunt trauma such as a slap, punch or kick, restriction of sleep, forced nakedness and humiliation.

- Sleep deprivation involved keeping detainees awake for up to 180 hours, usually standing or in stress positions, at times with their hands shackled above their heads. At least five detainees experienced disturbing hallucinations during prolonged sleep deprivation and, in at least two of those cases, the CIA nonetheless continued the sleep deprivation. CIA medical personnel treated at least one detainee for swelling in order to allow the continued use of standing sleep deprivation. The Istanbul Protocol Manual prohibits restriction of sleep, and positional torture using suspension, prolonged constraint of movement, and forced positioning.

- At least five CIA detainees were subjected to "rectal rehydration" or rectal feeding without documented medical necessity. While rectal rehydration is not explicitly forbidden in the Istanbul Protocol Manual, it does prohibit sexual violence to genitals, molestation, and "instrumentation."

- The waterboarding technique was physically harmful, inducing convulsions and vomiting. One man, for example, became "completely unresponsive, with bubbles rising through his open, full mouth." The Istanbul Protocol Manual prohibits asphyxiation, such as drowning, smothering, or choking.

- The CIA placed detainees in ice water "baths." Lack of heat at the facility likely contributed to the death of a detainee. The Istanbul Protocol Manual prohibits exposure to extremes of temperature.

- The CIA led several detainees to believe they would never be allowed to leave CIA custody alive, suggesting to one detainee that he would only leave in a coffin-shaped box. The Istanbul Protocol Manual prohibits threats of death.

- CIA officers also threatened at least three detainees with harm to their families—to include threats to harm the children of a detainee, threats to sexually abuse the mother of a detainee, and a threat to "cut [a detainee's] mother's throat." The Istanbul Protocol Manual prohibits threats of harm to family.

- Except when being interrogated or debriefed by CIA personnel, CIA detainees at the COBALT detention facility were kept in complete darkness and constantly shackled in isolated cells with loud noise or music and only a bucket to use for human waste. The Istanbul Protocol Manual prohibits solitary confinement, deprivation of light, deprivation of normal sensory stimulation, restriction of food, water, toilet facilities, bathing, medical care, and loss of contact with the outside world.

It is not only CIA personnel but members of the Armed Forces who participate in these actions.[40]

Mohamedou Ould Slahi, who was detained at Guantánamo from 2002 to 2016, was on the receiving end of many of these interrogation techniques.[41] In his diary, he says he asked some of his guards why they obeyed an unlawful order to stop him from praying. "I could have refused, but my boss would have given me a shitty job or transferred me to a bad place," the guard replied, "I know I can go to hell for what I have done to you." Elsewhere in his diary, Slahi remarks: "The Prophet Mohamed (Peace be upon him) said, 'God tortures whoever tortures human beings,' and as far as I understand it, the person's religion doesn't matter."[42]

---

40   *See*, U.S. Department of Justice, Office of the Inspector General, Oversight and Review Division, *A Review of the FBI's Involvement in and Observations of Detainee Interrogations in Guantánamo Bay, Afghanistan, and Iraq*, May 2008, Chapter Five, FBI Concerns about Military Interrogation at Bay, 77 (refers to "a major disagreement between FBI agents and the military regarding interrogation techniques") <http://www.justice.gov/oig/special/s0805/final.pdf>, accessed May 21, 2016.

41   Prolonged detention without charges is contrary to the following provisions of the International Covenant on Civil and Political Rights, Article 9, paragraphs 2, 3, and 4: "Anyone who is arrested shall be informed, at the time of arrest, of the reasons for his arrest and shall be promptly informed of any charges against him"; "Anyone arrested or detained on a criminal charge shall be brought promptly before a judge or other officer authorized by law to exercise judicial power and shall be entitled to trial within a reasonable time or to release. . . ."; and "Anyone who is deprived of his liberty by arrest or detention shall be entitled to take proceedings before a court, in order that that court may decide without delay on the lawfulness of his detention and order his release if the detention is not lawful." <http://www.ohchr.org/EN/ProfessionalInterest/Pages/CCPR.aspx>, accessed May 21, 2016.

42   Mohamedou Ould Slahi, *Guantánamo Diary*, Larry Siems, ed., (New York: Little, Brown and Company, 2015), 234 and 183. Numerous statements by Slahi are corroborated by official sources cited in footnotes by the editor of his diary. *See also*, Department of Justice, *Review of . . . Interrogations*, 122–28, "Concerns Raised Regarding Slahi's Interrogation." Those tactics "produced no intelligence of a threat neutralization nature." Ibid., 126. *See,* Department of Defense press release no. NR-371-16, "Detainee Transfer Announced," Oct. 17, 2016, <http://www.defense.gov/News/News-Releases/News-Release-View/Article/975922/detainee-transfer-announced>, accessed October 29, 2016:

> On July 14, 2016, a Periodic Review Board consisting of representatives from the Departments of Defense, Homeland Security, Justice, and State; the Joint Chiefs of Staff, and the Office of the Director of National Intelligence determined continued law of war detention of Slahi does not remain necessary to protect against a continuing significant threat to the security of the United States. As a result of that review, which examined a number of factors, including security issues, Slahi was recommended for transfer by consensus of the six departments and agencies comprising the Periodic Review Board.

And on October 17, 2015, Slahi was transferred from the detention facility at Guantánamo Bay to the Government of Mauritania.

Chapter 4.
Israel

ISRAEL BECAME RECOGNIZED AS A STATE AFTER WORLD WAR II AND THE HORRORS experienced by Jews during the Holocaust. On November 29, 1947, the United Nations General Assembly passed a resolution calling for the establishment of a Jewish State. The Declaration of the Establishment of the State of Israel was proclaimed on May 14, 1948.[1]

Israel has been engaged in military action since its founding. A partial list of Israel's wars and military operations includes:

- War of Independence (1948)
- Six-Day War (1967)
- First Lebanon War (1982–1985)
- First Intifada[2] (1988–1992)
- Second Intifada (2000–2005) and Operation Defensive Shield (2002)
- Second Lebanon War (2006)
- Operation Cast Lead (2008–2009)
- Operation Pillar of Defense (2012)
- Operation Protective Edge (2014)[3]

"Soon after the establishment of the State of Israel, the Israeli authorities created a military government to rule those areas of Israel most densely populated with Palestinians." The area under military government was divided into what were called "closed areas." Palestinians living in one closed area were not permitted to travel to another closed area without a special permit.[4] Thus, in apparent violation of the Hague Convention and the Universal Declaration of Human Rights,[5] "Palestinians who lived in one closed area and owned land in another closed area were prohibited

---

1   The Declaration of the Establishment of the State of Israel, May 14, 1948, <http://www. jewishvirtuallibrary.org/jsource/History/Dec_of_Indep.html>, accessed May 22, 2016.

2   The word "intifada" means "to shake off" in Arabic but is commonly translated into English as "uprising."

3   Jewish Virtual Library, "Israel Defense Forces: Wars and Operations," Table of Contents, http://www.jewishvirtuallibrary.org/jsource/History/wartoc.html, accessed May 22, 2016.

4   Al Haq, West Bank Affiliate of the International Commission of Jurists, "Perpetual Emergency: A Legal Analysis of Israel's use of the British Defence (Emergency) Regulations, 1945, in the Occupied Territories," Occasional Paper No. 6 (1989), 18 and sources cited therein.

5   Hague Convention IV, Regulations, Article 46 says, "Private property cannot be confiscated" and Article 50 says, "No general penalty . . . shall be inflicted upon the population on account of the acts of individuals for which they cannot be regarded as jointly and severally responsible." <http://avalon.law.yale.edu/20th_century/hague04. asp#art46>, accessed May 22, 2016. The Universal Declaration of Human Rights, Article

from entering the second closed area to cultivate their land. After several years without cultivation, the land was confiscated. . . ."[6]

In 1950, the United Nations Security Council passed a resolution calling on governments to take "no future action involving the transfer of persons across international frontiers or armistice lines without prior consultation. . . ."[7] Between 1950 and 1967, the UN Security Council called on Israel to allow Arab civilians to be allowed to return, and to stop military strikes on Syria, Jordan, and Egypt, and condemned loss of life and heavy damage to property in the southern Hebron area.[8]

The United Nations Relief and Works Agency (UNRWA) began operations in May 1950 to provide humanitarian relief to more than seven hundred thousand refugees and displaced persons who had been forced to flee their homes in Palestine as a result of the 1948 Arab-Israeli war. Anyone in Palestine who lost both home and means of livelihood as a result of the 1948 Arab-Israeli war qualified as a "Palestine refugee." UNWRA was expected to be short-lived but still operates refugee camps and provides education, health care, social services, shelter, and emergency aid to Palestine refugees in the Gaza Strip, West Bank, Jerusalem, Lebanon, Jordan and Syria.[9]

A week after the end of the Six-Day War in June 1967, the Security Council called upon the Government of Israel to "facilitate the return" of inhabitants who fled.[10] "Emphasizing the inadmissibility of the acquisition of territory by war,"[11] in

---

17 provides, "No one shall be arbitrarily deprived of his property." <http://www.un.org/en/universal-declaration-human-rights/index.html>, accessed May 22, 2016.

6   Al Haq, "Perpetual Emergency," ibid., 18.

7   UN Security Council Resolution 89, ¶ 6, November 17, 1950, <http://www.un.org/en/ga/search/view_doc.asp?symbol=S/RES/89(1950)>, accessed May 22, 2016. If you have the year and the number of the resolution, UN Security Council Resolutions can be found at <http://www.un.org/en/sc/documents/resolutions/>, accessed May 22, 2016. Therefore, only the number and date of UN Security Council Resolutions are annotated here.

8   For a list of Security Council Resolutions critical of Israel for violations of international law, 1948–2009, notably Resolutions 89, 93, 101, 106, 111, 119, 171, 228, 237, and 242, *see* "Jeremy R. Hammond, "Rogue State: Israeli Violations of UN Security Council Resolutions," Jan. 27, 2010, <http://dissidentvoice.org/2010/01/rogue-state-israeli-violations-of-u-n-security-council-resolutions/>, accessed May 22, 2016.

9   UNRWA was established by United Nations General Assembly resolution 302(IV) of December 8, 1949. Anyone whose normal place of residence was in Mandate Palestine during the period from June 1, 1946, to May 15, 1948, and who lost both home and means of livelihood as a result of the 1948 Arab-Israeli war qualifies as a Palestine refugee, as defined by UNRWA. UNRWA, "The United Nations and Palestinian Refugees," 1, 4, 5, <http://www.unrwa.org/userfiles/2010011791015.pdf>, accessed May 22, 2016. *See* <http://www.unrwa.org/> for current information.

10 Resolution 237 (1967). This and other resolutions cited are examples of many more.

11 Resolution 242 (1967); the inadmissibility of the acquisition of territory by war is reaffirmed in Resolutions 252 (1968), 267 (1969), 271 (1969), 298 (1971), 476 (1980), 478 (1980), 497 (1981), 681 (1990). However, in 1976, the US vetoed a resolution that

November 1967 the Security Council called for "withdrawal of Israel armed forces from territories occupied in the recent conflict."[12]

Violations of Internationally Recognized Human Rights

The UN Security Council has insisted that the Fourth Geneva Convention applies to all the Arab territories occupied by Israel in 1967. The international community, including the United States, considers Israel's authority in the occupied territories to be subject to the Hague Regulations of 1907 and the 1949 Geneva Convention relating to the Protection of Civilians in Time of War. The Israeli government considers the Hague Regulations applicable but denies the applicability of the Fourth Geneva Convention to the West Bank and Gaza (although stating that it observes many of the Convention's provisions).[13]

Numerous resolutions call on Israel "not to transfer parts of its own civilian population into the occupied Arab territories." For example, as early as 1969, the Security Council determined "that the policy and practices of Israel in establishing settlements in the Palestinian and other Arab territories occupied since 1967 have no legal validity and constitute a serious obstruction to achieving a comprehensive, just and lasting peace in the Middle East."[14] And in 1980, the Security Council called upon "all States not to provide Israel with any assistance to be used specifically in connexion [*sic*] with settlements in the occupied territories."[15]

In 1992, the Security Council strongly condemned the deportation to Lebanon of "hundreds of Palestinian civilians from the territories occupied by Israel since 1967, including Jerusalem," and demanded that all those deported be safely and immediately returned.[16] The Security Council insists that the Fourth Geneva Convention

---

among other things reaffirmed the principle of the inadmissibility of acquisition of territory by force. Draft resolution S/11940 (January 26, 1976), Security Council—Veto List, <http://www.un.org/depts/dhl/resguide/scact_veto_en.shtml>, accessed June 5, 2016.

12 Resolution 242 (1967), repeatedly reaffirmed by number, e.g. Resolution 1322 (2000). For resolutions calling for withdrawal from other Palestinian cities, *see* Resolutions 1402 (2000), 1435 (2002); calling for withdrawal from and cessation of military attacks on Lebanon, *see* Resolutions 279 (1970), 316 (1972), 450 (1979), 467 (1980), 517 (1982); and calling for withdrawal from Gaza, *see* Resolution 1860 (2009). <http://www.un.org/en/sc/documents/resolutions/>, accessed May 22, 2016.

13 UN Security Council Resolution 446 (1979); 2001 Country Report, Israel and the Occupied Territories, <http://www.state.gov/j/drl/rls/hrrpt/2001/nea/8262.htm>, accessed May 22, 2016.

14 Resolution 446 (1979); regarding Israeli settlements in the occupied Palestinian territories, *see also* Resolutions 452 (1979), 465 (1980), 471 (1980).

15 Resolutions 465 (1980), 471 (1980).

16 Resolution 799 (1992). For other resolutions concerning deportations from the occupied Palestinian territories, *see also* Resolutions 469 (1980), 607 (1988), 608 (1988), 636 (1989), 641 (1989), 694 (1991), and 726 (1992).

applies to all the Arab territories occupied by Israel in 1967, and has repeatedly called upon Israel to "abide scrupulously" with the Fourth Geneva Convention.[17]

In 2004, the Security Council reaffirmed ten resolutions between 1967 and 2003, referred again to Israel's obligations under the Fourth Geneva Convention, condemned the killing of Palestinian civilians in the Rafah area (in southern Gaza), and the demolition of homes in the Rafah refugee camp. It called on Israel to respect its obligations under international humanitarian law and, in particular, not to demolish homes.[18]

Also citing international humanitarian law, including the Fourth Geneva Convention, the Security Council expressed its alarm at severe restrictions on freedom of movement and goods, and demanded complete cessation of all acts of violence and expeditious withdrawal of Israeli occupying forces from Palestinian cities.[19]

Time and again, the Security Council has condemned Israel for its disregard for, even defiance of, UN General Assembly and Security Council resolutions and flagrant violations of the UN Charter.[20]

The U.S. Department of State reports each year on human rights practices in countries supported by U.S. military assistance.[21] The State Department reported in 2013 that

---

17 Resolution 446 (1979). For other resolutions reaffirming that the Fourth Geneva Convention is "applicable to the Palestinian territories, occupied by Israel since 1967, including Jerusalem, and to other occupied Arab territories" and/or calling for Israel to abide by the Fourth Geneva Convention, *see* Resolutions 271 (1969), 452 (1979), 465 (1980), 469 (1980), 471 (1980), 476 (1980), 484 (1980), 497 (1981) (Golan Heights), 592 (1986), 605 (1987), 607 (1988), 636 (1989), 641 (1989), 694 (1991), 726 (1992), 799 (1992), 1322 (2000), 1544 (2004).

18 Resolution 1544 (2004). For other resolutions concerning Palestinian refugees, *see* Resolution 521 (1982) condemning the massacre of Palestinian civilians in the Sabra and Shatila refugee camps (in Lebanon), and Resolution 1405 (2002) concerning reports of an unknown number of deaths and destruction in the Jenin refugee camp (in the West Bank).

19 Resolution 1435 (2002). *See also* Resolution 1860 (2009) condemning the escalation of violence and hostilities resulting in heavy civilian casualties in Gaza, and calling for unimpeded provision and distribution of humanitarian assistance including food, fuel, and medical treatment.

20 Resolutions 248 (1968), 252 (1968), 256 (1968), 265 (1969), 267 (1969), 280 (1970), 298 (1971), 316 (1972), 317 (1972), 332 (1973), 337 (1973), 446 (1979), 465 (1980), 467 (1980), 469 (1980), 476 (1980), and 478 (1980). On December 23, 2016, in Resolution 2334, the Security Council reaffirmed, in part, "that the establishment by Israel of settlements in the Palestinian territory occupied since 1967, including East Jerusalem, has no legal validity and constitutes a flagrant violation under international law and a major obstacle to the achievement of the two-State solution and a just, lasting and comprehensive peace."   <http://www.timesofisrael.com/full-text-of-unsc-resolution-approved-dec-23-demanding-israel-stop-all-settlement-activity/>, accessed December 28, 2016.

21 22 U.S.C. § 2304(a)(2) provides that, with some exceptions, "no security assistance may be provided to any country the government of which engages in a consistent pattern of

Human rights problems related to Israeli authorities included reports of excessive use of force against civilians, including killings; abuse of Palestinian detainees, particularly during arrest and interrogation; austere and overcrowded detention facilities; improper use of security detention procedures; demolition and confiscation of Palestinian property; limitations on freedom of expression, assembly, and association; and severe restrictions on Palestinians' internal and external freedom of movement.[22]

Torture and Other Cruel, Inhuman, or Degrading Treatment or Punishment

As we have seen in Chapter 2, the Convention Against Torture defines torture as consisting of severe physical or mental pain or suffering, intentionally inflicted by a person acting in an official capacity, for purposes such as obtaining information or a confession, punishment, intimidation, coercion, or discrimination.[23]

Israel admits that it uses what it calls a "moderate degree of pressure" when interrogating detainees. Guidelines on interrogation, recommended by the "Landau Commission" and adopted by Israeli authorities in 1987, have been controversial ever since:

- In 1994, the UN Committee Against Torture found "moderate physical pressure" completely unacceptable as a method of interrogation because it created conditions leading to the risk of torture.
- In cases considered by the Israeli Supreme Court in 1995 and 1996, it was argued that the interrogation methods being used did not cause severe suffering.
- The UN Committee rejected that idea since the government of Israel admitted that its interrogation techniques included hooding (putting a hood over a person's head), shackling in painful positions, causing sleep deprivation, and shaking, in violation of the Convention Against Torture.
- In 1999, the Supreme Court of Israel held that interrogation methods involving physical force violate Israeli law and the individual's constitutional right to dignity. The Court rejected the following interrogation methods: shaking, forcing detainees to crouch on the tips of their toes, painful handcuffing, seating suspects in the "Shabach" position and playing loud music

gross violations of internationally recognized human rights." <http://uscode.house.gov/view.xhtml?req=(title:22%20section:2304%20edition:prelim)>, accessed May 22, 2016.

22 United States Department of State, Bureau of Democracy, Human Rights and Labor, Country Reports on Human Rights Practices for 2013, "Israel and The Occupied Territories," The Occupied Territories, Executive Summary, <http://www.state.gov/j/drl/rls/hrrpt/2013humanrightsreport/index.htm?dynamic_load_id=220358&year=2013#wrapper>, accessed May 22, 2016.

23 Convention Against Torture, Art. 1.1.

while in that position, covering a suspect's head with a sack during interrogation, and prolonged sleep deprivation.

- In 2001, the government of Israel took the position that even if its interrogation techniques violated human dignity, they did not constitute
either torture or cruel, inhuman, or degrading treatment in violation of the
Convention Against Torture.

- In 2002, the UN Committee Against Torture, disagreed with the Israeli
Supreme Court.[24]

As discussed above, the Istanbul Protocol Manual on the Effective Investigation
and Documentation of Torture and Other Cruel, Inhuman or Degrading Treatment
or Punishment, issued in 2004, lists many methods of torture, including burns with
cigarettes, electric shocks; conditions of detention such as overcrowding or solitary
confinement, no access to toilet facilities, exposure to extremes of temperature; restriction of sleep, food, water, toilet facilities, medical care; deprivation of privacy;
humiliation; threats to harm the detainee or family; and psychological techniques
that break down the individual.[25]

According to the 2013 U.S. Country Report on Israel and the Occupied
Territories, human rights organizations reported that "physical interrogation methods" permitted by Israeli law and used by Israeli security personnel could amount to
torture. These included "beatings, forcing an individual to hold a stress position for
long periods, and painful pressure from shackles or restraints applied to the forearms."
Other Israeli detention practices included isolation, sleep deprivation, and psychological abuse, such as threats to interrogate spouses, siblings, or elderly parents or to
demolish family homes.[26]

Similarly, Israeli security forces were reported to abuse, and in some cases to
torture, children who were arrested on suspicion of throwing stones or to coerce
confessions. "Tactics included beatings, long-term handcuffing, threats, intimidation, and solitary confinement. In July the IDF [Israel Defense Forces] detained
a five-year-old child in Hebron suspected of stone throwing, and blindfolded and
handcuffed the child's father, although the father was not involved in the alleged
stone throwing."[27]

There are many forms of torture that involve tying or restraining the victim in
contorted, hyperextended, or other unnatural positions for minutes or hours that
cause severe pain and may produce injuries to ligaments, tendons, nerves, and blood

---

24   Manfred Nowak, "What Practices Constitute Torture? US and UN Standards," *Human
     Rights Quarterly* 28 (2006) 809–41, 824–27, <http://faculty.maxwell.syr.edu/hpschmitz/
     PSC354/PSC354Readings/NowakTorture.pdf>, accessed May 22, 2016.

25   Istanbul Protocol Manual, ¶ 145, <www.ohchr.org/Documents/Publications/
     training8Rev1en.pdf>, accessed May 22, 2016.

26   Country Reports on Human Rights Practices for 2013, "Israel and The Occupied
     Territories," The Occupied Territories, Section 1, c.

27   Ibid.

vessels. One of those is called "Palestinian" suspension.[28] Rather than use the description of positional torture in the Istanbul Protocol Manual, we turn to a vivid description by Lawahez Burgal in her oral history.

> I was bound in many positions. . . . First they put a sack on your face which is dirty with shit from the toilet. You can't breathe from that, and you can't see anything. . . . In one of the positions, you sit in a chair with one arm over the back of the chair tied behind your back, the other arm tied under the chair, and your feet tied behind another leg of the chair. Your hands are tied to one leg of the chair and your feet are tied diagonally across to the opposite leg of the chair, so that you are off balance. Hours! That means all your muscles here are affected. You get to the point where you want to die. Try it for ten minutes and imagine it for hours and days, this position.
>
> In another position, there is a pipe on the wall. They will tie your hands to the wall in a way that you are not standing and not sitting, but squatting with your knees bent, your back thrown forward, and your hands high up behind, also for hours or days.
>
> There is another position that was used on me also. They brought two towels and water. They put you squatting down and with your hands tied to the chair. If you are tired, and you fall to one side, you fall in the water. But your hands stay in the same place; they stretch but you fall. And if you want to lean back, there is a pipe that would strike your back.
>
> You are sitting like that and suddenly a policeman comes and goes [wham] on your head or on your back. . . .
>
> They put me in an isolation cell. . . . It was like a grave. It was a small room without windows, without light. . . . And I heard something walking, like mice, inside the cell.
>
> For the first time I felt I knew the meaning of death. I felt that everything was going to stop. I couldn't breathe. I couldn't talk. I couldn't do anything. . . . I was a dead person.[29]

These forms of torture leave few, if any, external marks but may produce chronic severe disability.[30]

What Lawahez Burgal described is an example of what the Manual says is one of the central aims of torture: "to reduce an individual to a position of extreme helplessness and distress." The Manual warns us of the consequences not only for the individual but for society.

---

28   Istanbul Protocol Manual, ¶¶ 159, 206(d), 207, 210.

29   Staughton Lynd, Sam Bahour, and Alice Lynd, eds., *Homeland: Oral Histories of Palestine and Palestinians* (New York: Olive Branch Press, 1994), 156–57.

30   Istanbul Protocol Manual, ¶ 210; *see also*, ¶¶ 207, 211 for details as to injuries.

[T]orture is a means of attacking an individual's fundamental modes of psychological and social functioning. Under such circumstances, the torturer strives not only to incapacitate a victim physically but also to disintegrate the individual's personality. The torturer attempts to destroy a victim's sense of being grounded in a family and society as a human being with dreams, hopes and aspirations for the future. By dehumanizing and breaking the will of their victims, torturers set horrific examples for those who later come in contact with the victim. In this way, torture can break or damage the will and coherence of entire communities. In addition, torture can profoundly damage intimate relationships between spouses, parents, children, other family members and relationships between the victims and their communities.[31]

Lawahez described the response of her son when she returned home: "For one week, my son didn't call me 'Mama.' I had left him alone and stopped feeding him and I went away. He didn't want to come to me because of that. . . . This hurt me a lot. . . . Now, he is very close to me. He doesn't like me to go anywhere without him. He is afraid, maybe, I will go and I will not come back."[32]

Arbitrary Arrest or Detention

Israeli military law applies to Palestinians in the West Bank, but Israeli civil law applies to settlers in the West Bank. According to the U.S. State Department, Israeli military courts have had a conviction rate of more than 99 percent for Palestinians.[33]

Israeli law provides safeguards against arbitrary arrest and detention, but key safeguards do not apply to Palestinian security detainees. Palestinian security detainees are subject to the jurisdiction of Israeli military law, which permits eight days' detention before appearing before a military court. There is no requirement that a detainee have access to a lawyer until after interrogation, a process that may last weeks. The maximum period for such a detention order, according to military law, is 90 days; however, detention can be renewed if deemed necessary. Denial of visits by family, outside medical professionals, or others outside the ISA [Israel Security Agency], the IDF [Israel Defense Forces], or the prison service occurred. NGOs [nongovernmental organizations] reported persons undergoing interrogations often were held incommunicado for several weeks. . . .[34]

---

31 Istanbul Protocol Manual, ¶ 235.
32 Lawahez Burgal in Lynd et al., *Homeland*, 157.
33 Country Reports on Human Rights Practices for 2013, "Israel and The Occupied Territories," The Occupied Territories, Section 1, d.
34 Ibid.

In military trials, prosecutors often present secret evidence that is not available to the defendant or counsel. The military courts use Hebrew. Various human rights organizations claimed the availability and quality of Arabic interpretation was insufficient, especially since most interpreters were bilingual Israelis performing mandatory military service.[35]

According to the United Nations Children's Fund, most Palestinian children under the age of eighteen who are arrested in the occupied territories are held in prisons within Israel and are prosecuted under military law.[36] Signed confessions, often coerced during interrogations and written in Hebrew, were used as evidence against Palestinian minors in Israeli military courts.[37] Palestinian children sixteen and seventeen years old are detained as long as adults, twice as long as Israeli children living in the West Bank. UNICEF reported that "mistreatment of Palestinian children in the Israeli military detention system appears to be widespread, systematic, and institutionalized."[38]

These practices are forbidden under internationally recognized human rights law. The Universal Declaration of Human Rights says that everyone is entitled to equal protection of the law, and no one shall be subjected to arbitrary arrest or detention.[39] The International Covenant on Civil and Political Rights says that anyone who is arrested shall be told at the time of arrest the reasons for the arrest and the charges against him.[40] The Fourth Geneva Convention says that persons who are detained or convicted in an occupied territory must serve their sentences within the occupied territory.[41] Such violations are part of a consistent pattern of human rights violations that has been going on for decades.[42]

All of the above violations—torture and other cruel, inhuman, and degrading treatment, and collective punishment—are aspects of the occupation of Palestinian territories by Israel. "Occupation is bad," says Salah Tamari in his oral history, "I don't care who the occupier is, be it Muslim, be it Christian, or be it Jewish. . . ."

> Even if the Jews came to our country as saints—they thought it was empty, they thought it was theirs—then they were confronted with a situation

---

35 Ibid.

36 Country Reports on Human Rights Practices for 2013, "Israel and The Occupied Territories," Israel, Section 1, d.

37 Ibid.

38 Ibid.

39 Universal Declaration of Human Rights, Articles 7, 9.

40 ICCPR, Article 9.2.

41 Fourth Geneva Convention, Article 76.

42 According to 22 U.S.C. § 2304(d)(1), "the term 'gross violations of internationally recognized human rights' includes torture or cruel, inhuman, or degrading treatment or punishment, prolonged detention without charges and trial, causing the disappearance of persons by the abduction and clandestine detention of those persons, and other flagrant denial of the right to life, liberty, or the security of person."

where they found a population. Those saints needed to control the population. After a while, they resorted to the same means that others before them resorted to: divide and rule; the stick and the carrot; collective punishment. Then, after a while, they were no longer saints.[43]

Proportionality and the Dahiya Doctrine

Israel's 1998 Manual on the Laws of War states: "Even when it is not possible to isolate the civilians from an assault and there is no other recourse but to attack, this does not constitute a green light to inflict unbridled harm on civilians. The commander is required to refrain from an attack that is expected to inflict harm on the civilian population that is disproportionate to the expected military gain."[44]

However, during the summer of 2014, the images shown to the world on television displayed an overwhelming disproportion between the deaths and suffering of Gazans and Israelis. Operation "Protective Edge" began in early July. On August 12, 2014, the United Nations Office for the Coordination of Humanitarian Affairs reported:

- 1,962 Palestinians had been killed, including at least 1,417 civilians, of whom 459 were children and 238 were women. The child fatalities exceeded the combined number of children killed in the conflicts in 2008–2009 and 2012.
- 67 Israelis had been killed, including 64 soldiers and three civilians including one foreign national.
- 335,000 people were hosted at UNRWA, government shelters and with host families.
- 16,700 homes in Gaza had been destroyed or severely damaged.[45]

There is no way to explain these numbers other than to recognize that Israel has targeted civilian institutions such as apartment buildings, medical facilities, and United Nations schools to which Gaza residents had fled for protection.

---

43 Salah Tamari in Lynd et al., *Homeland*, 68.
44 Israel, *Laws of War in the Battlefield, Manual*, Military Advocate General Headquarters, Military School, 1998, 40, quoted in ICRC Customary IHL under Rule 14, Military Manuals, Israel, <https://www.icrc.org/customary-ihl/eng/print/v2_rul_rule14>, accessed May 23, 2016.
45 OCHA, Highlights, 12 August 2014, <http://www.ochaopt.org/documents/ocha_opt_sitrep_11_08_2014.pdf>, accessed May 23, 2016. During the Israeli incursion into Gaza in December 2008–January 2009, the Israeli government reported that 1,166 Palestinian deaths resulted from Israeli military operations, including 295 noncombatant deaths; four Israeli civilians and ten soldiers were killed in combat or as a result of rocket and mortar fire. "Israeli human rights organizations reported a lack of protection for civilians during the Israeli incursion into Gaza. Among 1,385 estimated casualties, . . . B'Tselem reported that civilians accounted for 773, or more than half, of those killed." 2009 Human Rights Report: Israel and the Occupied Territories, The Occupied Territories, March 11, 2010, Section 1, a. <http://www.state.gov/j/drl/rls/hrrpt/2009/nea/136070.htm>, accessed May 23, 2016.

Israel's disproportionate actions appear to be pursuant to a strategy, known as the "Dahiya doctrine." Dahiya was a section of Beirut from which rockets were fired at Israeli cities during a thirty-four-day war in 2006. Israel responded by air raids that flattened Dahiya. In 2008, the commander of the IDF northern front was reported by Reuters to have said:

> What happened in the Dahiya quarter of Beirut in 2006 will happen in every village from which Israel is fired on. . . . We will apply disproportionate force on it (village) and cause great damage and destruction. From our perspective, these are not civilian villages, they are military bases. . . . This is not a recommendation. This is a plan. And it has been approved.[46]

These practices by the Israel Defense Forces violate the Fourth Geneva Convention and customary international humanitarian law. Combatants may not attack indiscriminately, may not cause harm to civilians that exceeds the military benefit of the attack, must take precautions before an attack to minimize civilian casualties, and must not use violence when its objective is disproportionate to the destruction it can be expected to cause.

Exemption from Military Service for Reasons of Religious Conviction

For decades, members of the Israel Defense Forces (IDF) have been confronted with orders to serve in a series of military actions and occupations in Lebanon, the West Bank, and Gaza Strip. Increasingly and prominently, young people facing military service, reservists, active-duty members of the military and veterans, have refused to serve or have denounced what they have come to believe are immoral or unlawful actions.

Israel is similar to the United States in that it exempts or postpones military service based on religious practice. Like the United States, Israel does not recognize selective conscientious objection. Unlike the United States, military service is compulsory for most Israeli men and women.

Under Israeli law, only women are exempted from military service for reasons of conscience. Article 39(c) of the Defence Service Law says, "A female person of military age who has proved . . . that reasons of conscience or reasons connected with her family's religious way of life prevent her from serving in defence service shall be exempt from the duty of that service." Article 40, "Exemption for reasons of religious conviction," requires practice as well as belief:

---

46 Reuters, "Israel Warns Hizbullah War Would Invite Destruction," *Ynetnews*, October 3, 2008, <http://www.ynetnews.com/Ext/Comp/ArticleLayout/CdaArticlePrintPreview/ 1,2506,L-3604893,00.html>, accessed May 23, 2016.

A female person designated for defence service who declares in writing . . . before a judge . . . [of a civil or rabbinical court,] (1) that reasons of religious conviction prevent her from serving in defence service and (2) that she observes the dietary laws at home and away from home and (3) that she does not ride on the Sabbath shall be exempt from defence service after delivering the affidavit, in the manner and at the time prescribed by regulations, to a calling-up office empowered in that behalf.[47]

Historically, full-time yeshiva students (men who study traditional religious texts and for whom "Torah is their calling") could be deferred or, in practice, exempt from military service.[48] The rationale was that ultra-Orthodox young men serve the nation through prayer and study, thus preserving Jewish learning and heritage, and that conscription threatens their community.[49] There has also been some question as to how effective such students would be in military service. They would encounter difficulties in adjusting to the military, and the military would have difficulties adjusting to them.

Thus, for example, the ultra-Orthodox do not recognize the Chief Rabbinate of Israel's certification that food is kosher, while they themselves disagree over recognition of a number of special kosher certifications by various rabbis. Similarly, other daily practices of theirs are likely to give rise to many difficulties in the IDF's ability to integrate them.[50]

After years of controversy, the Defence Service Law was amended in March 2014 so that yeshiva students will gradually be integrated into either the Israel Defense Forces or the National Civilian Service.[51]

---

47 Israel Ministry of Foreign Affairs, Defence Service Law—Consolidated Version 5746-1986, January 30, 1986, Article 39(c) and Article 40, <http://www.mfa.gov.il/ mfa/mfa-archive/1980–1989/pages/defence%20service%20law%20-consolidated%20 version--%205746-1.aspx>, accessed May 23, 2016.

48 GlobalSecurity.org, "Ultra-Orthodox/Haredi—Military Service," (no date), <http:// www.globalsecurity.org/military/world/israel/jew-haredi-idf.htm>, accessed May 23, 2016; and Batsheva Sobelman, "Cabinet Approves Changes to Israel's Draft Law," *Los Angeles Times*, July 7, 2013, <http://articles.latimes.com/2013/jul/07/world/la-fg-wn-israel-draft-20130707>, accessed May 23, 2016. Secondary sources are cited where primary sources are not readily available on the internet in English.

49 AP/Jerusalem Post/Knesset PR, "Jerusalem—Israel Passes Law Meant to Draft Ultra-Orthodox," March 12, 2014, <http://www.vosizneias.com/157999/2014/03/12/ jerusalem-israel-passes-law-meant-to-draft-ultra-orthodox/>, accessed May 23, 2016.

50 GlobalSecurity.org, "Ultra-Orthodox/Haredi—Military Service."

51 Global Legal Monitor [Global Legal Monitor is an online publication from the Law Library of Congress], "Israel: Amendment Law Imposes Military Draft and National Service Obligations on Yeshiva Students," (March 31, 2014), and sources cited therein, <http://www.loc.gov/lawweb/servlet/lloc_news?disp3_l205403917_text>, accessed May 23, 2016.

Israel's Policy on Selective Conscientious Objection

When military service is compulsory, as it was in the United States for many years and still is in Israel, some individuals or groups refuse induction into the military and others become objectors in the course of serving in the military. When numbers of objectors are small and cases are not publicized, individuals may be accommodated or not prosecuted. But when the numbers swell and there are notorious public refusals, policies become more clearly defined and enforced. Gad Elgazi was one of a group of twenty-seven high school seniors who published a letter in 1979 saying they would refuse to serve in the occupied Palestinian territories. Elgazi's request for exemption was denied and he served three consecutive one-month prison terms. He took his case to the Supreme Court of Israel, claiming discrimination inasmuch as the Ministry of Defense had previously granted exemptions. Counsel for the Israel Defense Forces (IDF) explained:

> Army authorities had given objectors a guarantee that they would be stationed according to their wishes, within the borders of Israel, as long as refusal was an isolated phenomenon. Now policy has changed. What had once been sporadic instances of refusal with which the IDF was prepared to live, has changed in character and become an organized protest whose aim is to turn the IDF . . . into the battleground for a kind of confrontation which the army cannot be associated with.

The Supreme Court of Israeli concluded: "No military organization can tolerate the existence of a general principle according to which individual soldiers can dictate their place of service, be it for economic or social reasons, or for reasons of conscience."[52]

In 1993, the Human Rights and International Relations Department of Israel's Ministry of Justice declared Israel's Policy on Selective Conscientious Objection pertaining to "soldiers who refuse to serve in specific locations (selective conscientious objectors)":

- "the needs of the IDF must take priority over the personal preferences of its soldiers";
- "each individual must abide by policies of the democratically elected government with which he might disagree";
- "soldiers of the IDF must serve where they are posted";
- "a soldier must serve 'when and where' so commanded."

---

52 Alek D. Epstein, "The Freedom of Conscience and Sociological Perspectives on Dilemmas of Collective Secular Disobedience: The Case of Israel," *Journal of Human Rights*, Vol. 1, No. 3 (September 2002), 305–20, 311, citing *Proceedings of the Supreme Court*, September 24, 1980, <http://www.openu.ac.il/Personal_sites/download/Alek/ 12%20Conscientious%20disobedience%20-%20JHR,%201,%203%20(2002).pdf>, accessed May 23, 2016.

The policy states:

> A soldier cannot be allowed to dictate which government policies he will respect nor where and under what circumstances he will serve. Israel does not recognize a right to "selective" objection, i.e., unwillingness to serve in specific places or capacities. The recognition of such a "right" runs contrary to basic conceptions of military order and discipline. Under any democracy's military law, refusal to comply with a military order constitutes grounds for criminal prosecution or disciplinary action. No army could function without the ultimate authority to order soldiers to serve in any location according to military necessity.

By way of rationale, the Israeli policy concludes with a quotation from the U.S. Supreme Court's rejection of selective conscientious objection in *Gillette v. United States* and a statement that disciplinary measures against selective objectors in Israel "are considerably more lenient than those taken by the United States and other Western democracies."[53]

Refuseniks

People who refuse to serve in the Israel Defense Forces (IDF), whether pacifists or selective objectors, are commonly called "refuseniks." Particularly during times of conflict in which the IDF attacked targets in Lebanon and the occupied Palestinian territories, men and women who would willingly defend Israel but believed that what Israel was doing was morally wrong or not in Israel's best interests, refused military service. Increasing numbers of Israeli teenagers, individually and in small groups, have publicly declared their refusal to serve in the IDF.[54] Furthermore, groups of conscientious objectors from several countries, including Greece, Turkey, Cyprus, Egypt, and Italy as well as Israel, are calling for breaking the cycle of violence between people of different nationalities or religion in the eastern Mediterranean region. These groups support refusal to participate in war for any reason. A statement by these groups concludes: "[W]e agree that our final goal is peace with justice for all. We all share a

---

53 State of Israel, Ministry of Justice, Human Rights and International Relations Department, "Israel's Policy on Selective Conscientious Objection" (May 25, 1993), <http://mfa.gov.il/MFA/AboutIsrael/State/Law/Pages/Israel-s%20Policy%20on%20 Selective%20Conscientious%20Objecti.aspx>, accessed May 23, 2016.

54 *See* List of hundreds of names posted by Mesarvot, <https://www.facebook.com/ mesarvot>, mostly in Hebrew. *See also*, Tair Kaminer, "No One Would Serve in the Israeli Army if They Knew," *Haaretz*, op-ed (Israel, March 29, 2016); and "Israel Should Let Conscientious Objector Serve Both Society and Her Conscience," *Haaretz*, Editorial (Israel, April 11, 2016), <https://portside.org/print/2016-04-14/no-one-would-serve-israeli-army-if-they-knew-israel-should-let-conscientious-objector>, accessed May 24, 2016.

common dream, and refuse to participate in its further destruction."[55] What follows are statements by various Israeli groups and individual refuseniks.

Shministim

Shministim is Hebrew for "twelfth graders" and refers to Israeli high school students who intend to refuse military service. Since 1970, groups of high school seniors who called themselves Shministim, have signed letters expressing their intention to refuse military service.[56]

Yesh Gvul

Yesh Gvul ("There is a limit!" in Hebrew) is an organization founded in 1982 in opposition to Israel's invasion of Lebanon. Thereafter, Yesh Gvul expanded its opposition to service in the occupied territories. It "was instrumental in providing information for prospective refuseniks regarding their rights, in launching broad-based protest activities in solidarity with reservists imprisoned for refusing call-up orders and even in mobilizing a degree of financial support for many imprisoned reservists, whose act of defiance exposed them to economic sanctions."[57]

Adam Keller

"I refused to do duty in Lebanon so they made me a dishwasher in a tank regiment. In 1988, at the beginning of the intifada, I went out one night and wrote on the tanks: 'Soldiers refuse to be occupiers and aggressors. Don't go to the occupied territories.'" Keller did three months in prison for having scrawled such graffiti on 117 tanks and other military vehicles.[58]

"A psychiatrist asked me what was my motivation. I told him it was the people in history who fought for right that motivated me. Then he said: 'Can we say you hear the voice of history?' That's how I got my discharge—he wrote on my report that I was hearing voices of history."[59]

Yuval Ophir-Auron

Yuval Ophir-Auron explained why he had a conscientious problem with enlisting in the army (presumably in 1989):

---

55 "Statement of conscientious objectors' groups from eastern Mediterranean region," March 10, 2016, <http://www.wri-irg.org/en/node/26267>, accessed May 24, 2016.

56 Primary sources are not readily available in English, but secondary sources corroborate one another. *See*, Michael R. Burch, "The Shministim: Israeli Refuseniks and Dissenters," <http://www.thehypertexts.com/The%20Shministim.htm>, accessed May 24, 2016.

57 "Yesh Gvul—There Is a Limit," <http://israeli-left-archive.org/cgi-bin/library?site=local host&a=p&p=about&c=yeshgvul&l=en&w=utf-8>, accessed May 25, 2016.

58 *The Guardian*, "I Realized the Stupidity of It," March 11, 2003, <http://www.refusingtokill. net/Israel/Irealisedthestupidityofit.htm>; and, Burch, "Shministim," which adds that on electricity pylons and doors of officers' toilet stalls, Keller wrote, "Down with the occupation!"

59 *Guardian*, "Stupidity."

For 41 years now, Israel has been imposing an occupation of lands that are not its own. . . . What I see is a country . . . in thrall to an insatiable hunger for another street, another tree to cram into its shattered borders. . . . I regard it as my moral duty to refuse serving in the army. My conscience does not allow me to join an organization that demolishes, by fiat of the state, the homes of innocent people, kills children who are not part of the armed fighting, and which prevents sick people from getting due treatment. . . .[60]

Jonathan Ben-Artzi

During the second Palestinian intifada, Jonathan Ben-Artzi, nephew of Benjamin Netanyahu (past and, at this writing, present prime minister of Israel), declared himself a pacifist and refused military service.

Jonathan Ben-Artzi went to France when he was fourteen years old. He visited some of the battlefields of World War I. Seeing "rows and rows of graves," he "realized the stupidity of it. So many lives sacrificed and they didn't really know what they were fighting for. . . ."

As a high school student, he wrote about pacifism. He refused to go on a trip through the occupied Palestinian territories: "I told the teacher I wouldn't go because it's not OK to have kids on a trip going through villages where [Palestinians] are trapped in their homes under curfew."

At the army induction center, he told the Colonel he had no intention of signing up. He was questioned by military officers on a "conscience committee." "Their decision was that I'm not a pacifist. It's an automatic decision. No one has ever been accepted as a pacifist. . . ." The military prosecutor said Ben-Artzi "was not a pacifist because 'the competent military committee has already reviewed his case' and decided he was not. The prosecutor added that to let Ben-Artzi go would 'undermine discipline in the army'."

Later, a brigadier general told Ben-Artzi that if he "agreed to enlist he would be granted 'an easy service, without a gun, uniform or military training'. A job would be found for him in a hospital. Ben-Artzi replied that he would do three years' service, but not in an organization dedicated to killing."

The army then "declared that Ben-Artzi was already conscripted and ordered the first court martial of a conscientious objector in three decades."[61]

---

60   Burch, "Shministim."

61   *Guardian*, "Stupidity." *See also*, Joshua Holland, "Meet Bibi Netanyahu's Refusenik Nephew Who Says That Israel Is an Apartheid State," lightly edited transcript of interview (August 6, 2012), <http://www.alternet.org/world/meet-bibi-netanyahus-refusenik-nephew-who-says-israel-apartheid-state>, accessed May 25, 2016. For a list of Israeli prime ministers, *see*, <http://en.wikipedia.org/wiki/List_of_Prime_Ministers_of_Israel>, accessed May 25, 2016.

Combatants' Letter

In 2002, fifty combat officers and soldiers signed what came to be known as the Combatants' Letter:

- We, reserve combat officers and soldiers of the Israel Defense Forces, who were raised upon the principles of Zionism, self-sacrifice and giving to the people of Israel and to the State of Israel, who have always served in the front lines, and who were the first to carry out any mission in order to protect the State of Israel and strengthen it.
- We, combat officers and soldiers who have served the State of Israel for long weeks every year, in spite of the dear cost to our personal lives, have been on reserve duty in the Occupied Territories, and were issued commands and directives that had nothing to do with the security of our country, and that had the sole purpose of perpetuating our control over the Palestinian people.
- We, whose eyes have seen the bloody toll this Occupation exacts from both sides,
- We, who sensed how the commands issued to us in the Occupied Territories destroy all the values that we were raised upon,
- We, who understand now that the price of Occupation is the loss of IDF's human character and the corruption of the entire Israeli society,
- We, who know that the Territories are not a part of Israel, and that all settlements are bound to be evacuated,
- We hereby declare that we shall not continue to fight this War of the Settlements.
- We shall not continue to fight beyond the 1967 borders in order to dominate, expel, starve and humiliate an entire people.
- We hereby declare that we shall continue serving the Israel Defense Force in any mission that serves Israel's defense.

The missions of occupation and oppression do not serve this purpose—and we shall take no part in them.

An organization by the name of Courage to Refuse continues to collect new signatories for this letter. "Its members, beyond refusing to serve in the occupied territories, take part in many demonstrations, cultural events and other activities of public education aimed to end the occupation and bring peace to Israel."[62]

---

62   Courage to Refuse, "About Us," <http://seruv.org.il/english/movement.asp>; and Combatants Letter, *Courage to Refuse*, <http://www.seruv.org.il/english/combatants_letter.asp>, accessed May 27, 2016.

Pilots' Letter

In September 2003, twenty-seven Israeli Air Force reserve pilots who described themselves as veterans and "active fighters, leaders, and instructors of the next generation of pilots," sent a letter to the commander of the Air Force declaring that they would defend Israel, but they were opposed to carrying out orders in the occupied territories that they believed were illegal and immoral.

> We, who were raised to love the state of Israel and contribute to the Zionist enterprise, refuse to take part in Air Force attacks on civilian population centers. We, for whom the Israel Defense Forces and the Air Force are an inalienable part of ourselves, refuse to continue to harm innocent civilians.[63]

Commandos' Letter

In December 2003, thirteen soldiers from the Israeli Defense Forces' most prestigious combat unit sent a letter to Prime Minister Ariel Sharon affirming that they would continue to defend Israel, but:

> We, citizens of Israel who fulfill our duty as reserve soldiers, fighters and officers, veterans of Sayeret Matkal, have chosen to walk at the head of our camp, as we have been taught. Out of concern for the future of Israel as a Jewish, Zionist, Democratic state, and out of fear for its moral character we declare that:
> - We shall no longer lend a hand in the occupation of the territories
> - We shall no longer take part in the deprivation of basic human rights from millions of Palestinians
> - We shall no longer serve as a shield in the crusade of the settlements
> - We shall no longer corrupt our moral character in missions of oppression
> - We shall no longer deny our responsibility as soldiers of the Israeli DEFENSE force.
>
> We fear for the fate of the children of this country, who are constantly subjected to an evil that is unnecessary, an evil in which we have participated. We have long ago crossed the line of those who fight for their own protection; we stand facing the border of those who fight to conquer another people. We shall not cross this border! . . . [64]

Maya Wind

Maya Wind joined the Shministim in December 2008 and refused to serve in the Israeli Defense Forces:

---

63   Courage to Refuse, "The Pilots Have Courage to Refuse" (September 25, 2003), <http://www.seruv.org.il/English/article.asp?msgid=55&type=news>, accessed May 27, 2016.

64   Courage to Refuse, "The Commandos Have Courage to Refuse," December 22, 2003, <http://www.seruv.org.il/english/article.asp?msgid=85&type=news>, accessed May 27, 2016.

We can no longer term our military a "Defense Force." A defense force does not conquer lands of another people. A defense force does not assist in the building of settlements on those lands. A defense force does not permit settlers to throw stones at Palestinian civilians, nor does it deny them access to their lands and source of livelihood. None of these are acts of a defense force. The occupation has no defensive advantages. On the contrary, the pointless occupation of millions of people only leads to radicalization of opinions, hatred and the escalation of violence. Violence is a cycle that feeds into itself. This cycle will not stop until someone stands up and refuses uncompromisingly to take part in it. This is what I am doing today. . . .

Maya Wind spent several weeks in detention and forty days in military prison before she was exempted from military service in March 2009.[65]

Danielle Yaor

Danielle Yaor is one of 150 signers of a statement by Israelis whose reasons for refusing to serve in the army are based on violations of international law and masculine domination of the Israeli army.

We, the undersigned, intend to refuse to serve in the army and the main reason for this refusal is our opposition to the military occupation of Palestinian territories. . . . In these territories, human rights are violated, and acts defined under international law as war-crimes are perpetuated on a daily basis. These include assassinations (extrajudicial killings), the construction of settlements on occupied lands, administrative detentions, torture, collective punishment and the unequal allocation of resources such as electricity and water. . . .

We refuse to aid the military system in promoting and perpetuating male dominance. In our opinion, the army encourages a violent and militaristic masculine ideal whereby "might is right." This ideal is detrimental to everyone, especially those who do not fit it. Furthermore, we oppose the oppressive, discriminatory, and heavily gendered power structures within the army itself. . . .

At age nineteen, she says, "I have to refuse to take part in the war crimes that my country does. . . . Since I was young we've been trained to be these masculine soldiers who solve problems by violence. I want to use peace to make the world better."[66]

---

65 Burch, "Shministim," <http://www.thehypertexts.com/The%20Shministim.htm>. *See also*, Bella Caledonia, "Exclusive: Interview with Maya Wind, an Israeli Peace Activist" (November 29, 2012), <http://bellacaledonia.org.uk/2012/11/29/exclusive-interview-with-maya-wind-an-israeli-peace-activist/>, accessed May 27, 2016.

66 David Swanson, "Israeli Chooses 'Honorable Life' Over Joining Military" (October 27, 2014), <http://davidswanson.org/node/4566>, accessed May 27, 2016.

Unit 8200 Letter

Unit 8200 is Israel's Intelligence Corps. On September 11, 2014, forty-three "veterans of Unit 8200, reserve soldiers both past and present," sent a letter to the prime minister, the military intelligence director, and the commander of Unit 8200, in which they declared: "we refuse to take part in actions against Palestinians and refuse to continue serving as tools in deepening the military control over the Occupied Territories."

> The Palestinian population under military rule is completely exposed to espionage and surveillance by Israeli intelligence. While there are severe limitations on the surveillance of Israeli citizens, the Palestinians are not afforded this protection. There's no distinction between Palestinians who are, and are not, involved in violence. Information that is collected and stored harms innocent people. It is used for political persecution and to create divisions within Palestinian society by recruiting collaborators and driving parts of Palestinian society against itself. In many cases, intelligence prevents defendants from receiving a fair trial in military courts, as the evidence against them is not revealed. . . .
>
> Millions of Palestinians have been living under Israeli military rule for over 47 years. This regime denies the basic rights and expropriates extensive tracts of land for Jewish settlements subject to separate and different legal systems, jurisdiction and law enforcement. This reality is not an inevitable result of the state's efforts to protect itself but rather the result of choice. Settlement expansion has nothing to do with national security. The same goes for restrictions on construction and development, economic exploitation of the West Bank, collective punishment of inhabitants of the Gaza Strip, and the actual route of the separation barrier.
>
> In light of all this, we have concluded that as individuals who served in Unit 8200, we must take responsibility for our part in this situation and it is our moral duty to act. We cannot continue to serve this system in good conscience, denying the rights of millions of people. Therefore, those among us who are reservists, refuse to take part in the state's actions against Palestinians. We call for all soldiers serving in the Intelligence Corps, present and future, along with all the citizens of Israel, to speak out against these injustices and to take action to bring them to an end. We believe that Israel's future depends on it.[67]

---

67   Leak Source, "Letter & Testimony from Israel's Elite Intelligence Unit 8200 Members Refusing to Spy on Palestinians" (September 13, 2014), <https://leaksource.wordpress.com/2014/09/13/letter-testimony-from-israels-elite-intelligence-unit-8200-members-refusing-to-spy-on-palestinians/>, accessed December 24, 2016.

According to media accounts in January 2015, members of Unit 8200 who signed the letter to Prime Minister Benjamin Netanyahu and top army chiefs in September were expelled and can no longer serve in the unit.[68]

Moral Injury and Conscientious Objection

Unit 8200 Testimonies

Several of the signers of the Unit 8200 letter offered personal explanations for their refusal to serve any longer in Israel's Intelligence Corps or to condone Israel's military control over the Occupied Territories.[69] Although they may not have used terms such as "moral injury" or "conscientious objection," what they say reminds us of individuals who do.

> After my discharge from the Intelligence Corps, I had a moment of shock while watching the film "The Lives of Others," about the secret police in East Germany. On the one hand, I felt solidarity with the victims, with the oppressed people who were denied such basic rights as I take for granted to be mine. On the other hand, I realized that the job I had done during my military service was that of the oppressor. My first reaction as a discharged soldier was that we do the same things, only much more efficiently.

The contradiction between morality and following orders became an issue for one of the signers of the Unit 8200 letter who had been a course instructor for soldiers assigned to the Palestinian arena:

> I gave a class called "Morality and Intelligence." . . . The Lieutenant A. affair was a major part of this class. . . . The report said the objective of that operation was to demolish a building empty of people, and that Lieutenant A.'s job was to make sure the building was indeed empty—when in fact the contrary was true. The objective was to bomb a building containing innocent people, and the Lieutenant was supposed to inform the unit when they were inside. We discussed this affair in class. Everyone said what they would have done in A.'s stead. . . . [T]he only conclusion reached was that in this unit there is no such thing as an illegal order. It is not we who decide what is moral and what isn't. Nowadays I realize that this is what

---

68 *See*, Reuters "Israeli intel unit drops soldiers who refused to spy on Palestinians," (January 26, 2015), <http://www.reuters.com/assets/print?aid=USKBN0KZ27F20150126>; and Jodi Rudoren, "Israel: Dissident Reservists Dismissed," *New York Times* (January 26, 2015), <http://www.nytimes.com/2015/01/27/world/middleeast/israel-dissident-reservists-dismissed.html?_r=0>, accessed May 27, 2016.

69 Leak Source, "Letter & Testimony." The following testimonies appear under the heading "Testimonies," after the list of signers of the letter.

the bombing pilot says too: "It's not for me to say what is moral and what isn't." Everyone passes the responsibility onto others. After deliberating a bit, as that was the method of the class, the final message was: "Do what you're told."

An Israeli veteran, who refused further service in the reserves, described an experience similar to that of American drone pilot Brandon Bryant (described above in Chapter 1):

[T]here was someone suspicious next to a weapons warehouse in Gaza and we thought he was our target. It had taken us a long time to find him. Judging by his location, the time and similar date, we concluded it was him. After we assassinated him it turned out that he was a kid. . . . I remember an image on the screen of him in an orchard, and the explosion on the screen, the smoke clearing and his mother running to him, at which point we could see he was a child. The body was small. We realized we had screwed up. It got quiet and uncomfortable. Then we needed to carry on as there were other things to do. . . .

This veteran explained, "In real time you can see maps and images from the helicopter, but you're sitting in an office so it's very easy to feel detached and distance yourself. Nor was it my job to ask questions. I was told what was needed and that's what I did."

I assumed a role in which people are called "targets." . . . I could urge my unit to take all kinds of measures. The attitude was "Why not?" "We can, so let's do it." . . . I chose to disconnect from it—to clock in my hours, and check out. . . .

An Israeli who served as a translator during "Operation Cast Lead" in Gaza wrote:

Upon the start of the operation something seemed wrong to me. Instead of attacking rocket and weapons caches in the Gaza Strip, as a preparatory defense measure for the campaign against Hamas, the Israeli Air Force attacked a parade of police officers. The assault killed 87 policemen. . . . Those were precious hours in which we should have been doing our jobs preventing the launching of rockets against Israeli civilians, and this did not serve that purpose. . . .

An Israeli reservist described the reactions of others in the room with him when they learned the results of bombing raids:

Throughout the operation I accompanied different teams engaged in collecting and translating intelligence on targets in the Gaza Strip—on both weapons and humans. I remember the overwhelming silence in the rooms from which we worked, seconds after the Air Force bombed those targets. A tense silence, hopeful of causing harm. When an attack was identified or executed, cheering and applause filled the room. . . . X's were marked on the facial composite sketches that adorned the walls of the rooms. No one asked about "collateral damage." I felt bad—it was very difficult to realize that no one was interested in who else had been hit. Throughout the campaign, hundreds of civilians were killed—men, women, and children—collateral damage. . . .

When senior leaders of the military wing of Hamas were targeted, the Air Force reported who had been harmed.

[T]ension filled the room in anticipation of finding out whether the people injured were the targeted objectives of the attack. When it became clear that they were other unrelated persons, cries of disappointment were heard, not because people had been killed arbitrarily, but because they weren't the people we were looking for. . . .

An Israeli assigned to collect "intelligence" on people who were accused of attacking Israelis, trying to attack Israelis, or desiring to harm Israelis, said he collected information on completely innocent people:

Any Palestinian is exposed to non-stop monitoring by the Israeli Big Brother, without legal protection. Junior soldiers can decide anyone is a target for the collection of information. There is no procedure in place to determine whether the violation of the individual's right is necessarily justifiable. . . . Any Palestinian may be targeted and may suffer from sanctions such as the denial of permits, harassment, extortion, or physical injury.

Another member of the 8200 Unit explained, you "fish out" an innocent person who might be recruited or squeezed into becoming a collaborator:

If you're homosexual and know someone who knows a wanted person . . . Israel will make your life miserable. If you need emergency medical treatment in Israel, the West Bank or abroad—we searched for you. The state of Israel will allow you to die before we let you leave for treatment without giving information on your wanted cousin. . . .

At the conclusion of my service in the army I was a commander and instructor for several months, teaching youth who had graduated from High

School and were being prepared to serve as translators for the Intelligence Corps. I repeatedly tried to raise these questions with them: is it legitimate to deem as a target any person who interests the Israeli security system, for whatever reason? The answer I received, time and again, was yes. Today I believe the answer is no.

Breaking the Silence

Breaking the Silence is an organization of veteran combatants who served in the occupied Palestinian territories. They collect and publish testimonies from young soldiers who have faced a civilian population on a daily basis in the West Bank, Gaza, and East Jerusalem.

> Soldiers who serve in the Territories witness and participate in military actions which change them immensely. Cases of abuse towards Palestinians, looting, and destruction of property have been the norm for years, but are still explained as extreme and unique cases. Our testimonies portray a different, and much grimmer picture in which deterioration of moral standards finds expression in the character of orders and the rules of engagement, and are justified in the name of Israel's security. While this reality is known to Israeli soldiers and commanders, Israeli society continues to turn a blind eye, and to deny what is done in its name. Discharged soldiers returning to civilian life discover the gap between the reality they encountered in the Territories, and the silence about this reality they encounter at home. In order to become civilians again, soldiers are forced to ignore what they have seen and done. We strive to make heard the voices of these soldiers, pushing Israeli society to face the reality whose creation it has enabled.[70]

Breaking the Silence collected testimonies from military personnel who were engaged in the war between Israel and Palestinian militants in Gaza during the summer of 2014 from which they concluded that many of the deaths were preventable and resulted from Israeli military policies. Here is a selection from one of those interviews under the title, *"From what we knew, that area was supposedly devoid of civilians."*

> I remember in Shuja'iyya there was one time I needed to interpret an attack that took place on a building or something like that. I opened up the footage, and it was all scorched, burned to the ground. Entire streets where one building is half-destroyed, the next one totally destroyed, the next one half-destroyed. Entire streets that were totally shelled, and I needed to verify a certain target that had clearly been obliterated. I opened up the footage

---

70 Breaking the Silence, "Israeli Soldiers Talk about the Occupied Territories," <http://www.breakingthesilence.org.il/about/organization>, accessed May 27, 2016.

and saw that it was taken right after the strike had been carried out, and there were lots of people there, and lots of ambulances, and a whole lot of smoke and lots of commotion. And from what we knew, that area was supposedly devoid of civilians.

[Question:] You said earlier that you did know the neighbourhood was supposed to be empty of civilians?

Yes. That's what they told us. They told us—maybe really so we wouldn't think the IDF [Israel Defense Forces] does immoral things—they told us the civilians had been informed via leaflets scattered in the area, and that it was supposed to be devoid of civilians, and civilians who remained there were civilians who apparently chose to be there.

[Question:] Who told you that?

The commanders, in off-the-record type conversations, or during all kinds of briefings. Just so we'd know, for our general knowledge, that this is what's going on. That there's no civilians supposed to be there, and any who are—are there because they chose to be. In conversations between us it was summed up as, "There's nothing we can do, war is war." You don't really talk about it—any discourse or opinions that are slightly "deviant" are pretty much silenced.[71]

Shachar Berrin

Shachar Berrin, an Israeli soldier, stood up wearing his IDF uniform, and spoke during the question and answer session at a debate on May 14, 2015, between a human rights activist and a pro-settler activist on the premise that the occupation is destroying Israel. Less than twelve hours after speaking, Berrin was ordered back to his base and charged with "taking part in a political meeting and in an interview [with] the media without permission from the army." Here are excerpts from what Berrin said:

I propose that what makes a country good isn't whether it is happy or not, it's about the ethics and morality of the country.

When soldiers, when we, are conditioned and persuaded on a daily basis to subjugate and humiliate people and consider other human beings as less than human, I think that seeps in, and I think the soldiers, when they go home . . . they bring that back with them.

. . . Just the other week, when some border police soldiers were rough with some Christian tourists, another soldier of mine, a colleague, said she couldn't believe what they were doing: "Come on, they are people, not

---

71   Alistair Dawber, "'From what we knew, that area was supposedly devoid of civilians': The testimonies of Israeli soldiers provided to Breaking the Silence," *The Independent*, May 4, 2015, <http://www.independent.co.uk/news/world/middle-east/from-what-we-knew-that-area-was-supposedly-devoid-of-civilians-the-testimonies-of-israeli-soldiers-provided-to-breaking-the-silence-10223374.html?>, accessed May 27, 2016.

Palestinians." And that, I think resonates through much of the soldiers in the occupied territories.

I personally serve in the Jordan Valley, and we can see it every day how soldiers talk about what they're doing, how they act, how they look at these people not as other human beings, not as someone who is equal, but as someone who is less than them.

And to think that, oh no, we can just leave that racism there, we can leave that xenophobia, they will only be racist, they will only humiliate Palestinians, of course not. . . .

A few weeks ago there was a border police soldier who was caught on camera beating up an Ethiopian Israeli in uniform. To say that we can just leave this all behind, is nonsense I think. I think that once you are conditioned to think something, you bring it back with you and it deeply affects Israeli society and causes it . . . to be more racist.[72]

Shachar Berrin was tried, convicted and sentenced to one week in prison before the program was aired on television. An Israeli journalist, Gideon Levy, commented,

This whole incident shows that when rapid, determined action is called for, the Israel Defense Forces knows how to act. When soldiers kill Palestinian children, the investigation is stretched out over years, gathering dust before usually going nowhere. . . . But if a soldier dares to attest publicly that his fellow soldiers are humiliating Palestinians, the IDF mobilizes rapidly to trample, punish and silence. That's what happened to Shachar Berrin.[73]

Berrin and other Israeli refuseniks do not use the term "moral injury," nor do they describe symptoms of suffering from moral injury. But they do describe participating in, seeing, or failing to prevent what they regard as immoral acts, and they convey a sense of betrayal of what Israel should stand for. They may not use the term "conscientious objection" but what they regard as immoral actions have led them to say No to such military service. By their acts these men and women are trying to break the cycle of violence.

---

72   Ben Norton, "Israel will imprison soldier, 19, for publicly criticizing the occupation," *Mondoweiss*, May 24, 2015, <http://mondoweiss.net/2015/05/imprison-criticizing-occupation>; excerpts no longer found. *But see*, Breaking the Silence, "Corporal Shachar Berrin on 'The New Arab Debates'," May 25, 2015, recording by Deutsche Welle, <https://www.youtube.com/watch?v=40cbB8Kxr9M>, accessed May 30, 2016.

73   Gideon Levy and Alex Levac, "Soldier Pays the Price for Criticizing the Israel Army," *Haaretz*, May 21, 2015, <http://www.haaretz.com/weekend/twilight-zone/.premium-1.657553>, accessed May 27, 2016, quoted excerpt no longer available without subscription.

PART II.
BEHIND BARS

Chapter 5.
Moral Injury among Prisoners

OUR EXPERIENCE LEADS US TO CONCLUDE THAT MORAL INJURY IS NOT LIMITED TO men and women who have engaged in warfare.

Since the end of the Vietnam War and the closing of steel mills in the Youngstown area, we have devoted ourselves to visiting and advocacy on behalf of prisoners. In 1998, Ohio opened its supermaximum security prison, the Ohio State Penitentiary in Youngstown, not far from where we live. We have spent a great deal of time with prisoners under conditions of supermax, maximum, and close security confinement. Some of these men (there are no women in those particular prisons) were sentenced to death, or life in prison, or very long sentences, for very serious crimes. In our view, some of them are suffering from moral injury.

We have written about a few of these men. In a conversation with Lessley Harmon, Alice said she thought it would be difficult for prisoners to do anything by way of atonement and reconciliation as long as they were locked up. Lessley agreed and told us the following:

> He had had a cellmate who said something like, "Lessley, you'll never know what it is like to have killed a man. I would do anything to breathe life back into that man. I can't talk to that man. If only there were some way I could talk to someone who loved that man, to ask forgiveness. But there is no way I can do that."
>
> Then Lessley went on to say that his cellmate was tormented particularly at night. In the morning he would get up and stay busy with activity all day to keep himself from thinking. To see him during the day and to hear him joking you would think he was happy, but as night came on and he had to go into the cell he became sad.
>
> Lessley said he had had seven or eight cellmates who had been murderers and they were all the same in this respect, that they used activity to keep themselves from thinking. Their sleep was fitful. One would wake in the night and scream or sit bolt upright in bed. If only there were someone they could go to and ask forgiveness then they wouldn't have to keep from thinking all the time, he concluded. . . .[1]

We got to know Glenn Benner when he was in the "honor block" on Death Row. He was sentenced to death in 1986 for raping and killing two young women, one of whom had been a childhood neighbor. Glenn's spiritual advisor said of Glenn:

---

1   Alice Lynd and Staughton Lynd, *Stepping Stones: Memoir of a Life Together* (Lanham, MD: Lexington Books, 2009), 168.

He felt unworthy of love. Every day he lived with knowledge of the terrible pain he had caused so many people by his actions. . . . He loved his family and carried the pain of knowing that he had let them down. In his shame he withdrew from them, feeling unworthy of the support and love they offered him. . . .

Glenn joined the Catholic Church and later was able to say to his family, "I love you, and I'm sorry." But when he had the opportunity to ask the parole board or the governor for clemency, he did not do so. He went willingly to the death house.

The family of one of Glenn's victims had questions they wanted to ask Glenn before he died. On the night before his execution, Glenn spoke at length on the phone with Rodney, his childhood friend and brother of one of the victims; they talked at length about the murder and reminisced about their lives. As Glenn was being readied for his execution, Rodney arrived at the prison. He had driven through the night to say one more thing to Glenn: "I forgive you."[2]

We shared with a group of prisoners Brian Willson's account that appears at the beginning of Part I of this book. One of the prisoners immediately got the point: "Yes, I did it. But that is not all that I am. I can still do good." Another man who was in prison for murder responded to Brian's account, "I know in my mind that I have to forgive myself but, in my heart, I'm not there yet."

During an attorney-client interview, another prisoner confided in us that it was he who had committed a certain murder and the man who was sentenced to death for that murder had nothing to do with it. It had been seven years since the murder and he had told no one before he spoke to us. He turned to one side, burst into tears, buried his head in his hands, and then looking up, blurted out, "It was me!" It seemed to us that he had to tell someone in order to lift that burden. He was later convicted by a court. Since then, based on good conduct, his security level has been lowered.

However, there is still a great deal that we don't know about what is needed to forgive oneself and to atone for moral injury. We talked with a man who has been in prison for thirty-six years for a murder he committed at the age of nineteen and several offenses committed while in prison. Some years ago, he met with a member of the murder victim's family who forgave him. But he still cannot forgive himself. He receives unconditional love from a widow old enough to be his mother, but that is not enough. He feels he has wasted his life and he has no hope that he can do any good for others in the future.

---

2   Ibid., 168–69, based on excerpts from "Meeting cools sting in heart, Man no longer believes in death penalty after seeing change in Glenn Benner II," by Carol Biliczky, *Beacon Journal,* Akron, OH, February 18, 2006; and conversations with Glenn Benner's spiritual adviser, Hilary Hughes. In a Christmas card to Alice and Staughton Lynd, received on December 24, 2016, Hilary Hughes wrote about what was most important to Glenn. "The greatest gift of all that he received was the gift of forgiveness from Rodney. . . . That melted him and reduced him to tears of relief and gratitude. His last message, passed to me and his family, was one of joy and hope. 'I have been forgiven!'"

Frameworks of Understanding

We must consider the connection between the experience of soldiers or veterans who feel isolated from other people and the experience of prisoners in solitary confinement. Professor Craig Haney is a leading specialist in seeking to understand the psychological effects of long-term solitary confinement. He explicitly states that solitary confinement is commonly used in brainwashing and certain forms of torture, and that "many of the negative effects of solitary confinement are analogous to the acute reactions suffered by torture and trauma victims, including post-traumatic stress disorder (PTSD)."[3]

Prof. Haney uses the term "social death" to describe what he found among prisoners held in long-term isolation at the Pelican Bay State Prison in California. Social death "consists of the near total . . . loss of meaningful contact, connections, and relations with other human beings." These prisoners were "different people because of it, people who had lost something not just in the world but in themselves."[4] Social death "undermined and even destroyed their relationships with others, and damaged their ability to function as social beings. Their identities have been transformed, and their personalities changed . . . and they have incurred significant amounts of pain and suffering along the way."[5]

Of course, there is the obvious difference that the prisoner in solitary confinement is compelled to live alone while the traumatized military combatant chooses to do so, both during military service and after it. But this apparent bright line distinction seems more ambiguous when viewed up close. "Social exclusion" can involve "self-isolation." As Prof. Haney describes it:

> [S]ome prisoners cope with the painful, asocial nature of their isolated existence by paradoxically creating even more distance between themselves and others. For some, the absence of others becomes so painful that they convince themselves that they do not need social contact of any kind—that people are a "nuisance," after all, and the less contact they have the better. As a result, they socially draw further from the world around them, receding even more deeply into themselves than the sheer physical isolation of solitary confinement and its attendant procedures require.[6]

---

3   "Expert Report of Craig Haney," Ph.D., J.D. , *Todd Ashker, et al. v. Edmund G. Brown, Jr., Governor, et al.*, Case No. 4:09 CV 05796 CW (United States District Court, Northern District of California, Oakland Division), 22, ¶ 34, <https://ccrjustice.org/sites/default/files/attach/2015/07/Redacted_Haney%20Expert%20Report.pdf>, accessed May 29, 2016.

4   Ibid., 57–58, ¶ 97.

5   Ibid., 103, ¶ 192.

6   Ibid., 28, ¶ 45.

Thus prisoners, like soldiers who have come to trust only other members of their platoon, may experience a "social death" that they have helped to create. For both groups of tormented human beings the ultimate act of self-isolation may be suicide.

The isolation of men sentenced to indefinite solitary confinement has aspects of moral injury. Professor Haney comments on the profound sadness of the many prisoners he has interviewed.

> Many of them seem to be grieving the relationships to family members and loved ones that they once had and now have lost . . . that they sense will never be recaptured or recreated. In other instances, the grief seems more generalized, as if they are grieving for a social self, a sense of who they once were, that they know is unlikely ever to be regained.

In either case, Haney concludes, these men are "grief-stricken over what has been lost or taken from them."[7]

There are other similarities between the experiences of isolated soldiers and isolated prisoners. For example, just as Dr. Shay found that veterans obliged to spend a year in combat were disoriented by the rotation of their officers every six months, so Professor Haney heard endless complaints about mental health staff who not only seem uncaring but also "change all the time."[8]

To be sure, prison guards carry the title of "officer" and, like blundering and unsympathetic military officers, are typically viewed by those they supervise with distrust and, sometimes, hatred. Indeed, Prof. Haney states:

> After more than four decades studying the dynamics of prison life, including countless conversations with correctional officers and observations made in correctional facilities throughout the country, I can unequivocally say that the dividing line between staff and inmates is nearly universally unbridgeable, in both directions. . . .[9]

An Unbridgeable Divide?

Unlike Prof. Haney, we have found that the divide between correctional officers and prisoners is not "nearly universally unbridgeable."[10]

At the Northeast Ohio Correctional Center, a private prison in Youngstown, two prisoners who were enemies were left unguarded in the same place at the same

---

7   Ibid., 70–71, ¶ 124.
8   Ibid., 97, ¶ 180, and 99, ¶ 183.
9   Ibid., 96–97, ¶ 178.
10   For an instance when a guard changed his attitude upon realizing that a prisoner had grown up in foster care under conditions as bad or worse than he himself had experienced, *see*, Bryan Stevenson, *Just Mercy: A Story of Justice and Redemption* (New York: Spiegel & Grau, 2014), 194–96, 200–202.

time. One attacked the other, wounding him grievously. A correctional officer told Staughton how he held the dying prisoner in his arms. The officer asked Staughton whether it would be acceptable for him to write to the dead man's mother and tell her how her son had died.

Alice recalls an interview with a prisoner at the Ohio State Penitentiary who was so disruptive that he was placed in a "pod" with no other prisoners. "There is this one guard," he said, "She can calm me down." Another prisoner, who had served in the military, said that mental health counselors were of no help to him, but there was one officer who had served in the military and he understood.

Mazin was one of forty-five hundred mostly Palestinian men held at the Ansar detention camp after Israel invaded Lebanon. Mazin recalled the following about his relationship with one of the Israeli guards:

> I trusted him and he trusted me. . . . We were not allowed to talk to the guards. But when he came, he called and then we talked. . . . One time he even provided us with bananas. We never had bananas at Ansar. He threw three bananas to me. It was a big deal. I divided them into six and shared them with my friends. . . .

Suggestive of moral injury, Mazin continued: "One of the soldiers at Ansar committed suicide. He could not stand what was going on. He said, 'What we are doing to the Palestinians right now is what happened to us in the past.'"[11]

An American prisoner with a violent history writes:

> It is the terrible truth that I have caused suffering. My fellow prisoners have caused suffering to their victims as well. Our victims have suffered, their family members have suffered, at the hands of those of us who are now incarcerated. This remains the truth we live with, but few realize that it is in the moments when we are treated fairly, humanely, or with compassion that we feel the greatest burden of conscience for the wrongs we have committed! It is when we receive courtesy, respect, and dignity that we reflect on our failures.[12]

He continues:

> It would be unfair for me to imply that all guards dehumanize prisoners. . . . Just like prisoners, many guards are loving, caring, compassionate people. I have seen many instances of these individuals showing courage and insight

---

11 Mazin in Lynd et al., *Homeland*, 120–21.
12 Carlito Cabana, "Prisons and the Dehumanizing Effects of Marginalization," unpublished paper.

in the management and care of those in custody. Over the years I have met guards who treated me like a person. Some have trusted me, told me about their lives, their families, their children. One guard's son was the first in his family to go to college (studying Criminal Justice) and the guard asked me to . . . critique his son's papers. When I went up for parole two guards wrote letters in support of my release.[13]

The problem is that these empathetic officers "are violating policy when they talk to a prisoner about life beyond the walls, when they support a prisoner's release plan, when they treat a prisoner as one of their fellow humans."

This prisoner goes on to explain,

[T]hese good guards, just like prisoners, are powerless to effect major change. . . . If they speak up, they face ostracism by fellow staff members. They risk being fired for fraternizing or being 'too friendly' with prisoners. There are no whistle-blower laws protecting guards, and they are not allowed to speak to the media except when officially authorized to do so.[14]

The obvious question becomes, What is to be done? Here another analyst of "social death," Dr. Lisa Guenther of the Vanderbilt University Department of Philosophy, says something that we describe more fully in the coming chapters.

[M]ovements of collective resistance among incarcerated and non-incarcerated men and women show that there are ways of resisting social death, even within the jaws of the penitentiary. Thanks to these movements of collective resistance, it still makes sense to speak of the "afterlives" of social death: not as the glorious redemption of the individual soul, but as the collective practice of refusal, resistance and solidarity.[15]

George Skatzes

Many of the men confined in the Ohio State Penitentiary had been in the Southern Ohio Correctional Facility (SOCF) in Lucasville, Ohio in 1993 during an eleven-day prison uprising.

George Skatzes (pronounced "skates") is a burly white man who was forty-seven years old at the time of the Lucasville uprising.

---

13   Ibid.
14   Ibid.
15   Lisa Guenther, "Social Death and Its Afterlives: A Critical Phenomenology of Solitary Confinement," *Academia* (2016), topic 7, <http://www.academia.edu/1883215/Social_Death_and_its_Afterlives_A_Critical_Phenomenology_of_Solitary_Confinement>, accessed May 29, 2016.

Skatzes had nothing to do with planning the Lucasville rebellion.[16] The occupation of L block began at approximately 3 p.m. on Sunday, April 11. That afternoon and evening, Skatzes busied himself with ensuring that three severely wounded correctional officers (Harold Fraley, John Kemper, and Robert Schroeder) and one gravely injured prisoner (John Fryman) were carried out to the yard where they could be retrieved by the authorities and given medical care.

Skatzes became one of the principal spokespersons for the rebellion. On that first afternoon of the uprising, Skatzes was approached by Muslim imam Carlos Sanders, a.k.a. Siddique Abdullah Hasan. Hasan (as prisoners call him) asked Skatzes to help him prevent the uprising from becoming a race riot between prisoners. In the gym that was part of the L cell block the whites were on one side and the African Americans on another, Skatzes was told. Skatzes went to the gym. He put his arm around the shoulders of a black man he did not know. He told the crowd that if the authorities were to invade L block to put down the rebellion, it wouldn't matter if you were white or black; the authorities would go after everything blue (the color of prisoners' uniforms).

The next morning, Monday, April 12, the prison authorities cut off all electricity and water to L block. Skatzes went out on the yard, accompanied by an African American Muslim named Cecil Allen. Using a megaphone, Skatzes asked for immediate negotiations to end the confrontation. The occasion was videotaped by the authorities and Skatzes can be heard to say: "Don't try to cut us down. We are as much interested in saving people's lives as you people are. We're here to try to take care of it peaceful and without any more violence than what you've already seen. We've got guards in here that are hurting and we're concerned about it just like you are. We don't want no more deaths than what's already been."

Prison spokespersons, responding to Skatzes from one of the towers surrounding the yard, deliberately stalled in the mistaken belief that this strategy would weaken the insurgents. As one of the state's negotiators testified: "the basic principle [was] to maintain a dialogue, to buy time, because the more time that goes on the greater the chances for a peaceful resolution to the situation."[17]

During the eleven days of the occupation Skatzes made regular rounds of L block, checking on the well-being of the hostages. He offered his own blood pressure medicine to one of them, Officer Buffington.

Two white correctional officers who were being held by the Muslim prisoners asked Skatzes if he could arrange for them to be transferred to the pod where he was

---

16 The following account of aspects of the eleven-day Lucasville, Ohio prison uprising in April 1993 is based on Staughton Lynd, *Lucasville: The Untold Story of a Prison Uprising*, second edition (Oakland, CA: PM Press, 2011), and Staughton Lynd, revised and edited by Alice Lynd, *Layers of Injustice: Re-examining the Lucasville Uprising* (Columbus, OH: CICJ Books, 2013).

17 Testimony of Howard Hudson, a member of the state's negotiating team, *State v. Sanders* (Ct. Com. Pl. Hamilton Cty.), Case Nos. B-953105 and C-960253, transcript, 2719, 2721.

sleeping, L-2. Skatzes did so, telling one of the officers to use his bunk while himself lying down at the cell's entrance to forestall any intruder.

On Wednesday, April 14, Skatzes spent most of the day on the telephone with David Burchett, a representative of the authorities. That evening the two men reached an agreed first step toward a settlement. The prisoners in rebellion would release two of the correctional officers they were holding as hostages. In return, the prisoners would have access to the media. The agreement Skatzes negotiated with Mr. Burchett ended with an exchange of good wishes and prayers that reminds one of the end of an episode of the TV series *The Waltons*.

Early the next morning, Thursday, April 15, a meeting of representatives of the different prison gangs involved in the revolt—the Sunni Muslims who had started the uprising, the Aryan Brotherhood or AB, and the Black Gangster Disciples—rejected the arrangement Skatzes had negotiated. The prison authorities would first have to turn the water and electricity back on. This accomplished, the prisoners would release one of their hostages. If the authorities rejected that proposal, the representatives of the gangs would meet again to decide whether to kill a hostage officer.

Skatzes was asked to go back on the telephone to deliver these new demands. He did so. While he was still on the telephone, pleading the need for the authorities to act quickly and warning that they were "wasting valuable time," hostage officer Robert Vallandingham was strangled by a rump group of prisoners and his body carried out to the yard.

When Skatzes learned after getting off the phone on April 15 that Officer Vallandingham had been killed, he got on his knees together with the two hostage officers he was protecting and a young member of the Aryan Brotherhood who would later testify against him. Skatzes said he did not know whether any of them would survive and prayed that all of them be protected by "the man upstairs."

That afternoon Skatzes once again went on the phone. The arrangement he had negotiated the night before was reinstated. In exchange for the release of two hostages, the prisoners would have two opportunities to address the general public, first by way of a radio message and then on television. Skatzes went out on the yard with hostage officer Darrold Clark, released him, and then briefly addressed the prison authorities, the prisoners in L block (who could listen on battery-powered radios), and the general public. In the course of his remarks Skatzes said:

> We hope there is no more violence, we hope there are no more unnecessary murders. We as a convict body send our condolences to Bobby's [officer Robert Vallandingham's] family. I can't pronounce his last name so I'll have to use his first.

Struggling to articulate as many demands as possible, Skatzes added:

> A man asked me to do him a personal favor. He asked me to bring a note out here to his people. I wasn't permitted to bring a note, that's fine. I will

say that Jeff Ratcliff sent his love to his mamma and his papa and his people and said that he is hanging in there strong. . . . [H]e's doin' good and I hope that we will have him out of here soon too.[18]

A week later, Ratcliff emerged from the ordeal unharmed. He testified at Skatzes's trial that Skatzes had saved his life.

When he concluded, Skatzes returned to a hero's welcome in L block, walking between two rows of lighted candles held by fellow prisoners. Later that evening, however, he was informed that he would be replaced as the prisoners' negotiator. The Muslims were disturbed that he had spent time in his radio address to assure Ratcliff's family that the guard would return to them safely.

George Skatzes suffered a variant of moral injury when he reflected on the ten "unnecessary" deaths that happened during the Lucasville uprising. In contrast to the 1971 riot at Attica, New York, where thirty-nine men were killed by the armed forces of the state and only four by prisoners,[19] all ten men killed during the Lucasville events (nine prisoners believed to be "snitches" and hostage officer Vallandingham) were killed by prisoners.

Skatzes blamed himself for the death of Officer Vallandingham, despite the fact that he had done everything he could think of to save him. At Skatzes's trial, he testified:

I talked to Bobby over in L-3 day room. I don't know what day it was, but I lit a cigarette for him and sat there on the floor and talked while he smoked that cigarette. . . . I give that man my word. I said, I'm going to do everything I can to make sure you are all right. It turned out the way it did. . . . I've had to live with this all that time. I let that man down.[20]

In the unsworn statement that he made to his jury before being sentenced to death, Skatzes said that he did not believe in activities like the Lucasville uprising.

I do want to say Lucasville was a bad thing. I ain't going to tell you no different. I'm not proud of what I seen down there. I don't like what I seen.

And, sadly enough, it seems like the Department of Corrections hasn't learned nothing from that and there's definitely a lesson to be learned, and wherever I go, I would like to be fortunate enough to be able to work with these people to help them maybe prevent another Lucasville. And that comes from my heart because I didn't like what I seen.

---

18   Radio address of George Skatzes, *State v. Skatzes* (Ct. Com. Pl. Montgomery Cty.), Case Nos. 94-CR-2890 and -2891, Exhibit 309A.

19   *See,* Heather Ann Thompson, *Blood in the Water: The Attica Prison Uprising of 1971 and Its Legacy* (New York: Pantheon Books, 2016).

20   *State v. Skatzes,* transcript, 5645–5646.

It is a mind-blower to . . . walk in that shower and see all of them boys all beat up . . . walk up in that cell and see Mugsy [Svette, an elderly victim] . . . or Bobby [Vallandingham] laying dead like that. . . .

There's got to be a way to prevent that from ever happening again. . . .[21]

Convict Race at Lucasville

Skatzes was hoping that an alternative "way" could be found to the violent prisoner uprisings at Attica in 1971, Santa Fe, New Mexico, in 1980, and Lucasville in 1993. In addition to the obvious negatives attending human relations in a maximum security prison, there are some positive elements as well. An individual prisoner who does not exhibit prejudice can make a difference. Even prisoners who testified for the state at Skatzes's trial after the negotiated surrender declared under oath that they had never known Skatzes to discriminate against blacks or Jews.

Moreover, prisoners in general are restricted in roughly the same ways whether they are white or black. Institutionalized forms of racial hierarchy or segregation are accordingly less prevalent. For this reason, prison is one of the few places in American society where there can be tested the late Howard Zinn's hypothesis that if members of racial or ethnic groups can experience "equal-status contact" over a significant period of time, prejudices will fall away.

Something like this happened during the eleven days that Lucasville prisoners in L block were out of their cells.

After the prisoners surrendered and the Ohio State Highway Patrol entered L block, they found a variety of graffiti on the walls. As a witness at trial, Sergeant Howard Hudson identified a photograph taken in the L corridor:

Q. On the wall on the right there appears to be something written?
A. Says, "Black and White Together."
Q. Did you find that or similar slogans at many places in L block?
A. Yes, sir.[22]

And, "188 is . . . inside the gymnasium, the wall to your left as you would enter from the corridor, there's a bulletin board with the words, 'Whites and blacks together,' painted on to it."[23]

Q. [What is photograph] 260?
A. 260, the words, "Convict unity," written on the wall of L corridor.
Q. Did you find the message of unity throughout L block?

---

21 Ibid., 6055–6056.
22 Ibid., 1922.
23 Ibid., 1978.

A. Yes. . . .

Q. Next photo?

A. 261 is another photograph in L corridor that depicts the words, "Convict race."[24]

We do not know which embattled prisoner wrote the words, "Convict race." But a fair translation would seem to be: "We are not members of a black race and a white race. We are members of a single convict race."

Prisoners at the Illinois and California counterparts to Lucasville appear to have carried the vision and practice of convict unity several steps further.

---

24 Ibid., 1993–1994.

Chapter 6.
Confronting Solitary Confinement
in Ohio and Illinois

ABOUT TEN THOUSAND PERSONS IN FEDERAL PRISONS, AND AT LEAST EIGHTY THOU-
sand persons in state and federal prisons combined, are presently held in solitary
confinement in U.S. prisons on any given day.[1] Typically such confinement in isolation is for an indefinite period of years.

In the contemporary United States, the practice originated at the federal penitentiary in Marion, Illinois. The Marion prison was built and opened in 1963 to take
the place of Alcatraz. In 1973, the first blocks of "control units" were created, in which
inmates spent twenty-two and a half hours a day in one-man six-by-eight-foot cells
designed to restrict contact with other human beings. In 1983 prisoners at Marion
stabbed and killed two correctional officers. The entire prison population was then
placed on permanent lockdown, or supermax, status. Prisoners ate alone in their cells
and, when let out for recreation, exercised by themselves.[2]

Super maximum security ("supermax") prisons in the United States have proliferated.
By 2004, more than forty states had some form of supermax housing, and by 2005, more
than eighty thousand prisoners were held in restricted housing.[3] By 2011–2012, nearly
20 percent of prison inmates and 18 percent of jail inmates had spent time in restrictive
housing (disciplinary segregation, administrative segregation, or solitary confinement)
during the past twelve months, and approximately 10 percent of all prison inmates and
5 percent of jail inmates had spent thirty days or longer in restrictive housing.[4]

---

1   *Time-in-Cell: The ASCA-Liman 2014 National Survey of Administrative Segregation
    in Prison*, The Liman Program, Yale Law School (revised August 31, 2015),
    <https://www.law.yale.edu/system/files/area/center/liman/document/asca-liman_
    administrativesegregationreport.pdf>, ii; letter of 126 organizations, including 39
    religious organizations, to President Barack Obama (October 1, 2015), <http://www.
    nrcat.org/about-us/nrcat-press-releases/1138-126-organizations-call-on-white-house-
    to-seek-elimination-of-prolonged-solitary-confinement>, accessed May 29, 2016.
2   Committee to End the Marion Lockdown, "From Alcatraz to Marion to Florence—
    Control Unit Prisons in the United States," 1992, <http://people.umass.edu/~kastor/
    ceml_articles/cu_in_us.html>, accessed June 5, 2016.
3   Vera Institute of Justice, "Prisons Within Prisons: The Use of Segregation in the
    United States," *Federal Sentencing Reporter*, Vol. 24, No. 1 (2011), 46–49, ISSN 1053-
    9867 electronic ISSN 1533-8363, <http://www.vera.org/sites/default/files/resources/
    downloads/prisons-within-prisons-segregation.pdf>, accessed June 1, 2016.
4   Bureau of Justice Statistics, "Use of Restrictive Housing in U.S. Prisons and Jails, 2011–
    12," Summary, October 2015, NCJ 249209, <http://www.bjs.gov/content/pub/pdf/
    urhuspj1112_sum.pdf>, accessed June 2, 2016.

Supermax Confinement in Ohio

Beginnings

In the mid-1990s, the Ohio state legislature decided to build a supermax prison in Youngstown. Hitherto one of the principal steelmaking locations in the United States, Youngstown had come on hard times when steelmaking facilities in the area closed in 1977–1980. Prisons were perceived as a substitute for lost employment. The Ohio State Penitentiary (OSP) was built in response to the eleven-day uprising at the maximum security prison in Lucasville in 1993.[5]

Criteria for transfer of prisoners to the 504-cell Ohio State Penitentiary were subjective and arbitrary.[6] There was no due process. A prisoner might be awakened at 4 a.m. in another Ohio prison, told that he was "going to Youngstown" that same day, and instructed to pack up. In June 1998, we paid the first visit to any prisoner at the new Youngstown supermax. He sat on a concrete stool in a small locked cubicle. A correctional officer sat outside the cubicle throughout the visit. Inside, the prisoner's feet were chained to the floor and he was handcuffed behind his back.

Initially, the property restrictions were also very severe: no socks, no T-shirts, no books other than two soft-cover religious books, no newspapers or magazines, no radio, no TV except for institutional programming. The only writing instrument allowed was comparable to the flexible plastic tube inside a ballpoint pen. "Never before in my life have I been in a place where I could not have a bar of soap," George Skatzes exclaimed. They were permitted only a small tube of liquid soap.

There was no outdoor recreation at OSP. When the director of the Ohio Department of Rehabilitation and Correction was asked in deposition why this was so, he answered that the Lucasville uprising of 1993 had begun on the recreation yard.

Medical care fell below minimum constitutional standards. A prisoner who experienced acute heart pain did not receive an EKG for five days, at which point he had to be life-flighted to the state capital for emergency care. Another prisoner complained repeatedly about intense pain from a tooth. Unable to obtain a response he extracted a thread from his blanket and used it to pull out the tooth himself.

What drove the situation toward change was a series of three suicides. Before the second man killed himself, he was taunted by guards who said, "When are you

---

5   The Ohio State Penitentiary was "[c]onstructed in reaction to the April 1993 riot at the Southern Ohio Correctional Facility at Lucasville. . . ." *Austin v. Wilkinson*, 189 F.Supp.2d 719, 722–23 (N.D. Ohio 2002).

6   The following description of life at the Ohio State Penitentiary when it first opened and in a lawsuit draws on the personal experience of the authors, correspondence with prisoners as well as visits to many, and a variety of documents. Written sources include Alice and Staughton Lynd, *Stepping Stones: Memoir of a Life Together* (Lanham, MD: Lexington Books, 2009), 144–49; and Staughton Lynd, *Lucasville: The Untold Story of a Prison Uprising*, (Oakland, CA: PM Press, 2011) 152–56.

going to do it?" A third suicide occurred in April 2000. In a letter to his family the man who took his own life said there was "no hope here" and "no love." The supermax had been open for two years.

After the second suicide at OSP in 1999, a member of the OSP administration telephoned us and asked what we thought OSP could do to give the prisoners more of a sense that life was worth living. Alice commented to Staughton after the phone call, "They should ask the prisoners rather than us."

She drafted a form that said, "If someone asked you, WHAT COULD OSP DO TO MAKE YOU FEEL YOUR LIFE IS MORE WORTH LIVING, what would you say?" She wrote a covering letter in which she said, you don't have to respond if you don't want to, if you do respond you don't have to sign your name, but say only what is OK for me to submit to the administration.

Alice sent the form to 100 prisoners at OSP who had already written to us. She received 110 responses. She divided the matters complained of into topics in a manner that would not disclose who had written what, and sent copies to the prison authorities. Here are some of the responses we received.

- They could begin to let me feel as if I *were* alive, because this is a very dead feeling place. I feel like an undead zombie in this place.
- They makes us feel less than a human being. They degrade us, take away our pride and break our spirits. They even take away our hope. What do we have left? Nothing.
- The *current* attitude of this place is very clear: We hate you inmates; you don't deserve anything, including being treated humanly; you're all just scum and we hope you never get out of here.
- [T]he institution is geared toward devaluing one's self worth by reducing one's life to a level of constant frustration, depression and loneliness. . . . Locked in a cell alone and nothing is done to help me cope or prepare me to re-enter general population or society. One's entire time spent here is done constantly battling frustration, depression and loneliness and when one leaves here it's a guarantee that they'll depart with an extremely high build up of those negative feelings.
- When you keep beating a dog what's that dog going to do? Bite you. What would that dog do if he had no hope and nothing to do? I will be released from here in November and you know what, I'm a very bitter man.
- By nature if you hate me it's only natural I hate back. How you expect us to act when get out—love thy neighbor. Society don't understand the whole big picture so how you expect prisoners to get out and love someone who has hated us. . . .
- OSP is a high-tech dungeon designed not to rehabilitate, but to dehumanize and drain our very souls. OSP's voice declares that this prison is a controlled and stable environment, but it provides no clue to outsiders about the perpetual inner-turmoil and hostilities.

- Since arriving at OSP I've been so humiliated, harassed, degraded, threatened, dehumanized that I have lost hope of getting out of prison until my maximum expiration date of 25 years. I may not even live to see my freedom.
- All these things . . . build aggression & people handle it in different ways. Some take their life while others build up such a hate for them that later on it could all come out & someone could get hurt. They bring you here, separate you, & eliminate all contact, thinking that it will mentally break you down, but in all essence it's creating a person who could possibly become very dangerous to himself or others.
- This situation has me so depressed that it is like I can just feel myself slowly slipping down into what seems to me a bottomless black pit. This cell feels like a tomb to me. I don't know how much more of this I can take. . . . I just can't handle it. . . .
- [T]his is a really "spooky" place, . . . giving the strongest man a strong sense of utter hopelessness, dark and gloomy.
- I don't know that anything (material) can be applied that would make me feel my life is more worth living. Every day I wake up with the knowledge that at some point during the day I am going to be humiliated, and that this little space in which I *exist* is going to be violated, and that whatever attempts I make towards maintaining my humanity will be challenged by an attitude of indifference that's designed to make me feel like an animal. And I would say it doesn't matter if you gave me all the televisions and commissary in the world; none of those (things) will make a difference if the willingness isn't there to treat me like a human being.
- I ask for the respect I give to the staff to be given back to me. Let me do my time in peace. That's all I need to do my time.

From another prison, we received a letter from a man who wrote to us about the lingering effects of having spent two years in solitary confinement:

This kind of treatment scars an individual for life. . . . To say that one loses his self-esteem and dignity is a gross understatement. . . . I have never felt like the same person since then, nor shall I ever, because I'm not the same person anymore. . . .

Even after 13 or 14 years, I can still feel the anger, resentment, and the hate. The loneliness and pain were at times more than I wanted to bear, and I often contemplated death, but revenge drove me on. Bizarre thoughts abound in a depraved and/or deprived mind—thoughts so scary that you dare not tell anyone else. At first, these thoughts scare you, but then through rationalization you justify them and they comfort you. Eventually you even start acting those thoughts out at any given opportunity. Your feelings become calloused and desensitized—you forget how to feel your pain and the pain of others as well.

You lose those human qualities and values that are so important to life. You stop punishing yourself with guilt, because what you did is far less than what is being done to you. You forget what compassion is, because none is shown to you. You're afraid to even dream, because all hope is gone. But worst of all, you lose your ability to forgive, and you learn how to hate with a passion that becomes your only driving force.

One prisoner at OSP wrote to his mental health counselor asking for a copy of *Man's Search for Meaning.*

Lawsuit

It took nearly three years to put together a legal team and to file a lawsuit challenging the conditions of confinement at OSP and the arbitrary decision-making process that led to placement and retention there. Jules Lobel, who taught civil rights litigation when Alice went to law school, and who was then vice president of the Center for Constitutional Rights, encouraged Alice to do the preliminary research. The Center for Constitutional Rights and the American Civil Liberties Union of Ohio agreed to cooperate, and volunteers associated with both of those organizations became involved.

Grievances and appeals filed by prisoners provided the skeleton for the class action complaint filed in federal court early in 2001. With regard to each topic Alice determined whether that issue had been widely complained about, and which prisoners had clearly defined the issues and fully exhausted their appeals. In the lawsuit the issues became causes of action, and the prisoners identified became the named plaintiffs.

The Complaint had 140 paragraphs and a page and a half Prayer for Relief. We believe that the degree of detail in the Complaint and its apparent authenticity contributed to the success of the lawsuit. Judge James Gwin signaled his attentiveness by scheduling opening arguments at OSP so that the named plaintiffs could listen.

Making Decisions about the Case

In a supermax prison, ordinary First Amendment practices such as group meetings and petitioning are forbidden. Person-to-person communication in the prison yard is not possible when group recreation out of doors is itself prohibited.

Despite the prison policy of keeping the men separated, the lawsuit required that they be assembled as a group to meet with their lawyers and make collective decisions. The warden made such meetings possible by using an empty "pod" of sixteen cells. We sat with Jules Lobel at a table in the open area at the center of the bottom tier. Each of the named plaintiffs was placed in a separate cell. The ports through which food trays were delivered were opened. After discussion, each prisoner voted by thrusting or not thrusting a forearm through the open slot.

After trial but before Judge Gwin had issued a ruling, the authorities proposed a settlement that would have made a decision by the judge unnecessary. The plaintiff prisoners, assembled for deliberation, unanimously rejected the proposal.

These meetings should be viewed as preliminary to direct action. The essence of supermax confinement is that it is solitary. Experts on the psychological effect of such confinement say that its typical result is an inability to function in social settings: a deficit in the ability to react to the small cues that every human being gives to his or her companions so as to forge and maintain bonds of friendship and solidarity. The plaintiff meetings required by the OSP class action helped those who took part to glimpse the possibility of a community of struggle.

Hunger Strikes

At a conference in Washington, DC, on the problems presented by supermax confinement, an attorney who was present remarked, "Prisoners in a supermax can't do anything." She had overlooked hunger strikes. Time out of mind, desperate prisoners all over the world have resorted to hunger strikes.

For several years before OSP opened in 1998, the "Lucasville Five" were confined together at the Mansfield Correctional Institution under conditions more harsh than those imposed on any other Ohio death-sentenced prisoners. They went on hunger strike in 1996 and 1997. These actions were unsuccessful in changing their conditions of confinement but they nurtured a spirit of solidarity. When the Five were transferred to OSP in May 1998, George Skatzes and Siddique Abdullah Hasan initiated another hunger strike. Hasan commented: "I chose to say on the fast to let them know that I was down with George's struggle too and I would not sit quiet and allow the system to mess over him. As anticipated, they got the message and know that we are one. . . ."[7]

A breakthrough came in January 2011. Only three men—Hasan, Keith LaMar, and Jason Robb—took part. Their hunger strike demanded, above all else, the opportunity to touch visiting relatives: in Robb's case, a sister he had not seen for many years because she lived in California; in LaMar's case, the little children of his cousin. After the men had gone less than two weeks without food, they were victorious. The warden signed a written agreement. Full contact visits, with the prisoner tethered by a chain to the floor but otherwise unencumbered, followed soon after.

The precedent of hunger striking that mattered most to the men confined at OSP (and later at Pelican Bay) was that of Bobby Sands, the Irish revolutionary who starved to death in May 1981.[8] Ten striking Irish Republican Army prisoners were allowed by the Thatcher government in Great Britain to fast to the death in prison.

Curiously, very small hunger strikes in Ohio involving only the men condemned to death after the Lucasville uprising in 1993 apparently helped to motivate the much larger hunger strikes of California supermax prisoners in 2011 and 2013.

---

7   Staughton Lynd, *Lucasville*, 150.
8   The life and death of Sands were brought to the attention of prisoners at OSP in Ohio and at Pelican Bay in California by Denis O'Hearn, author of *Nothing but an Unfinished Song: Bobby Sands, the Irish Hunger Striker Who Ignited a Generation* (New York: Nation Books, 2006).

The modicum of due process required by the Supreme Court in the OSP class action led prisoners in supermax confinement in many other states to write to us. They inquired as to what the court had decided and how it might affect their particular situations. One of these correspondents, Todd Ashker, would be a principal spokesperson for prisoners hunger striking at the Pelican Bay State Prison in California, where a later class action claimed that solitary confinement for more than ten years was cruel and unusual punishment, as will be described in Chapter 7.

What Was Won in Ohio

In the Ohio class action we began with two constitutional claims: one was based on cruel and unusual punishment, focusing mostly on medical and mental health issues; the other challenged the procedures for placement and prolonged retention under conditions of "atypical and significant hardship." The cruel and unusual punishment claims were settled so there is no legal precedent that could be used in other states. However, the changes in procedures became the law of the land.

Here is a summary of the procedural requirements won by prisoners in the Ohio class action lawsuit. Prior to placement at Ohio's highest level of security, the inmate must receive written notice with specific factual reasons, a hearing, and two levels of appeal. Specifically:[9]

- The inmate must have been found guilty, either by a court or by a Rules Infraction Board, of one of a limited number of serious offenses (almost always for offenses committed while incarcerated).
- The Notice of Hearing must tell the inmate what the factual basis is for placing him in high maximum security. A boilerplate statement that he "poses the highest level of threat to security" or comparable language is not sufficient. The disposition by a Rules Infraction Board, or the sentencing entry by a court, must be attached to the hearing notice.
- The inmate must be given the opportunity to appear and be heard by a Classification Committee. At the hearing he can present any relevant information, explanation, or objections to placement in high maximum security.
- The Committee makes a recommendation; the Warden reviews the Committee's recommendation and writes his own recommendation; and those recommendations go to the Chief of the Bureau of Classification for a final decision. At each level, the inmate must receive a written statement that includes the reasons for the recommendation or decision and the sources of information relied on. And, at each step before the final decision, the inmate can submit written objections.

---

9   This summary of the procedural requirements is based on opinions by the Supreme Court in *Wilkinson v. Austin*, 545 U.S. 209, 125 S.Ct. 2384 (2005), and by the federal trial court on remand, *Austin v. Wilkinson*, 502 F.Supp.2d 660 (N.D. Ohio 2006).

- Each inmate's security level is reviewed at least once a year. The procedures for retention are comparable to the procedures for placement in high
  maximum security: notice, hearing, written notice of reasons and sources of
  information relied on, and opportunity to appeal from the recommendation
  of the Classification Committee to the Warden and then to the Chief of
  the Bureau of Classification.

The Supreme Court emphasized the importance of telling the inmate what the
reasons were for placing him in high maximum security: "This requirement guards
against arbitrary decisionmaking while also providing the inmate a basis for objection
before the next decisionmaker or in a subsequent classification review. The statement
also serves as a guide for future behavior. . . ."[10]

These principles are critical for prisoners in solitary confinement outside Ohio
who want to know, "Why am I here? And what do I have to do to get out?"

Administrative Detention in Illinois

Tamms

In 1998, the same year that the Ohio State Penitentiary opened with 504 supermax
cells, the State of Illinois opened a 500-bed unit at the Tamms Correctional Center
to house prisoners regarded as the most disruptive and dangerous. Conditions
at Tamms were designed to be harsher than in any other segregation facility in
Illinois.[11]

Prior to the Supreme Court's ruling in the Ohio supermax case, a district court
had denied relief to prisoners at Tamms who were bringing some similar claims. But
after the Supreme Court specified what was required to place or retain a prisoner
in supermax confinement, a court of appeals reversed the district court and allowed
some of the Tamms prisoners' claims. Even though there were differences between
Tamms and the Ohio State Penitentiary, Illinois was required to provide procedures
for placement at Tamms comparable to those considered by the Supreme Court in
the Ohio case.[12]

The new procedures for placement at Tamms, consistent with the Supreme
Court's opinion in Ohio, appeared in a manual that was available to prisoners at
Tamms. Before transfer to Tamms, offenders were to receive written notice of the
reasons, an opportunity to appear and present statements and documents at a hearing, to be given an estimate as to how long they were expected to stay at Tamms, and
written notice as to the results of their hearing.

---

10   *Wilkinson v. Austin*, 545 U.S. at 226.
11   Illinois Department of Corrections, "Tamms Closed Maximum Security Unit: Overview
     and Ten-Point Plan," Executive Summary, September 3, 2009, <https://www.illinois.gov/
     idoc/facilities/Documents/TammsCMAXOverviewTenPointPlan.pdf>, accessed June
     2, 2016; and *Westefer v. Snyder*, 422 F.3d 570, 573 (7th Cir. 2005).
12   Ibid., 422 F.3d at 588–90.

In 2012, the governor of Illinois announced that Tamms would be closed due to budget cuts. The last five high security prisoners were transferred to the Pontiac Correctional Center at the end of December, and on January 4, 2013, Tamms was officially closed.[13] Some former Tamms inmates ended up in Administrative Detention at the Menard Correctional Center, a prison on the Illinois side of the Mississippi River, fifty miles southeast of St. Louis.

Pontiac and Menard are the oldest prisons in Illinois: Pontiac opened in June 1871 and Menard opened in March 1878.[14] They are antiquated and in disrepair.

Menard is the largest maximum security facility in Illinois. As of 2011, Menard's population was approximately 63 percent African American, 25 percent white, and 12 percent Hispanic. "The average inmate at Menard spen[t] roughly 21 to 22 hours a day locked in cells idle, with little or no activity or opportunity for normal social and human interaction."[15] As shown below, life in Administrative Detention is significantly more restricted.

Some Individual Stories

A few of the prisoners disclosed to us a little bit about their own personal histories. One man had been at Menard in 1997 before the supermax section of Tamms was opened. When Tamms opened in March 1998, he was transferred there and stayed until it closed. He was sent to Pontiac in December 2012. When he organized a hunger strike at Pontiac he was sent back to Menard. All of that time—seventeen years—he was under "No Human Contact Status."

> I have not shook someone's hand, or hugged someone since the middle of 1997. The ONLY human contact I ever receive is when the officers are putting handcuffs on me behind my back and then escorting me wherever I'm going.
>
> ... my last 12 years at Tamms were done w/out me receiving ANY major disciplinary reports. Yet they *still* won't let me out of isolation. ... I will never be released from isolation because of the things I did 20+ years ago.

Another man wrote in his diary that he had received a new ID card with the words "STAFF ASSAULTER" on it.

---

13   Wikipedia, "Tamms Correctional Center," <https://en.wikipedia.org/wiki/Tamms_Correctional_Center>, and, Amnesty International USA, "Tamms Supermaximum Security Prison Now Closed," January 10, 2013, <http://www.amnestyusa.org/our-work/latest-victories/tamms-supermaximum-security-prison-now-closed>, accessed May 31, 2016.

14   <http://www.illinois.gov/idoc/facilities/Pages/pontiaccorrectionalcenter.aspx>, and <http://www.illinois.gov/idoc/facilities/Pages/menardcorrectionalcenter.aspx>, accessed May 31, 2016.

15   John Howard Association, Monitoring Visit to Menard Correctional Center, June 21, 2011, <http://thejha.org/sites/default/files/Menard%20Report_2011.pdf>, accessed June 4, 2016.

Without having been given a disciplinary ticket, another prisoner was sent to Tamms in 1999 and remained there until it closed. He spent a year at Pontiac before he was sent to Menard. "Being at Tamms for all of that time kind of mess[ed] me up." He became sensitive to loud noise and bright lights. "I've also a problem with too many people around me and people touching me."

One young man said he had been incarcerated since he was a juvenile. He was housed in a one-man isolation cell at Tamms from the age of twenty to twenty-eight. At Menard, he requested one-man cell status: "I've been having a reoccurring nightmare that I'm given a cellie [cellmate] and that I seriously hurt him."

On the subject of double-celling, another prisoner explained that Menard

does not look to double bunk you with who they feel you'd best get along with. Menard has a policy of reviewing each individual's background looking for past or present affiliations, among other things. They then intentionally force you to accept somebody from an opposite past or present affiliation as a cellmate. A dangerous enough practice under normal circumstances. But we all know Administrative Detention is anything but normal circumstances. We are stuck in these rooms 24 hours a day, every day, with the exception of the two days we are permitted to go to the yard for a couple of hours.

Being confined to a cell 24 hours a day under the conditions of Administrative Detention is difficult enough by ourselves. Then add in another, who is dealing with the same stress, aggravation, frustration, and whatever else, and you have a recipe for disaster. Especially when you consider that in placing somebody of an opposite past or present affiliation in your cell, they are placing who even their records would show to be an enemy in your room, how could that be considered a safe practice? . . .[16]

Conditions of Confinement at Menard

Conditions at Menard are, as one prisoner wrote in a grievance, "harsher than general population or any facility now that Tamms supermax is closed." Menard was designed

---

16 *See* John Howard Association, 2013 Update Monitoring Visit to Menard Correctional Center, 2–3: "With double-cells as small as 4 feet 8 inches wide, inmates at Menard may experience the paradoxical psychological detriment of both being crowded and isolated." <http://www.thejha.org/sites/default/files/Menard%202013%20Update.pdf>, accessed June 2, 2016. That report contains the following footnote, 3 n.5:

    See e.g. Madrid v. Gomez, 889 F. Supp. 1146, 1229–30 (N.D. Cal. 1995) ("The combination of being in extremely close proximity with one other person, while other avenues for normal social interaction are virtually precluded, often makes any long-term, normal relationship with the cellmate impossible. Instead, two persons housed together in this type of forced, constant intimacy have an 'enormously high risk of becoming paranoid, hostile, and potentially violent towards each other.'")

with small open barred cells, meant to house one person at a time when most prisoners spent the day out of their cells, at work, school, or in common areas. The open bars were replaced with solid doors. Prisoners in solitary confinement spend all but approximately five hours a week locked in their cells.[17]

In a lawsuit filed in 2013, one of the prisoners in Administrative Detention at Menard described what he called unconstitutional conditions of confinement. He claimed that he had had no heat or hot water in his cell throughout an entire winter. The toilet leaked, causing foul odors in the cell and the plumbing did not function properly for several months. The housing wing was infested with mice, and many items in his property box were destroyed, contaminated with mouse feces, and smelled of mouse urine. Inmates in administrative detention did not have access to disinfectant to clean their cells.[18]

By 2014, prisoners had filed numerous grievances protesting lack of protection from the cold in winter months and lack of hot water in their cells for washing themselves or cleaning their eating utensils. The Department denied that these conditions existed. However, their own documents acknowledged that heat and hot water had been problems for two years. In response to one grievance, the counselor[19] wrote, "The pioneers showered, bathed & shaved in the cold without heat. They had no hot water." In response to another grievance, the grievance officer's report said, "The orientation Manual states you shall have water in your cell. It does not say hot water."

One grievant said the prisoners were forced to go to the yard in the winter and wait in the freezing cold for up to a half an hour until they were given "Community Coats." Another grievant requests that they "be provided with their own winter coat and not be forced to wear coats that have been worn by numerous other inmates and stink, and/or, are still wet with someone else's sweat. . . ."

Reasons for Placement in Administrative Detention

Prisoners were placed in the High Security Unit at Menard without notice or hearing. "I'm not being told why or who placed me here," a prisoner complained. In several cases, men remained in Administrative Detention after a disciplinary record had been expunged! One man told us, "We don't have any way to challenge [Administrative Detention]. I filed a grievance, and I was told that A.D. is an Administrative Decision and it's not grievable." The men in Administrative Detention at Menard asked for the kind of procedures that had been won at Tamms Correctional Center. A typical grievance stated:

---

17   Alan Mills, Alice and Staughton Lynd, "Statement for Senate Judiciary Subcommittee Hearing Reassessing Solitary Confinement II," February 25, 2014, 1.

18   *Shearrill v. Atchison et al.*, [S.D. Ill.] Case No. 13-cv-859.

19   A "counselor" is the first administrative staff person to review a grievance. See Illinois Administrative Code, Title 20, Sec. 504.810 (a): "An offender shall first attempt to resolve incidents, problems, or complaints other than complaints concerning disciplinary proceedings through his or her counselor."

I'm being treated as if I [was] put in Tamms with no reasons why[,] so I'm restricted phone privileges and visitation, audio-visual, showers & commissary. . . . How am I supposed to know I'm doing something wrong if I'm not given reasons why or the rule process. . . .

I request I be given all my privileges consistent with general population, also . . . to be given a hearing at which point I be informed of what, why and how I came to be placed in (A.D) to get a chance to present a defense to any allegations or accusations made and show justification in writing why I'm here.

The counselor responded: "You claim IDOC [Illinois Department of Corrections] has become judge, jury & executioner. We haven't executed anyone in Admin Detention program. This is an Administrative placement & as such is not grievable."

Another man said in a grievance, "Every time I ask if I could be given a reason why I was placed in [A.D.] I'm told that they don't know" or only the prison that sent him to Menard knows the reason. "I want my due process and be told why I'm placed in A.D. and be given a chance to defend myself." The counselor responded: "You have the right to ask. We have the right to deny answers to your questions."

Referring to the Ohio and Illinois court decisions, another prisoner put the following into a grievance appeal:

[T]he Supreme Court of the United States required adequate "Notice" of why an inmate is being placed in A.D.; notice of the charges must be given to grievant or other factual basis giving rise to my placement in A.D. high security unit. Grievant also must be given the opportunity to appear and be heard at an informal hearing to refute the charges and present any relevant information. Grievant also must be given written reason(s) for his placement and reason(s) for his continued placement in A.D. And grievant must be given the opportunity to appeal all adverse decisions of the Adjustment Committee and/or the Wardens.

Illinois Administrative Directive 504 does not include written notices of reasons, hearing, and opportunity to appeal placement or retention in Administrative Detention and thus violates grievant's due process of law.

Further, it is said that A.D. is not disciplinary, but grievant lost his audio-visual privileges, contact visits, property boxes and education privileges upon being placed in A.D. status. . . .[20]

---

20   Grievances by numerous prisoners were filed as exhibits in *Tillman v. Atchison et al.*, (S.D. Ill.), Case No. 13-cv-01125.

2014 Hunger Strike

We received a letter, written on Christmas Day 2013, telling us that men being held in Administrative Detention at Menard were planning a hunger strike and wanted our assistance in publicizing it.

The hunger strike began on January 15, 2014. "There are only about 25 to 28 inmates on the high security unit and most of us are on hunger strike. The rest are too fearful to do it because we've been told they'll never let us out of Administrative Detention if we complain too much." They filed emergency grievances "challenging their conditions of confinement at the high security isolation unit, i.e. no hot water, no coats, no cleaning supplies, filthy living conditions, rodent infestation, no access to mental health screening and/or treatment, and a complete lack of educational, life skills, substance abuse and behavioral incentive programs, etc."[21]

But, more fundamentally, they went on hunger strike because, unlike at Tamms, they were not told what they had allegedly done to warrant transfer to this highly restrictive unit. They were not given a hearing. They were not given any opportunity to defend themselves. They were not told what they were supposed to do to earn additional privileges, and they were not told what they had to do to be released from the unit. They were unable to obtain an official directive outlining what was required for them to move from one phase to the next such that they could be released from Administrative Detention and become reintegrated into a general population facility.

Twenty men participated in this hunger strike, some for more than thirty days. During that month, one prisoner informed us, fourteen disciplinary tickets were written targeted at nine of the hunger strikers, whereas between the fall of 2012 and the beginning of the hunger strike on January 15, 2014, less than half that many tickets were written. "This is just their way of getting back at us for exposing all their wrongdoings," he commented. And another man told us, "They are writing us tickets with the hope that it will stop us from continuing our fight. But instead all they're doing is adding wood to the fire."

Demonstration by Supporters

On Monday, January 27, the hunger strikers saw and heard about twenty people outside the prison, banging on homemade drums, holding signs and singing, "We support the hunger strike!" Several hunger strikers opened their windows and screamed: "Hunger Strike!" "No due process no peace," and "We Love You!" According to a "Brother in Struggle," the protesters "were out there in 12 degree weather" until the police came and told them to leave.

"Seeing them protest on our behalf was definitely a confidence booster," one of the prisoners told us. "The psychological effect on the prisoners is beyond explanation."

---

21 *Williams et al. v. Harrington et al.*, Circuit Court for Randolph County, Illinois, February 2014.

An assistant warden promptly "came to talk to us and told us the warden was coming back from a meeting in Springfield [presumably where he had been meeting with higher officials] and would come see us the next day to let us know about what was going to be done about all of our issues." However, when the warden came, instead of talking about solving any of their issues, he threatened everyone on the wing with shipping them out of the state if they continued their hunger strike.

The supporters came back on February 13. The second time the protesters came, the administration disciplined some of the prisoners. "Upstairs where I am at, 3 of us got tickets for yelling out of the window. . . . I was one of the guys who got a ticket. The police said that he gave me several direct orders to stop yelling out of my window. I told that Sergeant . . . I am not yelling out of my window because it is broken and I can not open it up at all." He was placed in segregation for three months and his property was taken.

As predicted, before the end of the hunger strike, one prisoner was removed from Menard and transferred to a prison in California, and others were later sent to Virginia, West Virginia, and New Mexico. Surprisingly, all of those men who had been in segregation for many years were released to general population in those distant prisons.

Windows Covered
On the morning of Saturday, April 12, 2014, maintenance workers installed metal boxes on the outside of the windows. "We can no longer see out the windows and barely any sunlight comes in."

> All of the windows in the High Security Unit are being covered (blocked) with a steel covering in retaliation of our hollering out to the protestors that marched outside the facility during our last hunger strike.
> We were told, "How you like your view now?"

Sadly, one of the prisoners whose view was blocked was one who wrote that he spent a lot of time looking out of his window, watching people working or looking at the Mississippi River, and there was no telling when he would see any of that again.

With summer approaching, the prisoners anticipated, "Not only will our air flow circulation be affected, but we . . . have steel doors. We will now be forced to live in what will amount to an extremely hot tomb." Later, one of the prisoners told us, "This summer has been torture! The cell has been extremely hot, especially since the cell I'm in is steel plated. The walls are steel not brick. Steel covered walls and a steel covered window is not a good combination."

At some point during the spring of 2014, their pens were confiscated and the prisoners were not permitted to purchase writing materials such as pens, paper, and white out. Men who had court deadlines were not able to write to their lawyers or the court. One prisoner wrote to the warden:

You censor our mail unnecessarily so that we can not hear. You instruct your [officers] to take our ink-pens so that we can not speak. You shutter our windows so that we can see, and I'm sure this is your ideal convict—one who can not hear, speak or see. You can shutter our windows, but you can NOT shutter our minds!

Special Response Team (a/k/a Orange Crush)

On April 12, a Special Response Team, known as the "Orange Crush" because their uniforms are orange, ran into the high security unit to conduct a shakedown. "We were strip searched and had handcuffs put on our wrists so tight it cut off the circulation to our hands. When we complained about this we were told to shut the fuck up and keep our heads down and eyes on the ground." They were escorted to the shower and called "Hunger Strike Bitches," and taunted by words such as, "When's the next hunger strike—tough guys? HA, HA, HA."

In the showers, as their heads were being shoved against the wall, they were told, "Put your fucking heads on the wall!" "I said put your fucking heads against the fucking wall!"

Prisoners in the upstairs showers heard screaming coming from the downstairs showers. "Quit slamming his head!" "Warden, investigate this!"

An assistant warden came to the upstairs shower asking if they had any questions. One at a time prisoners were escorted to talk to her in a hallway, although the other prisoners could hear their conversations. A prisoner asked whether any new rules were going to be implemented. She replied, "We aren't working on any rules, and you're not getting any rules." Another prisoner asked her why they were in Administrative Detention. "You all know," she said, along with some four-letter words. Sarcastically, she then asked, "Any mice? Find any mice?"

> Once back in our cells we realized . . . our pens were missing in order to prevent us from writing grievances. Our property was slung all over and some of it was destroyed. Also they took small things out of spite. Out of a deck of cards, one prisoner was missing one card. Out of a chess set, one prisoner was missing one chess piece.

Reports from downstairs were similar. When one prisoner told her he had no idea why he was in Administrative Detention and that he had not been informed either in writing or verbally, she stated, "Well I don't have to tell you anything for the safety and security of the institution." The prisoner then asked, "Why haven't we gotten any A.D. Orientation Manuals, or hearing to challenge our placement on A.D. or get a copy of our 90-day reviews, at least be present." Right now, they don't have any way to challenge A.D., he continued, but Pontiac gives the inmates in A.D. an orientation manual that explains the program. She responded: "We are not going to give none of you guys no orientation manuals or hearings, no matter what anybody says. If you don't know why you are here, then that's your problem."

We received reports both from a man who was physically assaulted by members of the Special Response Team and from other prisoners. An argument arose with the assistant warden over the conditions of confinement, and the effects of long-term isolation, especially for mentally ill inmates in administrative detention and disciplinary segregation. "What would you have a mentally ill person do?" the prisoner asked. She answered, "Follow our rules and do their time."

An officer took him back to the shower, and repeatedly banged his head on the wall while saying, "Put your head down." The officer punched the prisoner in his ribs and took his eyeglasses, then lifted the inmate's arms by the cuffs behind him, put his weight between the inmate's cuffed hands, told the inmate to get on his knees and, when he did not do so, kicked his feet from under him. "I was placed on my knees between an old out of compliance toilet and the shower bars. I stayed there until shakedowns were complete."

Meanwhile, the other prisoners were yelling to the assistant warden, "Y'all see this? He's banging his head on the wall." "Look, look, look, they are doing it again!"

The injured inmate fell asleep. When he tried to get up his head was hurting, he was dizzy and disoriented. His nose was bleeding. His eyes, wrists, back and neck were hurting. He says he asked for medical attention at least three times but was ignored or laughed at.

In reflecting on this experience, he stated that he was the third victim of an assault in administrative detention since the hunger strike. He wrote:

> I do fear for my safety, security and wellbeing. This unlawful, unwarranted and excessive use of force was completely unnecessary. The fact that it was done in front of the [assistant warden and intelligence officer] proves that they have *NO* moral standings, no standards and that all of our safety and security could be in jeopardy at any given time. . . . This is a dangerous time. . . . Grievances will not work. Mental health professionals are telling me I have to find a way to just deal with it! I can't any more! What am I supposed to do? I'm begging for an answer because I honestly do not know any more!!

Four days after the Orange Crush incident, on April 16, 2014, a new warden was appointed. In making the announcement the director of the Illinois Department of Corrections thanked the retiring warden, "especially [for] his stellar performance during the past 12 months of tremendous improvement at Menard Correctional Center. Safety and Security have never been better than during this time."[22]

---

22 According to an official press release dated April 16, 2014, Kim Butler was appointed
     to replace Rick Harrington as warden of Menard Correctional Center. <http://www.

A New Procedure

Contrary to previous statements by officials at Menard, the Illinois Department of Corrections issued a new Administrative Directive on Administrative Detention Placement, effective May 1, 2014. It provided that, except in exigent circumstances, an administrative detention hearing was to be conducted within thirty days *after* placement in administrative detention. The offender was to be afforded the opportunity to appear at the hearing to provide oral or written statements and documents relevant to his or her administrative detention placement. Recommendations to continue placement in administrative detention were ultimately to be approved by the director or his deputy. A written copy of the decision was to be provided to the offender. Every ninety days there was to be a review of each offender to determine whether continued placement in administrative detention is appropriate, and every six months the offender would have the opportunity to appear in person before the Review Committee.[23]

The 2014 hunger strikers wanted to know why they were in Administrative Detention, and they wanted to know what they had to do to get out of Administrative Detention. Although the Illinois Department of Corrections began to issue some notices, the notices still did not answer those questions.

Prisoners at Menard (and at Pontiac) sent us copies of the Notice of Administrative Detention Placement Review forms they received.[24] At the top of the notice, it says: "This document shall serve as notice of your upcoming review for placement in Administrative Detention by the Administrative Detention Review Committee."

It shows the Review Date for Initial Placement in Administrative Detention, or Continued Placement, or Transfer from Disciplinary Segregation. Next, it says:

> **Notice of Administration [*sic*] Detention Placement Rationale:** In order to prepare you for your Administrative Detention placement review, you are advised that the Department's rationale for your prospective or continued placement in Administrative Detention is based upon the following reason(s): . . .

But the reason may be no more than "Information was received that . . ." without any finding of guilt for a rule violation. The form then specifies,

> Copies of the following identified documents relied upon by Department administrators that may subject you to Administrative Detention Placement,

illinois.gov/idoc/news/2014/Pages/WardenMenardCorrectionalCenter.aspx>, accessed May 31, 2016.

23   Illinois Department of Corrections, Administrative Directive No. 05.12.101, Administrative Detention Placement. This Directive applied not only to Menard but also to Pontiac.

24   Notice of Administrative Detention Placement Review, DOC 0432 (Eff. 5/2014).

or continued placement, are attached to the Notice; however, portions may have been redacted based upon a finding that disclosure would compromise security or safety:

Every notice we have seen says "N/A," which we assume to mean "not applicable," in place of a list of documents; we know of no case where any documents were mentioned or attached.

Furthermore, the reasons given do not specify that the prisoner was found guilty of any particular offense on any particular date. In one instance, continued placement was recommended "due to his continued negative adjustment while in population and segregation, STG [security threat group, i.e., gang] activity, and orchestrating assaults on staff." The prisoner still does not know what evidence is being relied on or what he can say in self-defense. Did the review take into account incidents for which he was never found to have been responsible, or disciplinary tickets that were supposed to have been expunged from his record?

The written decision that the warden sends the prisoner at the end of the review is a memo that says no more than the following:

This memo is to inform [name and number] the Menard Administrative Detention Committee has reviewed your Administrative Detention placement and has voted to continue your placement in Administrative Detention on Phase 1. You will be reviewed again in 90 days.

2015 Hunger Strike

In September 2015, prisoners in Administrative Detention at Menard once again went on hunger strike. We received the following statement:

Here in A.D., everything is still the same. No one is being released and we are still not getting meaningful hearings. We are still not getting any written reasons or any new info relied on for the basis of the Committee's decision for our continued placement in A.D. We are still getting the same vague memos.

We now only get 1 day a week of out-of-cell exercise (yard). We are in our cells 24 hrs. a day, 6 days a week. We are being excessively confined in our cells. We are still not allowed to participate in any educational programs. Our mail is not being picked up or passed out 5 days a week, as they are supposed to.

We don't see any end to this indefinite isolation/solitary confinement. Due to these issues and more, we are going to go on hunger strike once again. We will be declaring a hunger strike on September 23, 2015. We will feel very thankful for your help in spreading the word.

Another prisoner sent us this list of "core demands":

- We demand an end to long term solitary confinement.
- We demand minimum due process at Administrative Detention Review Hearings by providing inmates with written reasons, including new information relied upon, for Committee's decision for our continued placement in A.D. and be allowed to grieve all adverse decisions. As it stands, the basis of the Committee's votes are kept secret.
- We demand more access to outside recreation for the sake of our physical and mental health. As it stands, we are confined indefinitely to these cages for 6 days out of the week, with the exception of one 5 hour day. This is unbearable.
- We demand that meaningful educational programs be implemented to encourage our mental stability, rehabilitation, and social development for the sake of ourselves and our communities that we will one day return to.
- We demand access to more visiting privileges. For most of our families traveling to Menard is like traveling to another state. Considering the distance, 2 hour visits behind plexiglass is insufficient. We should be allowed 5 or 6 hours. Moreover, our family members, including inmates, should be provided the human dignity and decency to purchase food items and refreshments from vending machines after traveling such great distances. This would benefit one's social development, as well as benefit prison staff environment.

On the third day of the hunger strike, supporters once again showed up in front of the prison.

> Even though we can't see them due to the covers that were placed on our windows, we were able to hear them. We were threatened by the major, lieutenant and staff members that if we said or yelled out anything to them they were going to write us tickets and "give us something to yell about." Officers were outside hollering to our supporters, telling them that it was all lies and we were *not* on hunger strike. Some of us yelled out and told our supporters that we *are* on strike and we started making noise to assure our supporters we were here and on hunger strike. They (officers) came and searched a cell to just make a mess and try to intimidate us.

Also that day, Wednesday, September 25, 2015, disciplinary reports were issued to each hunger striker for the offense of "Dangerous Disturbance" for declaring the hunger strike. Before the end of the week, however, the warden called out one of the hunger strikers and told him that if *all* of the hunger strikers would end the hunger strike before Monday, the disciplinary reports for having declared a hunger strike would be expunged. The warden offered to raise the commissary spending limit and, instead of five hours on the yard once a week, they would be able to go outside twice a week for two and a half hours. They would also be given more detailed reasons for their placement in Administrative Detention.

This offer put more than one of the men between a rock and a hard place. They had been given promises before, and had been disappointed. There was no basis on which to build a foundation of trust. Nothing was in writing. The only thing that would improve their overall situation was for the hearings to become meaningful. But if any individual did not come off the hunger strike, he could cause each and every one of the hunger strikers to spend a year in disciplinary segregation. By Sunday night, the hunger strike was over.

In October, everyone in Administrative Detention at Menard had a hearing. In November, seven of the men were moved to a "kick-out" gallery where their privileges were similar to those in general population. They could walk together to the yard and to chow. Their telephone, commissary and visiting privileges were restored. After thirty days without any incidents or hearing their names involved in what was considered Security Threat Group activity, they would be fully released into general population. The men who were moved out of the Administrative Detention galleries were told by the administration that, depending on how they did, they would determine the future of the guys coming behind them.

> The hate the C/Os have for us is clear as day as they see we are allowed to move about without cuff/chains. Some have made smart ass comments how we would be back in A.D. or how it's stupid to let us out and allowed to move around when just last week we were "dangerous." One incident is liable to put us back into A.D.

Meanwhile, one of the men said that those who were in the most restrictive phase of Administrative Detention and those in Disciplinary Segregation, gained no benefit from the settlement of the hunger strike. All of them had participated or it would not have happened, one of them wrote. "A lot of people were left stranded, while a certain fraction benefitted immensely. . . . I feel like we allowed them to divide and conquer with threats and promises!!"

Responding to that comment, a man who was released from segregation to "a different part of this concentration camp," wrote, "I'm still of the mind that even if our collective uprising forced the downpressors to 'release' just one of us from a torturous situation—for whatever reason—it's a small victory. . . . In our solidarity I found not just my humanity, but I found our collective humanity as well." Togetherness and unity, such as they had during the hunger strikes, is the key to freedom for the oppressed all over the world, he believes. "Our collective humanity was affirmed by ourselves in a system that constantly 'reminds' us that we're less than animals. . . . I gained my humanity and wrapped it in a sacredness that I will always defend. That's something!"

Incarcerated Lives Matter

After the 2015 hunger strike, one of the prisoners sent us a drawing he made showing all of the men together in what must have been an imaginary scene (because those men are never allowed to be together in the same space at the same time). In the background, one of the men was holding a sign that said, "Incarcerated Lives Matter." The drawing accurately depicted one of the 2014 and 2015 hunger strikers with the tattoo on his arm that says, "Never look down on a Man unless you're willing to pick him back up."

Here are a few reflections by the men who have been, or who remain in, Administrative Detention or Disciplinary Segregation at Menard.

> Dignity, integrity and loyalty all have a price. . . . Would you betray those whom you say you love for "another thing"? Many people *do*! . . . I've become accustomed to betrayal when I give my all.
>
> If you're not willing to fuck people over, do whatever it takes in the way of lie, steal and cheat or whatever else to make it to the top or "the next thing," you will surely have a hard life. . . . I'm afraid of life because I'm not willing to live that way, so I know my life will be hard. . . . I refuse to change who I am on account of what others are not. . . . We still must love, trust others, etc. . . .
>
> What you do between here and death is what matters.

Similarly, another man wrote:

> The roads ahead will be long and hard but through the process we shall endure, not because we want to but because we don't have any other choice! We stand to fight the powers that be armed with intelligence, dedication, determination, discipline, patience, [and] persistence. . . .

One of the prisoners who was sent out of state after the 2014 hunger strike says he learned a lot from going through that experience.

> I feel kind of sad about the people who I am around now. They do not do no prison activism. All they are worried about is doing drugs: 95% of the population are drug addicts and it is crazy how many young people are using serious drugs through needles. It makes no sense to me.
>
> I try to explain my journey to them and all they ask is why? I feel real alone at times and I try to stay to myself.

Back at Menard, and once again on hunger strike, one of the prisoners told us he was moved to a strip cell used for inmates who try to commit suicide or act crazy. He was housed between a guy that covered his head and face with feces, and a guy that masturbates in front of everybody. "It's weird," he writes, "I believe they thought this treatment would make me come off [hunger strike]. If they haven't noticed by now, I am different, different in that their attempts to bully me only drive me . . . [to] recognize that it's them actually running scared!" "It's funny," he continues:

> Everyone gets quiet when [another of the 2014 and 2015 hunger strikers] and I converse over the gallery. The men are interested. It's knowing what to do that stumps them. . . . I don't know if the talks of being unified have hit home, but people are listening! I even talk to the guy who had covered himself in poop. (Never look down on a man unless you are willing to pick him up.) I know people think it's strange. But, #1, I keep him calm. #2, people are noticing he's . . . well he's crazy. But he needs and deserves help. . . . I will leave no man behind unless he's unwilling to move. Incarcerated Lives Matter!

Chapter 7.
The Pelican Bay Hunger Strikes

THERE IS NO YELLOW BRICK ROAD TO FUNDAMENTAL SOCIAL CHANGE. NOTHING experienced by the generation that came of age in the 1960s, or by our current counterparts, the so-called millennials, permits the two of us, or anyone else, to point to a particular strategy, to a recommended party or movement, or to an imagined coalition of social forces, and say: "This is it. Take political path X or Y and all will be well." There are no guarantees.

On the other hand, there are experiences that it would be a shame to waste, to permit to be tossed into the dustbin of forgetfulness. There were Staughton's mountaintop months as coordinator of the Mississippi Freedom Schools in 1964, and Alice's experience in editing *We Won't Go*, a collection of firsthand accounts by persons who in a variety of ways refused to become soldiers in Vietnam. There was the effort to keep steel mills functioning in Youngstown and Pittsburgh under some form of worker-community ownership.

In the remainder of this book we want to begin remembering and reflecting on the massive hunger strikes by prisoners held in supermaximum security in California who, in 2011–2015, in effect abolished indefinite solitary confinement in the nation's largest state prison system. They needed a little help from their friends in the form of a class action lawsuit filed by the Center for Constitutional Rights. The two of us, Alice and Staughton Lynd, at the request of prisoners on the Short Corridor at Pelican Bay improvised an initial network of outside support that grew far beyond what we could provide from distant Ohio.

At this writing the thousands of men who took part in the hunger strikes of 2011 and 2013 are only partway along the road to freedom outside the bars. Moreover, it may never again be possible or appropriate to assemble into a single social force the elements of nonviolent direct action and legal support that made the road by walking it in California. Nevertheless, these nonviolent strugglers can justly claim to have "won."

We try to tell our part of the tale in the hope that it may offer some inspiration to the next assemblage of ordinary people who venture forth.

Pelican Bay

Pelican Bay State Prison in northern California opened in 1989.[1] Half of the prison holds prisoners in "general population" with outside areas for group recreation. The

---

1   Sources for the following sketch of the Pelican Bay Security Housing Unit include "Summary of *Ashker v. Governor* Settlement Terms," <http://ccrjustice.org/sites/default/files/attach/2015/08/2015-09-01-Ashker-settlement-summary.pdf>, accessed May 31,

other half of the prison contains an X-shaped cluster of buildings and barren ground known as the Security Housing Unit (SHU, pronounced "shoe"), where men were held in indefinite solitary confinement. Cells within the SHU are eight by ten feet. They have no windows. Food is delivered through a slot, or "port," in the cell door. A correctional officer at a central control booth controls the cell doors, pressing one button to allow one prisoner out for a shower and another for a period of solitary exercise.[2]

As of 2011, according to the California Department of Corrections and Rehabilitation, the average number of men in the SHU was 1,106. Five hundred thirteen men had been in the Pelican Bay SHU for more than ten years, and seventy-eight had been there for more than twenty years.[3]

Prisoners were confined in the SHU when alleged by the authorities to be members or associates of prison gangs. The procedure for attaching such a designation to an inmate, and thus, for placing him in the SHU, was extremely arbitrary. In one federal court case the evidence for involvement in a gang was the prisoner's possession of a design known as a "huelga bird." ("Huelga" is the Spanish word for "strike," and the huelga bird is a symbol popularized by the United Farm Workers union.[4]) Tattoos and greeting cards were also considered in determining gang involvement.

Reconsideration of a prisoner's placement in the SHU occurred only every half dozen years and was usually a paper proceeding that did not require the authorities to present new evidence. As perceived by prisoners, the only practical way to get out of the SHU was to "debrief," that is, to present testimony concerning the supposed gang associations of other prisoners.

2016; California Department of Corrections and Rehabilitation, Offender Information Services Branch, "Monthly Report of Population," as of January 31, 2013 (February 7, 2013), <http://www.cdcr.ca.gov/Reports_Research/Offender_Information_Services_Branch/Monthly/TPOP1A/TPOP1Ad1301.pdf>, accessed May 31, 2016; Corey Weinstein and Eric Cummins, "The Crime of Punishment: Pelican Bay Maximum Security Prison," in *Criminal Injustice*, ed. Elihu Rosenblatt (Boston: South End Press, 1996); Keramet Reiter, "Parole, Snitch, or Die: California's Supermax Prisons and Prisoners, 1987–2007," Institute for the Study of Social Change Working Paper (July 7, 2010).

2   Architects' drawings of the Short Corridor, and photographs of Todd Ashker's cell on the Short Corridor, are reproduced in Andrej Grubačić and Denis O'Hearn, *Living at the Edges of Capitalism: Adventures in Exile and Mutual Aid* (Oakland, CA: University of California Press, 2016), 210, 214–15.

3   *Ashker v. Brown*, Case No. 4-09-05796 (N.D. Cal.), Plaintiffs' Second Amended Complaint, ¶ 33.

4   *Lira v. Cate*, Case No. 3:00-cv-905 (N.D. Cal. 9/30/09), Doc. 456, Findings of Fact and Conclusions of Law; Order, 44 ("evidence at trial established that the Huelga bird is used by the United Farm Workers as their union symbol, and that it has become a symbol of Hispanic American culture"; and 49 ("expungement of plaintiff's gang validation records is an appropriate remedy").

Discontent at Pelican Bay expressed itself in a major lawsuit decided in 1995,[5] the upshot of which was that mentally ill prisoners should not be subjected to supermax confinement.

Beginning in 2011 a broad coalition of prisoners organized an enormously successful series of hunger strikes to draw attention to the human rights abuses endemic to the California solitary system. A class action lawsuit was also filed, and in 2015 the named plaintiffs agreed to a comprehensive settlement that fundamentally altered many aspects of the cruel and unconstitutional solitary confinement regime. One year after the settlement, Pelican Bay's long-term (more than ten years) solitary population had dropped 99 percent from 513 to 5. Between December 2012 and August 2016, California's entire solitary confinement population had fallen by 65 percent from 9,870 to 3,471.[6]

Todd Ashker

Todd Ashker was a leader of the three massive hunger strikes in California supermax prisons in 2011 and 2013. The authors' correspondence with Todd reveals that, up against the largest and one of the most oppressive prison systems in the United States, prisoners in California did find a comprehensive and successful "other way."

Todd Ashker was placed in solitary confinement on August 20, 1986. He was transferred to the SHU (Security Housing Unit) at Pelican Bay in May 1990. As a result of the three hunger strikes and a class action lawsuit he was finally moved to general population at another prison early in 2016. He had been in indefinite solitary confinement for over a quarter of a century.

The defining characteristics of what high security prisoners in California undertook is suggested by two things: first, the very large numbers of prisoners involved; second, the completely nonviolent character of their effort.

The Short Corridor Collective Representatives estimated the number of men who took part in the hunger strikes as 6,500 (hunger strike beginning in July 2011), 12,000 (hunger strike beginning in September 2011), and 30,000 (hunger strike beginning in July 2013).[7] The first two hunger strikes each lasted about three weeks and were suspended when there seemed some promise of successful negotiation with the authorities. The third hunger strike lasted approximately sixty days and ended because the more than forty men who had taken only liquids for the entire period

---

5   *Madrid v. Gomez*, 889 F.Supp. 1146 (N.D. Cal. 1995).

6   Center for Constitutional Rights, "California solitary confinement statistics: Year One after landmark settlement," [October 2016], <https://ccrjustice.org/sites/default/files/attach/2016/10/resource-PB-monitoring-stats.pdf>, accessed October 29, 2016.

7   Short Corridor Collective Representatives, "Statement Suspending the Third Hunger Strike," posted September 5, 2013, <https://prisonerhungerstrikesolidarity.wordpress.com/2013/09/05/statement-suspending-the-third-hunger-strike/>, accessed May 31, 2016.

were at the end of their physical endurance. By then, however, the class action lawsuit that would be successfully settled in 2015 was well underway.[8]

To say that a man "took part" of course does not mean that he went without food for the entire length of a particular hunger strike. This was especially so because most of the men in the Pelican Bay "Short Corridor" where the leaders of the strikes were housed were "in their 50s and 60s—a few are in [their] 70s."[9]

The Ideology of the Hunger Fasts

Ashker's letters to the Lynds offer a window into the thinking behind these historic actions.

In February 2010 Todd wrote that he had put "several of our friends" on notice of Denis O'Hearn's book on Irish hunger striker Bobby Sands,[10] adding: "I recently finished Thomas Paine's *Common Sense* and *Rights of Man*, and it was as if he was discussing events today!!! I took 4 pages of notes, as reminders & motivation!!!"[11] In a May letter, Todd reported that he had recently been reading a book of various writings by Howard Zinn entitled *The Zinn Reader: Writings on Civil Disobedience and Democracy* and commented, "Mr. Zinn was real sharp, and I took notes."[12]

Possibly influenced by Hispanic prisoners who made up the majority of inmates on the Short Corridor, Ashker was also reading about traditional Central American religion. In a December 2010 letter to the Lynds he reported: "Read some great books re Mayan cosmology and cosmic universe—which we're all linked to at the cellular level and due for a big advance in our evolution at a spiritual, higher consciousness level!"[13] Three weeks later he explained more fully:

> As I mentioned in my last note, I've been reading several books re Mayan history and their calendars/prophecies, as well as other books (e.g., "The Earth Chronicles by Z. Sitchin), and am certain we're in the midst of monumental events.
>
> One book I read a few months ago was *The Purposeful Universe: How Quantum Theory and Mayan Cosmology Explain the Origin and Evolution of*

---

8   The *Ashker v. Brown* Settlement Agreement, signed by attorneys for the parties on August 31, 2015, was approved by Judge Wilken on January 26, 2016. *See*, <https://prisonerhungerstrikesolidarity.wordpress.com/2016/01/27/historic-settlement-to-end-ca-indefinite-solitary-confinement-finalized-in-court/#more-8326>, accessed May 31, 2016.

9   Todd Ashker to Alice Lynd, March 6, 2011.

10   *See*, Grubačić and O'Hearn, *Living at the Edges*, 213, 215–16, 219, 226, regarding the impact of Bobby Sands on Todd Ashker and other prisoners on the Short Corridor at Pelican Bay.

11   Todd Ashker to Alice Lynd, February 18, 2010.

12   Ashker to Alice Lynd, May 16, 2010.

13   Ashker to Alice Lynd, December 5, 2010. *See also*, Grubačić and O'Hearn, *Living at the Edges*, 215–16, regarding the discussion that emerged from the study of Mayan cosmology by prisoners on the Short Corridor at Pelican Bay.

Life by Carl Johan Calleman, Ph.D. <www.bearandcompanybooks.com>. It's one of the best books I've ever read!!![14]

In previous prison uprisings in the United States, the intention of those involved may have been nonviolent but the rebellion quickly escaped the control of its supposed leaders. The three massive hunger strikes in California were intended to be, and remained, completely nonviolent. Four months before the first hunger strike Todd wrote, "We're all very serious about this protest and plan to keep it peaceful!"[15] Afterward, referring to the California Department of Corrections and Rehabilitation (CDCR), he exulted:

> The 2011 peaceful protest activity really shook CDCR up! Which is great and helped us gain their attention and some respect!! Obviously, prior to these actions they'd lost all respect for us, propagandizing [us as the] worst of the worst, gang problem catalysts for the whole state, etc., etc., while treating us like scum, dogging us out in various ways, every day![16]

In July 2012, halfway between the first and third hunger strikes, Todd reiterated: "Our cause is based on strictly *peaceful activity*!!"[17] In a reflective letter to the authors in November 2012, he explained his rejection of violence at greater length:

> I've been re-reading parts of a book I finished a few months ago called *Human Race Get Off Your Knees: The Lion Sleeps No More* by David Icke. It's got a chapter near the end which contains a good summary re peaceful protest [and] non-cooperation and includes reference to these actions being successful a few years past in Liberia. . . .
>
> I've been taking notes from the book because it is a very moving/motivating story with possible applications of use to our outside supporters!
>
> Icke includes points re violent protest plays right into the trap of the oppressors and quotes Martin Luther King: "The limitation of riots, moral questions aside, is that they cannot win and their participants know it. Hence, rioting is not revolutionary but reactionary because rioting invites defeat. It involves an emotional catharsis, but it must be followed by a sense of futility."
>
> It's certain that a combination of peaceful protest—non-cooperation—inside and outside will be successful in forcing real reform in these prisons!![18]

---

14   Ashker to Alice Lynd, December 26, 2010.
15   Ibid.
16   Todd Ashker to Staughton and Alice Lynd, October 25, 2011.
17   Todd Ashker to Staughton and Alice Lynd, July 22, 2012 (emphasis in original).
18   Todd Ashker to Staughton and Alice Lynd, November 18, 2012.

A final aspect of Todd Ashker's thinking about what he and his colleagues accomplished has to do with the proper place of prison protest within the wider context of changing the whole society. Spokespersons for prisoners in California held in indefinite solitary confinement declared, in suspending their longest hunger strike in September 2013, that they were members of "the working class poor warehoused in prisons."[19] Later that month Todd wrote to us:

> I've been having some dialogue with various men up here re need to shift our mentality from a focus on race—because such is a form of divisiveness— and we are all similarly situated, subject to very hard times, poor prospects, etc., etc., irregardless of race!
>
> It's a class war people can no longer ignore: the elitists, which I believe is a fascist group with a global police state agenda vs. the working class poor, which includes a majority of prisoners. It is the "prisoner class." And until people come together, across racial lines, collectively, for the benefit of all similarly situated people, we will not be effective!!
>
> We need to have awareness of, and respect for, the differences of the races, historically, culturally, and presently. People of color have been and are still subject to racist policies and practices.
>
> It's also true that poor whites are getting more of the short end each day. The line between the two is blurring!!
>
> The powers that be need the two to remain at odds, divided, distrustful and warring with each other. They manipulate continued conflict the same way they do in these prisons!!
>
> I've been including working class poor/prisoner class references in my statements.
>
> I've always associated myself with the working class poor. I grew up in poor neighborhoods. We had the bare necessities, and so I began stealing at age six.[20]

Our goal, Todd wrote in December 2013, is to see our movement expand "beyond these prison walls, and help to unify the working class poor and people of conscience under the common cause of human rights."[21]

In characterizing the victory over indefinite solitary confinement in California as a victory for "human rights," Todd Ashker was in step with international bodies charged with defining the rights of prisoners. In February 2014, Amnesty International submitted to a committee of the United States Senate the recommendation that "solitary or

---

19   "Statement Suspending the Third Hunger Strike," posted on September 5, 2013.

20   Todd Ashker to Staughton and Alice Lynd, September 29, 2013.

21   Statement sent to Alice Lynd, January 22, 2014, by Carole Travis on behalf of Todd Ashker.

isolated confinement, whether for disciplinary or administrative purposes, is imposed only as a last resort and for the minimum period possible," and the recommendation that "No prisoner should be held in prolonged or indefinite isolation."[22] The latest revision of the "Standard Minimum Rules for the Treatment of Prisoners" (now known as the "Mandela Rules" in honor of the former South African political prisoner and later president, Nelson Mandela) was adopted by the United Nations General Assembly in December 2015. Rule 43 prohibits *indefinite* solitary confinement, *prolonged* solitary confinement, and collective punishment. Rule 44, particularly applicable to solitary confinement in supermaximum security prisons in the United States, specifies:

> For the purpose of these rules, solitary confinement shall refer to the confinement of prisoners for 22 hours or more a day without meaningful human contact. Prolonged solitary confinement shall refer to solitary confinement for a time period in excess of 15 consecutive days.[23]

The Agreement to End Hostilities

The nonviolent character of the California hunger strikes was the more remarkable because violence between ethnic groups and gangs, sometimes encouraged by correctional officers, had been characteristic of California prison life. Ashker estimated that there were about 210 prisoners in the Short Corridor: 35 white, about 20 black, the rest [155] Mexican.[24] Appropriately the "main representatives" of the protest activity included one white man, one black man, and two Hispanic men. Hence also the importance of the "Agreement to End Hostilities" issued by the Pelican Bay State Prison Security Housing Unit (PBSP-SHU) Short Corridor Hunger Strike Representatives in August 2012. The text of the Agreement read as follows:

AGREEMENT TO END HOSTILITIES

Aug. 12, 2012

To Whom it may concern and all California Prisoners:

---

22 Amnesty International, "Submission on 'Reassessing Solitary Confinement—The Human Rights, Fiscal and Public Safety Consequences," Hearing before the Senate Judiciary Subcommittee on the Constitution, Civil Rights and Human Rights, February 25, 2014.

23 Resolution adopted by the General Assembly on 17 December 2015, 70/175, *United Nations Standard Minimum Rules for the Treatment of Prisoners (the Nelson Mandela Rules)*, <http://www.un.org/en/ga/search/view_doc.asp?symbol=A/RES/70/175>, accessed June 3, 2016. The United States has gone partway along this same path but stopped short of absolute prohibition. *See*, Department of Justice, "Report and Recommendations Concerning the Use of Restrictive Housing," Executive Summary (updated March 30, 2016), <https://www.justice.gov/restrictivehousing>, accessed June 3, 2016.

24 Todd Ashker to Alice Lynd, April 24, 2011.

Greetings from the entire PBSP-SHU Short Corridor Hunger Strike Representatives. We are hereby presenting this mutual agreement on behalf of all racial groups here in the PBSP-SHU Corridor. Wherein, we have arrived at a mutual agreement concerning the following points:

1. If we really want to bring about substantive meaningful changes to the CDCR system in a manner beneficial to all solid individuals, who have never been broken by CDCR's torture tactics intended to coerce one to become a state informant via debriefing, . . . now is the time for us to collectively seize this moment in time, and put an end to more than 20–30 years of hostilities between our racial groups.

2. Therefore, beginning on October 10, 2012, all hostilities between our racial groups . . . in SHU, Ad-Seg, General Population, and County Jails, will officially cease. This means that from this date on, all racial group hostilities need to be at an end . . . and if personal issues arise between individuals, people need to do all they can to exhaust all diplomatic means to settle such disputes; do not allow personal, individual issues to escalate into racial group issues!!

3. We also want to warn those in the General Population that IGI will continue to plant undercover Sensitive Needs Yard (SNY) debriefer "inmates" amongst the solid GP prisoners with orders from IGI to be informers, snitches, rats, and obstructionists, in order to attempt to disrupt and undermine our collective groups' mutual understanding on issues intended for our mutual causes (i.e., forcing CDCR to open up all GP main lines, and return to a rehabilitative-type system of meaningful programs/privileges, including lifer conjugal visits, etc. via peaceful protest activity/noncooperation e.g., hunger strike, no labor, etc. etc.). People need to be aware and vigilant to such tactics, and refuse to allow such IGI inmate snitches to create chaos and reignite hostilities amongst our racial groups. We can no longer play into IGI, ISU, OCS, and SSU's old manipulative divide and conquer tactics!!!

In conclusion, we must all hold strong to our mutual agreement from this point on and focus our time, attention, and energy on mutual causes beneficial to all of us (i.e., prisoners), and our best interests. We can no longer allow CDCR to use us against each other for their benefit!! Because the reality is that collectively, we are an empowered, mighty force, that can positively change this entire corrupt system into a system that actually benefits prisoners, and thereby, the public as a whole . . . and we simply cannot allow CDCR/CCPOA—Prison Guard's Union, IGI, ISU, OCS, and SSU, to continue to get away with their constant form of progressive oppression and warehousing of tens of thousands of prisoners, including the 14,000 (+)

plus prisoners held in solitary confinement torture chambers [i.e. SHU/ Ad-Seg Units], for decades!!!

We send our love and respects to all those of like mind and heart . . . onward in struggle and solidarity . . .

Presented by the PBSP-SHU Short Corridor Collective:
Todd Ashker, C58191, D4-121
Arturo Castellanos, C17275, D1-121
Sitawa Nantambu Jamaa (Dewberry), C35671, D1-117
Antonio Guillen, P81948, D2-106

And the Representatives Body:
Danny Troxell, B76578, D1-120
George Franco, D46556, D4-217
Ronnie Yandell, V27927, D4-215
Paul Redd, B72683, D2-117
James Baridi Williamson, D-34288, D4-107
Alfred Sandoval, D61000, D4-214
Louis Powell, B59864, D1-117
Alex Yrigollen, H32421, D2-204
Gabriel Huerta, C80766, D3-222
Frank Clement, D07919, D3-116
Raymond Chavo Perez, K12922, D1-219
James Mario Perez, B48186, D3-124[25]

There can be little doubt that the Short Corridor prisoners, and the thousands of other California prisoners who acted with them, considered the Agreement an achievement almost on a par with the abandonment of indefinite solitary confinement. On August 21, 2015, nine Pelican Bay prisoners, five of whom were also signers of the Agreement, issued a statement. They began by characterizing the settlement of the lawsuit as "a monumental victory." Our movement, they continued, "rests on a foundation of unity: our Agreement to End Hostilities." They went on to say that they hoped the Agreement would "inspire not only state prisoners, but also jail detainees, county prisoners and our communities on the street, to oppose ethnic and racial violence." The "prisoners' human rights movement," the signers asserted, "is awakening the conscience of the nation to recognize that we are fellow human beings." And so, as they celebrated, these spokespersons also recognized "that achieving our goal of fundamentally transforming the criminal justice system and stopping

---

25   Agreement to End Hostilities, August 12, 2012, <https://prisonerhungerstrikesolidarity. files.wordpress.com/2015/03/agreement-statement-to-youth.pdf>, accessed May 31, 2016.

the practice of warehousing people in prison will be a protracted effort. We are fully committed to that effort, and invite you to join us."[26]

There is some evidence that young people outside the bars are listening. "The following youth (so far)" issued a statement two months after promulgation of the Agreement to End Hostilities. During the 2011 hunger strikes, they said, "People from all 'sides'—blacks, whites, Asians, Sureños and Norteños—put all politics behind and came together to demand their human rights." The men of Pelican Bay, they said, "After doing so much time . . . have realized that they are being recycled over and over through the same dead-end system."

Accordingly the three signers challenged "the youth in the streets, schools and lock-ups throughout California to do the following." Their manifesto included these demands:

1. End all the killing and drama between hoods, crews, and races. Declare a temporary cease fire and work toward building lasting truces.
2. Take the same mentality and skills we have used to hustle drugs, bang our hoods and promote our crews to unite in a powerful movement to demand dignity, respect and equality for all our people. . . .
4. Demand an end to the War on Gangs—including the CalGang Database that labels people (as young as ten) as gang members without their knowledge or right to appeal. . . .

And they ended: "Spread the word to unite all hoods, all barrios, all crew and all cliques, all cells, all dorms and all units—from the Nickerson Gardens to Estrada Courts, from the PJs to the Y.A., from TJ to Pelican Bay, to the Bay Area and back down to Sac Town—let everyone know, as youth of California we are NOT DOWN WITH THE LOCK DOWN!!!"[27]

---

26 "Statement of plaintiffs on settlement of Ashker v. Government of California," August 31, 2015, <https://ccrjustice.org/statement-plaintiffs-settlement-ashker-v-governor-california>, accessed May 31, 2016.

27 "Statement to the Streets and All Youth Lock-Ups," [October 10, 2012], <https://prisonerhungerstrikesolidarity.files.wordpress.com/2015/03/agreement-statement-to-youth.pdf> [second document], accessed May 31, 2016.

Chapter 8.
Nonviolent Direct Action and
Lawyering as Partners

IN THIS CONCLUDING CHAPTER WE WIDEN THE LENS A LITTLE AND TRY TO COMPARE what happened in California with the successes and failures of two other movements for social change in recent times. These are the civil rights movement, culminating in 1965 with the direct action at Selma and the federal voting rights statute, and the efforts of the labor movement to surmount certain serious concessions made at the very inception of the CIO in the late 1930s.

Here our emphasis also shifts from negative to positive. We ask, How can the bitterness of defeat and humiliation be overcome in a manner that is sustained? and how can compassion, comradeship and hope be protected and nurtured?

The example provided by recent events in the California prison system is based on the conception that in a lawsuit, lawyer and client should be equal partners who accompany one another, each contributing a particular kind of expertise. It is also an example of important social change achieved through nonviolence, in contrast to uprisings at Attica, New York in 1971, Santa Fe, New Mexico in 1980, and Lucasville, Ohio in 1993, when a total of eighty-six persons died and negligible change in conditions of confinement appears to have resulted.[1]

We think that a similar strategy or combination of tactics could be utilized in a wide variety of oppressive settings.

The Civil Rights Movement

Direct action, even when nonviolent, and lawyering by established institutions dedicated to social change, are often regarded as mutually exclusive. Organizations like the National Association for the Advancement of Colored People (NAACP) and AFL-CIO trade unions have discouraged direct action initiated from below as an unpredictable and destabilizing force. Thus the NAACP persistently counseled African Americans not to resort to controversial direct action like the Montgomery, Alabama bus boycott, which it regarded as a "wildcat movement," to quote the suggestive description by historian Taylor Branch.[2]

Successful campaigns in the civil rights movement required both nonviolent direct action and litigation. The mistaken assumption that nonviolent direct action

---

1   *See,* Thompson, *Blood in the Water,* 567: "Forty years after the uprising of 1971, conditions at Attica were worse than they had ever been."

2   Taylor Branch, *Parting the Waters: America in the King Years 1954–63* (New York: Simon and Schuster, 1988), 144.

and litigation are opposing, mutually exclusive methods of struggle has caused this critical lesson of history to be forgotten.

Montgomery

Consider the successful campaign to integrate bus service in Montgomery, Alabama. Nonviolent direct action and the courts were entwined from the very beginning in Montgomery.

On Thursday, December 1, 1955, Rosa Parks was arrested for refusing to move to the back of a bus. That night, Professor Ann Robinson met with colleagues at Alabama State College. They drafted a letter calling on African Americans "to stay off the buses on Monday," the day Mrs. Parks would appear in court.[3]

On Monday, December 5, there were next to no African American bus riders, but five hundred persons jammed into the courthouse to make sure that Mrs. Parks was released after posting bond. In his sermon that first evening of the campaign to the crowd at and outside the Dexter Avenue Baptist Church, a young preacher, Dr. Martin Luther King Jr. said: "Standing beside love is always justice. Not only are we using the tools of persuasion—but we've got to use the tools of coercion." More than six years later, Dr. King repeated this idea in a speech in Atlanta. Marchers and boycotters, he said, "should not minimize work through the courts. But . . . legislation and court orders can only declare rights. They can never thoroughly deliver them. Only when the people themselves begin to act are rights on paper given life blood."[4]

In the end the Montgomery movement forged a synthesis. Without abandoning the boycott, it decided to file suit in federal court, and won.

Resort to the courts was not dictated by biology, as in a hunger strike. The breakdown of negotiations with the white community and the strain of providing an estimated twenty thousand rides a day had the same effect. Before the Montgomery boycott the longest bus boycott in the Deep South had been in Baton Rouge, where it lasted two weeks. Five weeks into their similar action, leaders of the Montgomery movement reached for what Dr. King had called a second set of "tools."

The moment that nonviolent direct action and litigation converged in Montgomery was dramatic. City officials had asked a state court to enjoin the Montgomery Improvement Association car pool as an unlicensed municipal transportation system. Any attempt to continue the boycott while the action was pending in court ran the danger of triggering contempt convictions and imprisonment for the movement leaders.

---

3   Here and throughout this account of the Montgomery bus boycott we have followed Taylor Branch, *Parting the Waters*, chapter five. At the time, we were living in an intentional community in the hills of northeast Georgia. Another member of the community visited Montgomery and asked if there was something the Macedonia Cooperative Community could do to help. "Rest and Recreation" for a few of the weary walkers was the answer. After Ms. Aurelia Browder and her daughter spent two weeks in the mountains with ourselves and our colleagues, Staughton drove Mrs. Browder back to Montgomery.

4   Branch, *Parting the Waters*, 141, 598.

On November 13, 1956, a hearing on the city's motion was held in state court. During a recess, an AP reporter handed Dr. King a note. The United States Supreme Court had affirmed the judgment of a lower federal court in the lawsuit filed by the bus boycotters holding bus segregation in Alabama to be unconstitutional. The boycott had been successful. As Branch says, "it was over."

Throughout the Montgomery campaign and afterwards, Dr. King, on behalf of the Montgomery Improvement Association, maintained an uneasy relationship with Roy Wilkins of the NAACP. Dr. King "publicly criticized the NAACP for scorning the boycott." Not long after, however, he wrote to Wilkins thanking the older man for the NAACP's "fine contribution" to the Montgomery effort. King was invited to address the 1956 convention of the NAACP but Wilkins and Thurgood Marshall opposed numerous resolutions that favored the nonviolent methods of the bus boycott. According to Branch, when King, cornered by reporters, was asked "whether he thought nonviolent methods might help desegregate the schools," he replied that "he had not thought about it much but that they probably could do so." Annoyed, Marshall declared that "school desegregation was men's work and should not be entrusted to children." Wilkins and Marshall finally engineered passage by the convention of a resolution calling merely for the executive board to give "careful consideration" to the use of the Montgomery model.[5]

What made the difference between this all-too-familiar jostling for influence between organizations and what happened in Montgomery was that the rank and file of the Montgomery movement never gave up direct action. They never stopped walking to work (or traveling by means of an improvised transportation system) instead of taking a bus.

The Student Nonviolent Coordinating Committee

The Student Nonviolent Coordinating Committee (SNCC) recruited a full-time staff from young men and women many of whom had been bloodied and imprisoned in two previous campaigns: sit-ins in facilities serving the public that began in Greensboro, North Carolina, and Nashville, Tennessee, in 1960, and the 1961 Freedom Rides on behalf of non-segregated seating in interstate bus travel.

These campaigns sought to enforce a victory that was declared a constitutional right in the course of prolonged direct action (the right to be served by a facility ostensibly open to the public) or had apparently been won on paper but required direct action before it could be enforced in the Deep South (the Freedom Rides).

Prompted by local NAACP leaders in Mississippi and by the Kennedy Administration, beginning in 1961 SNCC focused its efforts on voter registration.

---

5   For the NAACP and the Montgomery boycott, see Branch, *Parting the Waters*, 163 (scorning the boycott and fine contribution); 176 (offering major NAACP support after the Kings' house was bombed); 186 (NAACP invites King to address its convention after the Dexter Avenue church purchased a $1,000 life membership in the NAACP); 189–90 (NAACP convention and Marshall comment).

This led to the disillusionment experienced by delegates of the Mississippi Freedom Democratic Party (MFDP) at the national Democratic Party convention in Atlantic City in August 1964, when the convention refused to seat the MFDP delegates.

One way to characterize that disillusionment, and the disintegration of SNCC that followed, is to view the MFDP strategy as one-sidedly dependent on the equivalent of legal action in court, namely, the willingness of the national Democratic Party to seat black as well as white delegates from Mississippi. There was no course of direct action held in reserve to respond to President Lyndon Johnson and President Walter Reuther of the United Automobile Workers when these two conspired to deny members of the MFDP seats as delegates. Stalwart MFDP delegates like Fannie Lou Hamer might enthrall the convention Credentials Committee with stories of their persecution back home. But many of these delegates had left Mississippi for the first time in their lives to attend the convention and were unfamiliar with the parliamentary rigmarole of such bodies. They were poorly positioned to improvise an effective rejoinder to Roy Wilkins, Bayard Rustin, their nominal attorney Joseph Rauh, and other political pros who urged them to accept the inadequate "compromise" proposal of President Johnson and his supporters. The so-called compromise provided that two MFDP delegates would be selected by President Johnson and seated at the convention as at-large delegates. The president stipulated that he would not choose as a delegate to be seated "that illiterate woman," Ms. Hamer.

The delegates and their SNCC supporters said No, and rode the buses back to Mississippi with no clear idea of what to do next.

The task of achieving the vote thus fell back into the hands of Dr. King and the Southern Christian Leadership Conference (SCLC).

Selma

The great civil rights confrontations did not always begin as in Montgomery with non-violent direct action initiated from below, and the intervention of federal courts was often an obstacle rather than a help. In Albany, Georgia, efforts to build momentum were obstructed by an injunction issued by U.S. District Court Judge J. Robert Elliott, who held that "Negro protest marches denied Albany's *white* people equal protection by draining police manpower and other public resources out of white neighborhoods."[6] In Greenwood, Mississippi, in early 1963, Burke Marshall of the Justice Department knew that any threat of federal court action was "a bluff" because any federal lawsuit would go, at least initially, "before a federal judge in Mississippi whom Marshall already had described to Robert Kennedy as an unscrupulous segregationist."[7] And on the eve of the climactic encounter in Birmingham, Republican Nelson Rockefeller criticized Kennedy for appointing Southern judges "of well-known segregationist views," giving rise to a situation in which the only

---

6   Branch, *Parting the Waters*, 609 (italics in original).
7   Ibid., 721.

hopes of the Department of Justice "for racial justice through the courts" were Eisenhower appointees.[8]

Nonetheless, it remains a fact that the civil rights movement was most successful, not when it operated without federal support as was so often the case with the Student Nonviolent Coordinating Committee, but when local activists and federal lawyering achieved some degree of rapprochement. This is what happened in Selma, Alabama, in 1965, when the Southern civil rights movement required a conjunction of brave and in part tragic direct action from below, and the protective intervention of a federal court.[9]

The story of Jimmie Lee Jackson's murder during a night march near Selma, and of James Bevel's call for a fifty-four mile march from Selma to Montgomery, the state capital, need not be repeated here. For our purposes it is enough to recall the three-act structure of the drama that began on March 7, 1965, with the first attempt to cross the Edmund Pettus Bridge en route to Montgomery.

Participants in that first march had no government support of any kind. Agents of the State of Alabama lined up at the far side of the bridge to prevent their passage, and did so with overwhelming force, showering the unarmed crowd with tear gas, and riding down the marchers on horseback.

Dr. King and his associates called for another attempt to march to Montgomery two days later. But on the morning of March 9 the leaders were informed that federal judge Frank Johnson was signing a court order to prohibit another march until further notice.

Judge Johnson had cast the deciding vote to protect the Montgomery bus boycott in 1956. Should he be defied, the march organizers wondered, or should they somehow postpone the bridge crossing scheduled for that day in hope that he might change his mind? Messengers from the Department of Justice promised support if a confrontation could be delayed.

Apparently unsure of what to choose until the last possible moment for decision, Dr. King told the marchers on the bridge to turn around and return to Brown Chapel, their point of departure. Experienced organizers from SNCC were at first perplexed, then outraged, by what seemed to them an unexplained betrayal.

That evening the Reverend James Reeb was set upon by white vigilantes and mortally wounded. There followed a week of demonstrations in Selma, Montgomery and Washington, DC, framed by worldwide publicity. Congressional leaders urged President Lyndon Johnson to speak to the Congress, and on Monday, March 15 he delivered his famous "We shall overcome" address. Two days later Dr. King was again at a courthouse when an aide pushed through the crowd to whisper to him that Judge Johnson had just ruled that, in King's words, "we have a legal and constitutional right to march from Selma to Montgomery."

---

8   Ibid., 700.
9   Here we have followed Taylor Branch, in his *At Canaan's Edge: America in the King Years, 1965–68* (New York: Simon and Schuster, 2006), chapters 5–9.

The foregoing, desperately summarized, is the story of how the civil rights act of 1964 and the voting rights act of 1965 came into being. Neither one was the product solely of nonviolent direct action, or of federal court litigation alone. Enactment of both laws required a combination of nonviolent action and federal litigation.

The Labor Movement

Between 1932 and 1935, the United States Congress enacted the Norris-LaGuardia Act, the National Industrial Recovery Act, and the National Labor Relations Act (NLRA, or Wagner Act), declaring the organization of trade unions to be a fundamental right and extending the protection of the federal government to concerted activity for mutual aid or protection. Specifically, section 7 of the National Labor Relations Act, enacted in 1935, still provides:

> Employees shall have the right to self-organization, to form, join, or assist labor organizations, to bargain collectively through representatives of their own choosing, and to engage in other concerted activities for the purpose of collective bargaining or other mutual aid or protection.[10]

The Right to Strike

Many books describe the intricate interaction between direct action from below and lawyering from above that prompted and followed enactment of these laws.[11] General strikes in Minneapolis, San Francisco, and Toledo, and a nationwide strike of cotton textile workers, were the most visible evidence of the rank-and-file upsurge before passage of the NLRA. After the Act became law there ensued the occupation of the General Motors complex in Flint, Michigan. Acting through the Committee (later Congress) of Industrial Organizations (CIO), and a variety of improvised local entities, workers in steel, automobile assembly, rubber, meatpacking, electrical equipment, and other areas of the economy made use of the new legal tools to organize trade unions.

At the heart of these activities was the issue of the right to strike. Section 13 of the NLRA as originally enacted provided: "Nothing in this Act shall be construed so as either to interfere with or impede or diminish in any way the right to strike." Years

---

10   Enacted in 1935 as the National Labor Relations Act (NLRA) this statute was amended in 1947 and is now known as the Labor Management Relations Act (LMRA). In 1947, language was added giving employees the right to refrain from the above-described activities. The NLRA is sometimes referred to as the Wagner Act because Senator Wagner of New York was its principal sponsor.

11   See Jeremy Brecher, *Strike!*, revised, expanded, and updated edition (Oakland, CA: PM Press, 2014); *"We Are All Leaders": The Alternative Unionism of the Early 1930s*, ed. Staughton Lynd (Urbana: University of Illinois Press, 1996); *Workers' Struggles, Past and Present: A "Radical America" Reader*, ed. James Green (Philadelphia: Temple University Press, 1983), Part Two.

later Leon Keyserling, principal draftsperson of the NLRA, described the reason for putting this residual guarantee of the right to strike in the Act.

> There was a definite reason. First, because [Senator] Wagner was always strong for the right to strike on the ground that without the right to strike, which was labor's ultimate weapon, they really had no other weapon. That guarantee was a part of his thinking. [And it] was particularly necessary because a lot of people made the argument that because the government was giving labor the right to bargain collectively, that was a substitute for the right to strike. . . .[12]

The preservation and protection of the right to strike intended by the drafters of the Wagner Act did not survive long. Three causes worked to undermine it.

First, the courts were hostile to strikes as a disorderly way for settling conflicts better resolved in the courts or by arbitration. Disregarding the explicit language of Section 13 of the Act, the Supreme Court handed down a decision finding that it was not an unfair labor practice for the employer "to replace the striking employees with others in an effort to carry on the business" and then, when the strike was over, to retain the scabs rather than recall the strikers.[13] Henceforth replacement, which is to say, discharge, of workers who have gone on strike was prohibited only if those denied reemployment were found to have been singled out because of union activity.

A second reason that the right to strike withered under the National Labor Relations Act was World War II. CIO unions that had been recognized by the employer voluntarily gave up the right to strike for the duration of the war, substituting the grievance and arbitration process for walking off the job. The most radical CIO organizers were members of Marxist groups, of which the Communist Party was by far the largest and most influential. The Party strongly supported the no-strike pledge so as not to interfere with wartime production that might help the Soviet Union, then a wartime ally of the United States.

The third reason strikes came to be disfavored had to do with the preferred practices of John L. Lewis, president of the United Mine Workers, which financed and largely dominated the fledgling unions of the CIO. Lewis imposed on the new unions the template of collective bargaining he had established in his own union.

Militant direct action was favored only until the incipient union was recognized by the employer as exclusive bargaining agent for the appropriate workers. Then in almost all the new CIO unions the union agreed to surrender, or "waive," the right to strike for the duration of the collective bargaining agreement. Howard Zinn states:

---

12 Kenneth M. Casebeer, "Holder of the Pen: An Interview with Leon Keyserling on Drafting the Wagner Act," *University of Miami Law Review*, Vol. 42 (November 1987), 353.

13 *National Labor Relations Board v. Mackay Radio & Telegraph Co.*, 304 U.S. 333, 345 (1938), <https://supreme.justia.com/cases/federal/us/304/333/case.html>, accessed June 5, 2016.

In the spring of 1937, a *New York Times* article carried the headline "Unauthorized Sit-Downs Fought by CIO Unions." The story read: "Strict orders have been issued to all organizers and representatives that they will be dismissed if they authorize any stoppages of work without the consent of the international officers. . . ." The *Times* quoted John L. Lewis, dynamic leader of the CIO: "A CIO contract is adequate protection against sit-downs, lie-downs, or any other kind of strike."[14]

At war's end self-help activities from below, small and large, continued to be disfavored. Strikes tended to become ritualistic affairs that occurred only when the no-strike clause expired together with the contract as a whole. An employer under such a contract could predict when a strike, should there be one, would occur, and prepare for it by stockpiling quantities of its products so as to continue to serve customers even if production ceased for a time.

One Issue at a Time

There are new movements in United States trade unionism that hold promise for combining direct action with supporting activity in the law, just as occurred in California supermaximum security prisons.

Instead of seeking a single resolution of issues in a comprehensive collective bargaining contract, the new style of unionism would proceed one issue and one struggle at a time.

This was the situation when the United Electrical Workers was coming into being in the area around Pittsburgh. These factories had entertained a significant presence of the Industrial Workers of the World in the years before and during World War I, and labor relations in the first days of the CIO replicated the preexisting industrial practice. A particular issue would arise on the shop floor, management and union would come to an understanding about it, and a notice to that effect would be posted.[15]

The most dramatic example of this approach known to the authors occurred at Inland Steel in East Chicago, Indiana in 1937–1941. John Sargent, first president of the eighteen-thousand-member local union of the Steel Workers Organizing Committee at Inland, told the story as follows.

[I]n 1937 there was a strike called on Little Steel. . . . We did not win a contract. . . . What we did get was an agreement through the governor's office that the company would recognize the Steelworkers Union and the

14   Howard Zinn, *A People's History of the United States: 1492–Present* (New York: HarperCollins, 1999), 401.

15   Ronald W. Schatz, *The Electrical Workers: A History of Labor at General Electric and Westinghouse, 1923–60* (Urbana: University of Illinois Press, 1983), 73.

company union and any other organization that wanted to represent the people in the steel industry. . . . [W]e had no contract with the company. But the enthusiasm of the people who were working in the mills made this settlement of the strike into a victory of great proportions.

Without a contract, without any agreement with the company, without any regulations concerning hours of work, conditions of work, or wages, a tremendous surge took place. . . . The union organizers were essentially workers in the mill who were so disgusted with their conditions and so ready for a change that they took the union into their own hands.

. . . Without a contract we secured for ourselves agreements on working conditions and wages that we do not have today, and that were better by far than what we do have today in the mill. For example as a result of the enthusiasm of the people you had a series of strikes, wildcats, shut-downs, slow-downs, anything working people could think of to secure for them-selves what they decided they had to have. If their wages were low there was no contract to prohibit them from striking, and they struck for better wages. If their conditions were bad, if they didn't like what was going on, if they were being abused, the people in the mills themselves—without a contract or any agreement with the company involved—would shut down a department or even a group of departments to secure for themselves the things they found necessary.[16]

Concerted activity for mutual aid or protection can take place even in the ab-sence of a union. For example, piecemeal, single issues can be won by workers through administrative agencies.

Alice once interviewed two workers in a non-union shop who were endangered by deafening noise, such that they could not hear when it was necessary to com-municate. She wrote down what they told her on a complaint form, they took the complaint form back to their shop, about forty workers signed it, and they sent it in to the Occupational Safety and Health Administration (OSHA). OSHA inspectors came, found hearing loss among the workers, and ordered the company to enclose the compressor with soundproofing. After that, "You could hear a pin drop!"

In another instance, an order to the employer from the National Labor Relations Board, provided language that was later incorporated into a collective bargaining agreement.

In yet another shop where the workers were exposed to toxic chemicals without protection, Alice drafted a National Institute for Occupational Safety and Health

16 *Rank and File: Personal Histories by Working-Class Organizers*, ed. Alice and Staughton Lynd, updated edition (Chicago: Haymarket Books, 2011) 107–8. See also the account of Nick Migas, grievance man for the open hearth during the period described by Sargent, 165–75.

(NIOSH) complaint. Not realizing that NIOSH would respond that they could not be bothered with a complaint involving only about seventy-five workers, the employer immediately put hoods over the vats, and gave the workers protective clothing. The chairman of the union's safety committee said they won what he had been trying to get for twenty-five years!

$15 an Hour

A second significant new movement, for a minimum wage of $15 an hour, synthesizes elements that showcase the benefits of direct action and lawyering in combination. For the time being, major established unions like the Service Employees International Union (SEIU) have set aside the objective of "representing" a given group of workers by becoming their exclusive bargaining representative as a matter of law.

Instead, these big unions have poured money derived from the dues of other, better-paid union members into facilitating effective action for particular immediate objectives by the most vulnerable and poorly paid workers in the United States economy. Among the protagonists who have stepped forward are Starbucks baristas, home health aides, restaurant waitresses, hotel workers, and Walmart warehouse employees.

These service workers are more often Latin American, African American, or Asian, and more often women, than the generality of employees. They have seized on new organizing opportunities that sponsorship by an established union makes possible: attending national conferences of other workers like themselves so as to select common organizing targets, designating particular "days of action" such as the Friday after Thanksgiving, coordinating with community groups to seek higher minimum wage ordinances, and the like.

All this activity is exploratory and fragile. The SEIU, for example, may very well at some point seek to envelop the new labor activists within the deadening bureaucratic framework of conventional unionism.

But there are enormous potential positives. These workers offer services to consumers who can readily boycott a particular provider. Often they are recent immigrants from Latin America who bring with them the residue of ancient communal traditions. They may reside in the same neighborhoods as persons who speak the same language and share a similar cultural background, so that their solidarity has the three-dimensional aspect also experienced by seamen and miners who are together twenty-four hours a day. In the country from which they came to the United States, belonging to a union may have required a more dangerous and demanding choice than doing so in the United States. It is these poorly paid men and women, whose English may be imperfect and who perforce must often live in the shadows, who represent the hope of the labor movement in the United States.

In all the workers' struggles sketched above, the functional equivalent of court injunctions protective of civil rights is Section 7 of the NLRA. It is the worker's First Amendment. Strikes and related activities such as picketing, leafleting, and the wearing of insignia such as union buttons, when appropriately respectful of restrictions as to time, place, and manner, may be viewed as nonviolent expressions of the fundamental rights to speech and assembly.

A difficulty arises for the attorney or union representative when it is feared that direct action by the workers may frighten a judge, arbitrator, or NLRB administrator into siding with the employer. Staughton twice became aware of planned occupations of steel company administrative buildings before they occurred. In one instance, not yet having filed a lawsuit, he spoke from the escalator connecting the first two floors of the national U.S. Steel headquarters in Pittsburgh, reporting to the crowd on planned legal actions. In a second instance, the lawsuit having been filed but the parties not yet having met the judge, he carefully stayed outside the occupied company headquarters. In retrospect, it was probably unnecessary for him to have done so and he thereby forfeited the opportunity to join those inside the building in making tactical decisions.

A court may find a rank-and-file worker or a prisoner to be a more reliable witness than a company supervisor or prison administrator. At a hearing in the Ohio prisoners' class action, a deputy warden testified that it was possible to schedule time outdoors for every prisoner. Lawyers for the prisoners then called as a witness a prisoner who explained, in effect, yeah, it's March and they haven't shoveled the snow all winter and all we have to wear on our feet is thin canvas shower shoes! The judge wrote in his opinion: the prison's "dubious snow-shoveling and lackluster provision of warm garments for the winter months cut in favor of the Plaintiffs."[17]

It must always be remembered: Direct actions planned and carried out by those immediately affected may annoy a senior officer (as in war), a prison administrator (as in prison hunger strikes), or a judge, arbitrator, or NLRB decision-maker (as in civil rights and labor struggles). However, action from below may send a message as to how much those about to lose their livelihoods, or those imprisoned alone for many years, or those directed once again to engage in a military maneuver they know to be potentially lethal, really care; and how much they may be prepared nonviolently to do in order to make their point.

Accompanying
One final point: In order for nonviolent direct action and lawyering to work together in the strategy described in this chapter, they can only do so if they treat each other as equals, like two hands.

From the lawyer's standpoint, he or she cannot defer to whatever the client may propose. The rules of practice require an attorney to be satisfied in his or her own mind that any tactical move suggested by the client has a basis in fact and law. If it does not, the planned maneuver is "frivolous" and in an extreme case the lawyer can be barred from practicing if he or she pursues what the client wants.

---

17   *Austin v. Wilkinson*, Case No. 4:01-CV-071 (N.D. Ohio), Order (July 28, 2005, Doc. 580).

A subtle variation of this dilemma may arise if the lawyer says to the client words to the effect. "If we do X as you wish, the other side will very likely respond with Y, and then where will we be?" We have known a client at this point in the dialogue with his lawyer to become angry, maintaining: "It is your job to represent *me,* I don't care what the other side thinks!" Hopefully, over time as with this client of ours, it will come to be recognized that it is a part of the lawyer's responsibility to anticipate the tactical responses of the opposing party.

The flip side, the sunshine beyond these storm clouds, comes with mutual recognition that the nonviolent protagonist and his or her legal representative *each bring expertise to the table.* In order for there to be two mutually reinforcing "hands," there must be mutual recognition that client and attorney each offers a different kind of knowledge and experience to the task of resolving the problems at issue.

The closest we can come to describing the special joy that can result when this melding of lives takes place, is to go back to a scene previously described. Lawyers and clients in the OSP class action needed to meet together, as one group, to decide whether or not to settle the case. The warden made available a single "pod" or living area with two tiers of eight cells each. The named plaintiffs in the class action, one to a cell, sat before the open slots through which food is handed in so as to be able to vote, which they did by thrusting a forearm through the slot.

Pros and cons were discussed and it was time to decide. One man said, "This proposal would benefit me personally, but it won't solve the problem." A federal judge was leaning on us hard to say Yes to the State's inadequate proposal. The risk, of course, was that if we said No we might end up with nothing. In the end it was the clients' decision. All those opposed to the State's offer were asked to so indicate. More than a dozen hairy arms immediately appeared through the food slots. All our clients had rejected the authorities' proposal.

For the sake of completeness we asked if there was anyone who wished to vote Yes. One of the arms re-appeared. The man who voted both ways was essential to our case. At a different Ohio prison he had been standing in the chow line when another prisoner hit him, from behind, with a heavy industrial spatula. The victim of this blow was sent to the hospital and then he—not the man who hit him—was transferred to the supermax! It was a dramatic instance of the arbitrary way these decisions were being made.

In his best Quaker manner, Staughton asked the man who voted both ways if he realized that he had voted both Yes and No. Then, from an upper tier, came a solitary voice: "Maybe that's what happens when you get hit on the head with a spatula!"

The whole pod collapsed in laughter.

We were a community again. We told the judge No, and he ruled in our favor.

Conclusion

As we prepared the manuscript of this book for the publisher, we wrote to several of the "ordinary" people who are extensively quoted, seeking permission to use what had been originally intended as private correspondence. In doing so we summarized the content of the book as follows:

> People may experience moral injury after they did, or saw, or failed to prevent something that deeply offends their sense of right and wrong. They may not know what it is that makes them feel that way, but the sense of mankind as to what is and is not morally permissible has been expressed in international law and other declarations of fundamental human rights. Rather than rioting, prisoners are now using hunger strikes as a way of insisting on their right to be treated humanely.

Let that stand as a summary of the argument in the previous eight chapters.

The reader may still be puzzled by our insistence that something negative—the infliction of an injury—should be understood as also immensely positive. What is positive is that human nature is not infinitely malleable; that there is a line distinguishing impermissible from permissible conduct that even many volunteers for the military are not prepared to cross; that even so-called "hardened" criminals may draw back from inflicting violence on especially vulnerable persons, such as wounded hostages or children. This latent empathy in some soldiers and prisoners holds out hope that it may be discovered in most. We cannot give up on the possibility of change.

In this Conclusion we offer further inferences from the evidence that the reader may wish to consider.

Both Victims and Executioners

Years ago the French-Algerian writer Albert Camus projected the modest goal that people on the Left should strive to be neither victims nor executioners. What we see as we draw close to the actual experience of soldiers and prisoners is that many have been *both* victims of arbitrary administrators *and* perpetrators of violence. Dr. Shay's clients told him story after story in which common soldiers squeezed the trigger but the order to do so, or the commands that placed them in a situation where they perceived no other alternative, came from higher military authority.

This is not a minor problem affecting only a few persons. Dr. Shay, writing in a book published in 1994, said: "more than twenty years after their military service" about "three-quarters of a million heavy combat veterans from Vietnam are still alive . . . of whom a quarter million are still suffering" from the persistence of severe traumatic experiences.[1]

It is essential to acknowledge that what distresses the one in three who suffer in this way is not merely that superior officers took advantage of their dependent status. It is more complicated than that. These veterans feel that, yes, they were mistreated by higher-ups in the chain of command, *but also that, as a result, they committed acts for which they are now deeply regretful and ashamed, and for which they seek forgiveness.*

Thus it is an oversimplification to suggest that one set of people (officers in the military, and prison administrators and guards) are the only guilty parties and that another group (enlisted men and prisoners) are altogether innocent. The evidence obliges us to concede that in these episodes of "people's history," the people—such as the veterans who have come to Dr. Shay for help—may also have blood on their hands.

This analysis applies to prisoners as well as veterans. Some prisoners are completely innocent, just as some of the soldiers now suffering from moral injury never killed anyone. But many, perhaps most, of the prisoners who are confined at high levels of security and now lead hunger strikes and draft declarations to end hostility between gangs, somewhere along the line engaged in serious violence themselves.

Dr. Shay's analogy to Greek classics rings true. As in the theater of ancient Athens, in approaching the suffering of those damaged by an unjustified war or by an unfair criminal justice system, we come into the presence of tragedy. Modern warfare requires of the infantryman the gift of his or her life, if not in the form of death in combat then in the form of personal disintegration when the warrior comes home. The penal systems of the United States every year release men and women from whom—whether they are exonerated or have done their time—they have taken away life in a different way. This is tragedy!

Moral injury, if not overcome, can lead to an individual giving up, turning to drugs and alcohol or suicide. But moral injury can also demand that one turn one's life around. It offers hope by way of resistance to the use of violence that offends a sense of decency.

Individuals and Collective Action

The initiatives by ordinary people described in these pages share the obvious fact that they were very often solitary actions: of individual soldiers determined to stop killing, or of individual prisoners who managed to hold on to the idea that "thoughts are free" during decades of solitary confinement.[2] The message taught by their actions is that

---

1   Shay, *Achilles in Vietnam*, xix–xx.
2   Imprisoned German workers in the mid-19th century created the song "Die Gedanken Sind Frei" (Thoughts Are Free). In English translation the first and last verses go:

even among those society has invited to do its fighting for it, or judged deserving of punishment and neglect, there is an inner ethical core that these persons seek to protect and express. They impact the world not so much by organizing others, but by their example.

There is a cluster of experiences associated with moral injury that are beyond doubt the experiences of individuals. "Conscience" is indisputably something possessed and exercised by individuals. Equally individualistic is a certain kind of shame, as when a person inwardly suffers over something done or thought that no one else knows about. A sense of shame can remind the individual of the self that person wishes to be.

Accordingly, we do not see history as made only by groups of discontented persons. We believe that history from the bottom up needs to find space for individuals like those who take center stage in this book.

Remember Dave Dillard, the man who brought together surviving members of the company in which he served in Vietnam? First, he went alone to the Vietnam Memorial in Washington. (Other veterans also go regularly to the Memorial. One group has initiated the practice of leaving letters at the wall, written to a veteran or group of veterans whom the writer knew personally but who were killed.) Then, using the internet, Dillard slowly brought into being periodic gatherings of Delta Company members who were still alive. Was this sequence of events the work of an individual or a group? Clearly, both. Like the warp and woof of a weaving, individuals and groups join their energies to create occasions of mutual aid.

Breaking the Cycle of Violence

As World War II approached, David Dellinger refused to register for Selective Service and served a year and a day at the federal prison in Danbury, Connecticut. The prison was racially segregated and David's first trip to "the hole" came about when he sat down next to an African American man at a prison movie. After his

---

Thoughts are free,
Who can discover them?
They fly by like shadows in the night.
No man can know them,
No hunter can shoot them,
Come what may, thoughts are free.

And should I be thrown
Into a dark dungeon,
It will be useless for them to do so.
For my thoughts can burst the fetters,
And cleave the walls in two.
Thoughts are free.

release, he received another draft call, refused to cooperate, and was sent to the more rigorous federal prison in Lewisburg, Pennsylvania, for two more years.[3]

Soon after David arrived at Lewisburg, he and four other prisoners went on a hunger strike. One of the demands was an end to the censorship of mail. After about three weeks the warden came to his cell and told him that his wife was dying from complications connected with her pregnancy, adding: "She has sent a message telling you to go off the strike so that she can die in peace." After agonized reflection David decided the warden was lying. The warden *was* lying. The strike ended a few weeks later when "we won on the question of censorship," and David received a pile of letters in which his wife reported that she was doing fine and fully supported the hunger strike.[4]

Also at Lewisburg, David Dellinger passed through an experience that, as in Brian Willson's similar case, he had difficulty talking about for the rest of his life. A fellow conscientious objector, twenty years old and slightly built, came to David and said that three other prisoners had decided to make him their sexual "boy" and would be coming to his cell that night.

As soon as lights were out, David stationed himself outside his friend's cell and waited. Four men showed up, including a man named Steele. He "had the coldest, most steely eyes and voice that I had ever seen or heard." Desperately, David engaged them in conversation about every subject he could think of. Finally the men drifted off except for Steele. And Steele, when he finally understood the situation, said, "You'd let someone stick a shiv into *you* to save *him*. [Expletive deleted]." From then on, David Dellinger narrates, "we were all friends."[5]

David Dellinger demonstrated what Barbara Deming described as using "two hands."[6] David was extending one hand as he made conversation in a friendly way with those who came to use violence. But by standing in front of the cell of the man he was protecting, it was as if he was holding up his other hand like a stop sign, telling the other prisoners, you are not going in there to harm that man.

Barbara Deming explains, we must assure our adversaries that they need not be afraid of us, at the same time we insist that things have to change. By our actions, we must communicate the urgency of our conditions; we act out our objections to violations of our rights.

---

3   *See* David Dellinger, *From Yale to Jail: The Life Story of a Moral Dissenter* (New York: Pantheon Books, 1991), 82.

4   Ibid., 119–24.

5   Ibid., 152–57.

6   *See,* Barbara Deming, "On the Necessity to Liberate Minds," in *We Are All Part of One Another: A Barbara Deming Reader* (Philadelphia: New Society Publishers, 1984), talk delivered in June 1970; and "On Revolution and Equilibrium," reprinted in Staughton Lynd and Alice Lynd, eds., *Nonviolence in America: A Documentary History*, revised and expanded edition (Maryknoll, NY: Orbis Books, 1995).

Because the human rights of the adversary are respected, though his actions, his official policies are not, the focus of attention becomes those actions, those policies, and their true nature. The issue cannot be avoided. The antagonist cannot take the interference with his actions personally, because his person is not threatened, and he is forced to begin to acknowledge the reality of the grievance against him.[7]

She continues, it is as if we have two hands upon our adversary, "the one calming him, making him ask questions, as the other makes him move."[8] We try to shake him out of former attitudes and force him to appraise the situation in a way that takes into consideration our needs as well as his. It becomes in his own interest to adapt himself to change, and fear for himself does not prevent him from doing so.[9]

David Dellinger and Barbara Deming devoted years of their lives to opposing warfare and championing civil rights; and they spent time behind bars in the process. As Barbara said in 1970, "The machinery of things-as-they-are is a machinery of death." Our task is to "waken men's minds, *to keep them from postponing and postponing all real thought about our condition*," and to communicate "not merely with words but above all by our actions."[10] Nonviolent actions by individuals and small groups can bring about change.

We aim to carry on the messages of these departed friends.

---

7   Deming in *Nonviolence in America*, 416.
8   Ibid.
9   Ibid., 419.
10 Deming, *We Are All Part of One Another*, 201.

Index

About the Authors

ALICE LYND WAS A DRAFT COUNSELOR AND TRAINER OF DRAFT COUNSELORS DURING the Vietnam War. In 1968, she published *We Won't Go: Personal Accounts of War Objectors*. She later became first a paralegal and then a lawyer. After retirement from practicing labor law in the wake of plant shutdowns, she became an advocate for prisoners sentenced to death and/or held for years in solitary confinement at Ohio's supermaximum security prison. Among her publications is an article published in the University of Toledo Law Review, "Unfair and Can't Be Fixed: The Machinery of Death in Ohio."

Staughton Lynd is an historian, lawyer, activist, and author of many books and articles. Howard Zinn hired him to teach at Spelman College, a college for black women, during the early 1960s. He was coordinator of the Freedom Schools in Mississippi during the summer of 1964. As an outspoken opponent of the Vietnam War, he became unemployable as a university professor and became a lawyer. In Youngstown, Ohio, he fought for and lost the fight against plant shutdowns and for worker/community ownership of the mills. Among Staughton's books are *Lucasville: The Untold Story of a Prison Uprising* (second edition, PM Press, 2011); *Accompanying: Pathways to Social Change* (PM Press, 2012); and *Doing History from the Bottom Up* (Haymarket Books, 2014).

Staughton and Alice, with Jules Lobel, spearheaded a class action that went to the Supreme Court of the United States, establishing due process rights of prisoners held in prolonged solitary confinement. Joint publications by the Lynds include *Nonviolence in America: A Documentary History* (second edition, Orbis Books, 1995); *Stepping Stones: Memoir of a Life Together* (Lexington Books, 2009); and with Sam Bahour, *Homeland: Oral Histories of Palestine and Palestinians* (Olive Branch Press, 1994).

PM Press was founded at the end of 2007 by a small collection of folks with decades of publishing, media, and organizing experience. PM Press co-conspirators have published and distributed hundreds of books, pamphlets, CDs, and DVDs. Members of PM have founded enduring book fairs, spearheaded victorious tenant organizing campaigns, and worked closely with bookstores, academic conferences, and even rock bands to deliver political and challenging ideas to all walks of life. We're old enough to know what we're doing and young enough to know what's at stake.

We seek to create radical and stimulating fiction and non-fiction books, pamphlets, T-shirts, visual and audio materials to entertain, educate, and inspire you. We aim to distribute these through every available channel with every available technology—whether that means you are seeing anarchist classics at our bookfair stalls; reading our latest vegan cookbook at the café; downloading geeky fiction e-books; or digging new music and timely videos from our website.

PM Press is always on the lookout for talented and skilled volunteers, artists, activists, and writers to work with. If you have a great idea for a project or can contribute in some way, please get in touch.

PM Press
PO Box 23912
Oakland CA 94623
510-658-3906
www.pmpress.org

FRIENDS OF PM

These are indisputably momentous times—the financial system is melting down globally and the Empire is stumbling. Now more than ever there is a vital need for radical ideas.

In the many years since its founding—and on a mere shoestring—PM Press has risen to the formidable challenge of publishing and distributing knowledge and entertainment for the struggles ahead. With hundreds of releases to date, we have published an impressive and stimulating array of literature, art, music, politics, and culture. Using every available medium, we've succeeded in connecting those hungry for ideas and information to those putting them into practice.

Friends of PM allows you to directly help impact, amplify, and revitalize the discourse and actions of radical writers, filmmakers, and artists. It provides us with a stable foundation from which we can build upon our early successes and provides a much-needed subsidy for the materials that can't necessarily pay their own way. You can help make that happen—and receive every new title automatically delivered to your door once a month—by joining as a Friend of PM Press. And, we'll throw in a free T-shirt when you sign up.

Here are your options:
- $30 a month: Get all books and pamphlets plus 50% discount on all webstore purchases
- $40 a month: Get all PM Press releases (including CDs and DVDs) plus 50% discount on all webstore purchases
- $100 a month: Superstar—Everything plus PM merchandise, free downloads, and 50% discount on all webstore purchases

For those who can't afford $30 or more a month, we have Sustainer Rates at $15, $10, and $5. Sustainers get a free PM Press T-shirt and a 50% discount on all purchases from our website.

Your Visa or Mastercard will be billed once a month, until you tell us to stop. Or until our efforts succeed in bringing the revolution around. Or the financial meltdown of Capital makes plastic redundant. Whichever comes first.

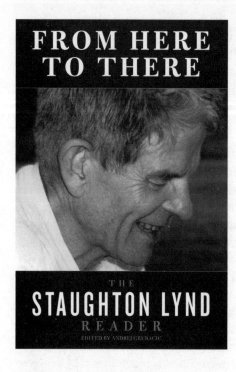

From Here To There
The Staughton Lynd Reader
Staughton Lynd
Edited with an Introduction by
Andrej Grubacic
$22.00 • 978-1-60486-215-7
9 by 6 • 320 pages

From Here To There collects unpublished talks and hard-to-find essays from legendary activist historian Staughton Lynd.

The first section of the *Reader* collects reminiscences and analyses of the 1960s. A second section offers a vision of how historians might immerse themselves in popular movements while maintaining their obligation to tell the truth. In the last section Lynd explores what nonviolence, resistance to empire as a way of life, and working class self-activity might mean in the 21st century. Together, they provide a sweeping overview of the life, and work—to date—of Staughton Lynd.

Both a definitive introduction and further exploration, it is bound to educate, enlighten, and inspire those new to his work and those who have been following it for decades. In a wide-ranging Introduction, anarchist scholar Andrej Grubacic considers how Lynd's persistent concerns relate to traditional anarchism.

> "*The Staughton Lynd Reader* is a veritable treasure chest. Lynd shows unparalleled respect for rank-and-file movements. If you're interested in broad social change and meaningful democracy, you simply must read Staughton Lynd."
> —Daniel Gross

Lucasville
The Untold Story of a Prison Uprising, 2nd ed.

Staughton Lynd
Preface by Mumia Abu-Jamal
$20.00 • 978-1-60486-224-9
8.5 by 5.5 • 256 pages

Lucasville tells the story of one of the longest prison uprisings in U.S. history. At the maximum-security Southern Ohio Correctional Facility in Lucasville, Ohio, prisoners seized a major area of the prison on Easter Sunday, 1993. More than 400 prisoners held L block for eleven days. Nine prisoners alleged to have been informants, or "snitches," and one hostage correctional officer, were murdered. There was a negotiated surrender. Thereafter, almost wholly on the basis of testimony by prisoner informants who received deals in exchange, five spokespersons or leaders were tried and sentenced to death, and more than a dozen others received long sentences.

Lucasville examines the causes of the disturbance, what happened during the eleven days, and the fairness of the trials. Particular emphasis is placed on the interracial character of the action, as evidenced in the slogans that were found painted on walls after the surrender: "Black and White Together," "Convict Unity," and "Convict Race."

An eloquent Foreword by Mumia Abu-Jamal underlines these themes. He states, as does the book, that the men later sentenced to death "sought to minimize violence, and indeed, according to substantial evidence, saved the lives of several men, prisoner and guard alike." Of the five men, three black and two white, who were sentenced to death, Mumia declares, "They rose above their status as prisoners, and became, for a few days in April 1993, what rebels in Attica had demanded a generation before them: men. As such, they did not betray each other; they did not dishonor each other; they reached beyond their prison 'tribes' to reach commonality."

STAUGHTON LYND

ACCOMPANYING
PATHWAYS TO SOCIAL CHANGE

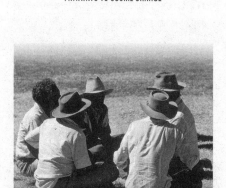

"This is a book rooted in years of hands-on experience, a must-read for anyone who believes a better world is possible."
—MARGARET RANDALL

Accompanying
Pathways to Social Change
Staughton Lynd
$14.95 • 978-1-60486-666-7
8 by 5 • 176 pages

In *Accompanying*, Staughton Lynd distinguishes two strategies of social change. The first, characteristic of the 1960s Movement in the United States, is "organizing." The second, articulated by Archbishop Oscar Romero of El Salvador, is "accompaniment." The critical difference is that in accompanying one another the promoter of social change and his or her oppressed colleague view themselves as two experts, each bringing indispensable experience to a shared project. Together, as equals, they seek to create what the Zapatistas call "another world."

Staughton Lynd applies the distinction between organizing and accompaniment to five social movements in which he has taken part: the labor and civil rights movements, the antiwar movement, prisoner insurgencies, and the movement sparked by Occupy Wall Street. His wife Alice Lynd, a partner in these efforts, contributes her experience as a draft counselor and advocate for prisoners in maximum-security confinement.

"Since our dreams for a more just world came crashing down around us in the late 1980s and early 1990s, those of us involved in social activism have spent much of the time since trying to assess what went wrong and what we might learn from our mistakes. In this highly readable book, Lynd explores the difference between organizing and accompanying. This book is a must-read for anyone who believes a better world is possible."
—Margaret Randall